To my sister Elaine for her tenacity and courage.

COLEG SIR GAR	
Cypher	02.11.02
005.74	£29.99

Key Recommendations: Part 3

✔ **Use models**. Skillful modeling has many benefits for purchasing and developing applications, including better quality, reduced cost, faster time to market, and better performance.

Build applications via models. Conceive your models first, and then develop the application. Do not construct models as an afterthought.

Use a structural model. Functional and process models are useful for scoping an application, but are not suitable for designing a database.

Standardize names. Use a naming convention and approved keywords to improve model readability and application consistency.

Do not obsess with choosing a notation. The choice of a notation is a secondary decision. The most important issue is that you use models, and learn to use them well.

✔ **Do not use IDEF1X for conceptual modeling**. It is better to prepare an ER model and switch to IDEF1X notation for relational database design.

Recognize that modeling is difficult. Be proactive and help your staff learn to model.

✔ **Carefully structure discussions with users**. Actively consider different interaction techniques.

✔ **Generate database designs**. Use a tool to generate database designs. Check the quality of the resulting code until you are confident of the accuracy of the tool.

Deliberately choose an approach for identity. Use existence-based identity for most RDBMS applications.

✔ **Address normal forms**. You will automatically satisfy normal forms (aside from deliberate violations) by preparing a sound model.

✔ **Carefully choose dimensions**. Reconsider a data warehouse model if facts have fewer than 5 or more than 15 dimensions.

✔ **Incrementally build a data warehouse**. Use the bus architecture and build one data mart at a time.

✔ **Normally use the star structure**. Use another structure only when there is a compelling reason.

✔ **Don't rewrite operational applications for a data warehouse**. Repair of operational databases should be a separate issue justified on its own merits.

A Manager's Guide
to Database Technology:
Building and Purchasing
Better Applications

MICHAEL R. BLAHA
OMT Associates Inc.
Chesterfield, Missouri 63017

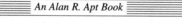
An Alan R. Apt Book

Prentice Hall, Inc.
Upper Saddle River, New Jersey 07458

Library of Congress Cataloging-in-Publication Data

Blaha, Michael.
A manager's guide to database technology : building and purchasing better applications
/ Michael Blaha.
p. cm.
ISBN 0-13-030418-2
1. Database management. 2. Application software. I. Title.

QA76.9.D3 B56 2000
005.74--dc2 100-062441

Publisher: *Alan Apt*
Editorial assistant: *Amy Todd*
Production editor: *Audri Anna Bazlen*
Vice president and editorial director, ECS: *Marcia Horton*
Executive managing editor: *Vince O'Brien*
Managing editor: *David A. George*
Assistant vice-president of production and manufacturing, ESM: *David W. Riccardi*
Art director: *Heather Scott*
Art editor: *Adam Velthaus*
Cover design: *John Christiana*
Creative director: *Paul Belfanti*
Manufacturing manager: *Trudy Pisciotti*
Manufacturing buyer: *Pat Brown*
Marketing manager: *Jennie Burger*

Prentice
Hall

© 2001 by Prentice Hall
Prentice-Hall, Inc.
Upper Saddle River, New Jersey 07458

Printed in the United States of America
10 9 8 7 6 5 4 3 2 1

ISBN 0-13-030418-2

Prentice-Hall International (UK) Limited, *London*
Prentice-Hall of Australia Pty. Limited, *Sydney*
Prentice-Hall Canada Inc., Toronto
Prentice-Hall Hispanoamericana, S.A., *Mexico*
Prentice-Hall of India Private Limited, *New Delhi*
Prentice-Hall of Japan, Inc., *Tokyo*
Pearson Education Asia Pte. Ltd.
Editora Prentice-Hall do Brasil, Ltda., *Rio de Janeiro*

Contents

Preface

If you've taken the trouble to open this book, chances are you're involved with some aspect of software development or purchase. You've probably also experienced the software crisis—software takes too long to build, has uneven quality, and costs too much. A few firms have managed to use software systems to enhance their business and give them a competitive edge. But many more are still coping with inferior systems that end up hobbling or even sabotaging their goals.

Unfortunately, the whole situation is worse than it has to be. There's no shortage of techniques for combatting the software crisis, but many organizations seem unwilling or unable to use them.

I believe "a failure to communicate" is a big part of the reason. Computing technology is complex and has idiosyncratic jargon, which makes it difficult to explain or understand. Managers have an even harder time because they must deal not only with the software but also with human and organizational issues. They have neither the time nor the patience to wade through technobabble and irrelevant details.

This is particularly true for database systems, which are a special kind of software. Databases are critical, because they provide the memory of an organization. With sound databases, you can readily get the information you need to execute business strategies. With flawed databases, you can't find customers, you lose orders, and the organization fails to capitalize on its collective knowledge.

The marketplace is full of books on software development, but the level of detail is crushing. There is little or no attention to strategy and managerial concerns about how applications should be organized and how they fit together. In contrast, this book takes a broad look at technology and focuses on databases. You need databases that are flexible, sound, and efficient for successful applications.

What You Will Find

This book covers key aspects of database technology and provides practical tips that managers can use immediately. It has five main parts.

- **Part 1: Introduction**. Explains some basic terms and sets the book's context.

- **Part 2: Data Management Technology**. Helps you decide whether to use a database for a particular application. If you use a database, you must choose a paradigm and couple the database to your application. The emphasis is on relational databases, which are the dominant technology for new applications.

- **Part 3: Database Design Technology**. Shows how to model and design a database for an application you build and gives you insight for understanding the database of a product you may want to purchase. Separate chapters address operational (transaction oriented) and analytical (data warehouse) applications.

- **Part 4: Software Engineering Technology**. Presents software engineering, which is a systematic approach to development. Software engineering is needed for repeated success and for coping with differences in individual skill levels.

- **Part 5: Advanced Technology**. Covers special topics. Distributed databases are important for scalability, performance, and effective hardware use. Reverse engineering lets you seed the model for new applications and assess the quality of existing applications. Integration issues arise with suites of applications. The book concludes by discussing the significance of object-oriented technology for databases.

Who Should Read This Book?

The primary audience is managers. Nevertheless, several kinds of persons can benefit.

- **Managers**. The book is for managers who are concerned about software and want to understand the world of Information Systems (IS) and Information Technology (IT).

- **Technical staff**. They can learn more about the concerns of their manager, as well as broaden their computing background.

- **Business staff**. They can deepen their understanding of the capabilities and limitations of computing.

- **University courses**. Some professors may find the book suitable for business (MBA) and computing courses.

This book is intended for both large (Fortune 500) and small firms. I qualify my advice when a firm's size really matters. For the most part, I assume that a firm is building or purchasing software. Nevertheless, a vendor may find this book helpful in understanding their customers' point of view.

Acknowledgments

I thank the many reviewers who took the time to read manuscripts and give me their thoughtful comments: Ian Benson, Jim Blaha, Dave Curry, Kathi Davis, Bill Huth, Chris Kelsey, Sham Navathe, Bill Premerlani, Hwa Shen, Steve Sherman, and Rod Sprattling. The comments of Jim Blaha, Chris Kelsey, and Steve Sherman were particularly thorough and incisive.

Thanks also to Nancy Talbert, who edited the final manuscript improving its readability and organization, and to Alan Apt and Toni Holm of Prentice Hall, who facilitated the book's production and distribution.

I took some of the material from *Object-Oriented Modeling and Design for Database Applications* (1998, Prentice Hall), which I co-authored with Bill Premerlani.

Finally, I thank the many managers who helped me write this book. Some helped me directly by reviewing the book. Others helped me indirectly over the years by bringing me problems, asking me questions, and clarifying my thinking.

Contact Information

If you have any questions or comments, please contact me. I would like to hear if this book has helped you and about your experiences. Send e-mail to blaha@acm.org or blaha@computer.org, or visit my Web site at www.omtassociates.com.

Part 1

Introduction

Many organizations fail to connect business requirements with software development and acquisition. This disconnect is especially troublesome for database applications because they are pervasive and critical to the operation of a business. The resulting applications are slow, buggy, hard to maintain, and awkward to evolve.

Chapter 1 provides some insights into how business needs drive software development. Chapter 2 gives some background on the types of database applications and the basic concerns of procurement, maintenance, and removal.

1

The Business of Software

Database applications are the lifeblood of a business. Databases are endemic in all major organizations. They record our purchases, payments, and credit worthiness. They track the arrival and departures of airline flights. They even appear in advanced research such as the decoding of the human genome.

The approach to procuring (building or purchasing) database applications is much different than that for other types of applications. Database applications have many distinctive issues: Large quantities of long-lived data must be accessed in different ways. There is a need to coordinate the effects of multiple users and applications. Many databases are self-descriptive and publish their structure in a system catalog.

In principle, databases are application independent; any application can access their data. In practice, most databases are built for a specific application. Multiple application databases can lead to redundant data. But given that applications are motivated by business needs that occur at different times and are sponsored by different organizations, such duplication can be difficult to avoid.

Two Scenarios

The following two experiences illustrate how the quality of a database can make, or break, an application.

A Success

During one consulting engagement, I met with a small group of developers to review their design for an application and to verify that their development practices were sound.

They began the review by explaining the motivation and requirements for the application. The firm was a service business, and they were wary of being overtaken by competitors if they did not add capabilities. The developers had thoroughly modeled their application and carried it forward into the database design. Their model was sound, and their database design was solid. It was apparent that management had assembled a team of skilled developers who understood modeling and databases well.

The developers were writing programming code to support their business logic and user interfaces. They were using an object-oriented language and were understandably concerned about how it would work with a relational database. They had devised a reasonable architecture to couple programming code to the database.

The end result was that their application ran well. It was flexible, extensible, and fast. They had a modest number of bugs and met their scheduled delivery dates. The successful application helped maintain the company's business position and keep competitors at bay.

A Failure

Another time a client asked me to evaluate a product sold by a prominent Fortune 500 company. The vendor had a great market vision, and the product supposedly had many impressive features. The vendor understood the business requirements well, and my client was enthusiastic.

The first hint of a problem came during installation. The documentation was confusing and it took my client's support staff several weeks to install the product, only to find that it was buggy and slow. An experienced developer attended their training course and found it confusing. I decided to reverse engineer the database to understand the product better.

I was surprised to find that the database had been poorly designed. Even though the vendor was a large, credible company and understood the requirements well, they mishandled the database. The database looked as if it had been designed by a programmer new to databases. In later discussions, the vendor confirmed my suspicions. It had never occurred to them that database design was difficult and that a bad design could cause so much trouble. It was no wonder that the software ran slow and was confusing. My client rejected the product.

The upshot is that the vendor wasted a few million dollars in developing and marketing a flawed product. This could have been readily avoided with early attention to modeling and careful database design. A few months of time from a talented database designer could have saved them much rework, increased the quality of their product, and boosted sales. The product was temporarily withdrawn from the market, fixed, and is now being sold again.

In This Book

In many cases, a little time and a deeper understanding of database technology can save a firm millions of dollars. The developers in the failure scenario didn't understand what it took to produce a sound database design and didn't realize that their design decisions would ultimately doom the product. I wrote this book in the hope that managers can avoid these kinds of costly mistakes. It is a *guide* to *database applications* primarily for *managers*.

- As a **guide**, it describes database technology in terms of the key ideas and concepts and suppresses fine detail. The emphasis is on techniques, processes, and advice for more effective practice. I deliberately avoid much product commentary, because such information becomes quickly dated. However, the principles covered will help you perform your own product assessments for your particular situation.

- As a guide to **database applications**, it addresses applications that are dominated by a database. These kinds of applications are typically of most importance to business and of most concern to managers. The focus is on relational database technology, covering both operational and analytical applications. Operational applications involve the routine and critical operations of a business. Analytical applications enable decision support and involve data warehouses. The book covers both software development and the purchase of applications.

- As a guide for **managers** who want to understand the world of Information Systems (IS) and Information Technology (IT), it limits technical detail to what is needed to make business decisions. Technologists can read it to learn more about management concerns.

2

Database Applications

A *database* is a permanent, self-descriptive store of data that is contained in one or more files. A *database manager* (also called *database management system* or *DBMS*) is the software that manages access to a database. Oracle, SQL Server, DB2, MS-Access, and IMS are examples of commercial database managers.

A *database application* uses a database manager to handle its long-lived data. Database applications include systems such as financial, personnel, payroll, inventory, sales, marketing, manufacturing, engineering, and customer service. Most database applications are either operational or analytical. The basic concerns are how to procure, maintain, and remove them.

Operational and Analytical Applications

Operational applications involve the routine and critical operations of a business and must process transactions rapidly. Order processing is an example of an operational application. A *transaction* is a group of commands that succeeds or fails as an indivisible unit of work; an entire transaction is written to a database, or nothing is written. Operational transactions tend to be simple, access few records, and have a response time within seconds. Because the operations are fundamental to the business, the database must be kept current, intact, and reliable. As Figure 2.1 shows, many users can simultaneously read and write from the same database. Most operational databases store only the most recent data, and an update overwrites any prior value.

In contrast, analytical applications emphasize complex queries that read large quantities of data and enable organizations to make strategic decisions. Consider a

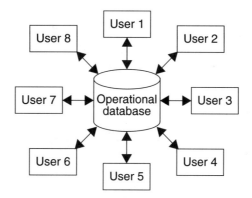

Figure 2.1 Operational applications. Many users quickly interact with a database.

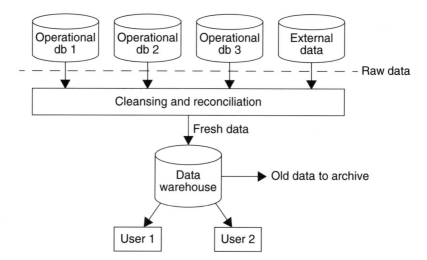

Figure 2.2 Analytical applications. Users query a database that reconciles
and accumulates operational extracts.

supermarket that analyzes sales data to find products with correlated sales. As Figure
2.2 shows, analytical applications execute against a data warehouse, which combines data from multiple sources. A data warehouse acquires its information from
periodic feeds from operational databases and external data sources. Most data
warehouses store data parameterized by time, so users can query past data and detect
temporal trends. Analytical applications tend to have few updates, other than the periodic feeds.

Table 2.1 compares both categories of applications.

Criterion	Operational applications	Analytical applications
Purpose	Support routine clerical tasks via rapid transaction processing	Explore for trends and patterns to enable managerial decisions
Data timeliness	Current data	Historical data
Database size	Megabytes to gigabytes	Gigabytes to terabytes
Number of users	10–1000	10–100
Update frequency	Multiple updates per second	Usually daily or weekly mass updates
Update scope	A few records	Can be much of the database
Database availability	High	Occasional downtime is tolerable
Query complexity	Short and simple	Variable size and can be complex
Query response	Seconds	Minutes

Table 2.1 Comparison of database applications. Operational and analytical applications have different characteristics.

Procuring Applications

Typically, business experts initiate an application. They set tentative requirements by considering customer needs, opportunities for profit, and synergy with other business activities. Once needs are defined, there are three options for obtaining an application.

- Purchase a commercial off-the-shelf application.
- Build an application within your organization.
- Outsource application development.

Purchase a Commercial Off-the-Shelf Application

When you purchase a commercial off-the-shelf (COTS) package from a vendor, you rely on that vendor's efforts and vision. If your application is a general capability that many other firms also need, there's a good chance you can buy suitable software.

■ **Advantages**. A vendor can reduce your expense by amortizing development effort across multiple customers. You can also use an existing vendor application immediately and thus reap quick benefits, as opposed to waiting for new development. Finally, an existing product is a known quantity without development risk.

■ **Disadvantages**. Applicability is an important issue. You must determine whether a COTS application has the necessary functionality. Can you modify your business practices to fit the application? How much flexibility and customizability does the application provide? You should also consider the difficulty of integrating a COTS application with other software. Different vendors have divergent quality, style, and conceptual bases, which can make integration difficult.

Most businesses evaluate purchased software on the basis of four criteria: functionality, user interface, cost, and vendor stability. None of these criteria address software quality. For database applications, you can assess the database quality and infer the software quality. (Chapter 20 discusses how to evaluate vendor products, but you may need the material in previous chapters as background.)

Warning! Many COTS packages have user-definable fields and forms, and it is acceptable to use them to a limited extent. However, it is not a good idea to purchase a COTS package and modify it heavily. *Use a COTS package with minimal modification, or don't use it at all.* There are the obvious issues of cost and customization time. In addition, modification impedes your ability to accept vendor upgrades.

Build an Application within Your Organization

If you build an application within your organization, you rely on your own efforts and vision.

■ **Advantages**. You tightly control every aspect of an application—both its conceptual basis and its realization. Your staff thoroughly understands the application and has the knowledge to evolve it for future needs.

■ **Disadvantages**. Most firms lack the resources to build all applications in-house. A core staff services critical needs. Outside resources augment the core staff and are adjusted as business ebbs and flows. Thus for most firms, you may build some applications, but you cannot build them all.

You can increase your productivity and quality by adopting the practice of excellent software development firms, which build applications indirectly through models. Models provide a formalism for thinking about the difficult aspects of an application and let you defer details. *Think carefully and deeply before becoming enmeshed in the minutia of programming and databases.*

Outsource Application Development

With outsourcing, you still control the requirements for an application. However, you rely on an external party to reduce your requirements to a working system.

■ **Advantages**. With this approach, you can have a limited in-house computing staff and still readily adjust to varying demands for software. You can reduce overhead and incur additional cost only when there is direct business benefit.

■ **Disadvantages**. The success of your application depends partially on external developers. Also it can be difficult to compensate external developers properly for their efforts. A fixed-price contract invites cutting corners and reducing quality to meet budget and schedule pressures. A time-and-materials contract incurs expense, and interim accomplishments can be difficult to measure.

You will be most successful if you define the proper interface between your firm and external developers. Keep modeling and database design in-house. They take only a fraction of the total development effort, but involve the most intense thought. These are the crown jewels of your applications. Outsource the tedious and time-consuming activities of programming and user-interface construction.

Warning! This recommendation differs from the typical approach of delivering a set of functional requirements and letting external developers build the software any way they want. *Make sure external developers actually use your model and database design.* You can enforce the use of your model and database design with contract language and periodic reviews.

Comparison of Options

Table 2.2 summarizes the trade-offs of the procurement options. Firms typically handle most deployment issues themselves—user training, interfaces to other systems, and initial database loading are highly individualistic.

Vendor software normally has the lowest development cost, because effort is spread across multiple customers. Outsourced development normally has the highest cost, because contract developers are more expensive than in-house developers.

An existing vendor application clearly has the least deployment time and development risk. In-house development often takes the most time, because staffing is limited. Outsourced development has the most development risk, because you lack control of the entire project.

The downside of vendor software is that it fits your business only approximately and may fit poorly with your other software. With in-house software, your staff can ensure that all requirements are met and that the new software complements existing software.

You can assure the quality of vendor software by inspecting the database used in their product as an indicator of the overall quality. For in-house and outsourced development, you can assure quality by building software via models.

Criterion	Purchase a COTS application	Build within your organization	Outsource development
Development cost	Lowest	Medium	Highest
Deployment time	Lowest	Highest	Medium
Development risk	Lowest	Medium	Highest
Applicability risk	Highest	Lowest	Medium
Fit with other software	Worst	Best	Medium
Maintenance strategy	Rely on vendor	Rely on staff's understanding of software	Rely on staff's understanding of models
How to ensure quality	Assess database quality	Build the software via models	Specify to vendor via models

Table 2.2 **Application procurement options**. The procurement options have different trade-offs.

Maintenance

An established firm must not only add applications for new business needs, but also maintain existing applications. You should rely on vendors to maintain their software. Your developers should be able to maintain in-house software if they keep sufficient documentation. Your developers should also be able to maintain outsourced software if they control the models that the contractors build against. Maintenance involves many routine issues that this book does not address, but I do have some advice.

- **Audit data quality**. About half the database applications (in-house development, outsourced development, and COTS) that I have seen have severe flaws. Many of these are poorly conceived (lack of modeling); others are poorly implemented (inadequate database design).

    Ideally, your organization should redevelop any severely flawed applications. Unfortunately, this is often impractical. If the flawed application is a vendor product, you may lack a suitable alternative, and you defeat the purpose of vendor software by rewriting it. If it is an in-house application, you may simply not have the time and funding to rewrite it.

Even if you can't rewrite a flawed application, your developers can prepare a proper model of the application and note important constraints that the database does not enforce. They can then write test programs that check the database for data that violate the constraints. Support staff can periodically run the test programs and report any noncompliant data. Users can then use application forms and commands to fix the errors.

■ **Document legacy software**. You can use reverse engineering to understand legacy software. (See Chapter 19.) For in-house and outsourced applications, a reverse-engineered model provides documentation that can help guide software evolution. You can gradually improve the software in conjunction with routine maintenance and enhancement.

Removing Obsolete Applications

Applications become obsolete for different reasons. Some applications are tied to old hardware that is expensive to operate and difficult to repair. An extreme example is the U.S. air traffic control system, which is bound to computers from the 1960s. Other applications become unwieldy, as they are successively patched over time; this aging can be exacerbated by obsolete languages and missing source code. Still other applications have archaic user interfaces, date problems, rigid telephone number formats, and various other limitations. A firm must discard obsolete software so that the staff can focus maintenance efforts on the remaining vibrant applications.

The removal of applications often bedevils corporations. Users may be accustomed to an old application and reluctant to learn new software. Many old applications have had their performance tweaked over the years and have rich features, even if their architecture or platform is no longer viable. An application that is useful, but not quite good enough, can impede the deployment of a replacement.

Removing old applications is mostly a matter of logistics and overcoming user inertia. However, if you use models and software engineering principles to guide your new applications, you will be able to build and deploy them more quickly, simplifying the logistics. In addition, old software may go away, but the data often persist. The techniques in this book will make it easier to convert data from the old to the new system.

Chapter Summary

Database applications provide the memory of a firm, retaining customer data, pricing details, requests for products and services, employee salaries, and many other kinds of data. Database applications vary in their characteristics, ranging from applications that involve routine and critical operations (operational) to applications that are used to analyze strategies and trends (analytical).

The software inventory must be carefully managed. Applications are added as new needs arise; these applications may be purchased or developed with some combination of in-house and outside resources. Existing applications, some of which are deeply flawed, must be maintained. Obsolete applications must be removed.

✔ **Assess vendor products fully**. Reverse-engineering techniques (see Chapter 20) let you evaluate the database quality and infer the software quality.

✔ **Limit customizations of vendor software**. User-definable fields and forms can seem inviting, but you should limit their use, because they expend time and funds and impair your ability to accept vendor upgrades.

✔ **Define the proper interface to external developers**. Don't just give them business requirements and let them build the software any way they want. Instead, keep the critical tasks of modeling and database design in-house, and outsource the tedious and time-consuming activities of programming and user-interface construction. Make sure that external developers actually use your model and database design.

✔ **Audit data quality**. You largely have to accept existing applications as they are. However, you can periodically check the database and use normal application input to repair any errors.

Major recommendations for Chapter 2

Part 2

Data Management Technology

Part 2 explains database technology and the decisions you must make whether you develop the software or purchase it.

Chapter 3 presents major architectural issues that you must address. The chapter focuses on several basic architectures that are common in database applications.

Chapter 4 surveys data management paradigms. Most database applications store their data in a database, but files and groupware are viable alternatives.

Chapter 5 examines different kinds of databases (relational, multidimensional, object-oriented, object-relational, hierarchical, and network) and provides advice for their use.

Chapter 6 looks at the dominant database paradigm—relational databases—in more depth, defining basic concepts and identifying subtle capabilities. It also revisits object-relational databases.

Part 2 concludes with a discussion of data processing in Chapter 7. There are several ways to couple programming code to databases and improve performance.

When you've read Part 2, you will understand the broad issues involved with data management and be ready for Part 3, which gets into design details.

3

Architecture

An *__architecture__* is the high-level plan or strategy for building an application. This chapter first discusses several common architectures for database applications (tiered architectures, TP monitor, and Web architecture) and then presents a simple approach for resolving remaining issues.

The focus is on logical architecture, as opposed to physical architecture. The concern is about the way software is organized, rather than how computers and other hardware are physically connected with networks.

Tiered Architectures

Architectures can have any number of tiers. They may place data management, application logic, and the user interface into separate processes or combine them in some manner.

One Tier

The simplest way to develop an application is just to write code for whatever is needed. Such a *__one-tier architecture__* (Figure 3.1) combines data management, application logic, and the user interface into a single executable file.

Many old data-processing applications have a one-tier architecture, such as Cobol programs that store data in fixed-format records. These programs perform calculations on data and display results on a screen or as a printed report. Many modern applications also have a one-tier architecture. For example, some PC applications built on the MS-Access database manager deliver data, code, and the user interface in a single file.

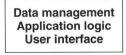

One tier

Figure 3.1 One-tier architecture. A one-tier architecture packages
an entire application into one executable file.

A one-tier architecture has the advantage of simplicity. The user executes a single file to obtain functionality. Such applications are usually straightforward to develop, and the performance is good.

However, maintenance can be complex, because the dissimilar technologies of data management, calculation, and user interface are entwined. Only one person at a time can use a one-tier application. It is difficult for one-tier applications to provide a common look and feel, since each has a custom user interface.

 Consider a one-tier architecture for small (less than three months of development effort) and throwaway applications.

Two Tiers

A ***two-tier architecture*** (Figure 3.2) organizes an application into two layers. One layer focuses on the user interface; the other on data-management services. Application logic may be in either or both layers.

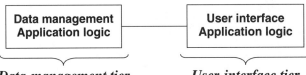

Data-management tier   *User-interface tier*

Figure 3.2 Two-tier architecture. A two-tier architecture separates data
management from the user interface, but combines them with
application logic.

The two-tier architecture is often used in conjunction with ***client-server computing***. The user-interface tier is the ***client***, which sends queries. The data-management tier is the ***server***, which sends data in response to the queries. Client-server technology provides a means for distributing work across machines and coordinating the results.

As Figure 3.3 shows, multiple clients can access a server. For example, one client may present data as a table; another as a graph. Similarly, one client can access multiple servers, for example, to combine data from two databases. Clients and servers may run on the same or different machines, be written in various languages, and use different operating systems.

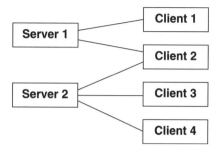

Figure 3.3 Client-server computing. A server can have multiple clients and a client can access multiple servers.

The terms *__fat client__* and *__fat server__* are often used in conjunction with client-server computing. A fat client places most of the application logic with the user-interface tier. A fat server places most of the application logic with the data-management tier. Application logic is usually skewed toward one tier or the other.

Many applications have a two-tier architecture. For example, the standard programming language interface of a major database manager such as Oracle yields two tiers. The server handles the data; the client provides application logic and the user interface. Special database statements in the client precompile to server calls.

You can even use a two-tier architecture with a simple database manager, such as MS-Access, if you create one database for the tables (the server), and another for the application logic and user interface (the client). The client refers to the tables, connecting the two tiers.

Client-server computing requires some sophistication in assigning work to clients and servers. Developers must state queries precisely so that excessive data are not passed over the communications network. For example, for a database of phone numbers, users probably shouldn't be allowed to browse an entire country. Instead, you could require that they provide part of a name or a category. With database queries, you should include some kind of filter to reduce the transmitted data (such as specify a *where* clause for an SQL query).

 Client-server applications should state queries precisely to avoid transmitting excessive data.

A two-tier architecture offers many benefits.

■ **Economy**. You can use inexpensive machines (such as PCs) for clients and more robust machines (such as UNIX workstations) for servers.

■ **Scalability**. Typically, you can add hardware as additional users are brought on-line. You need not replace the existing computers and network infrastructure.

■ **Familiarity**. You can choose client hardware that users are familiar with. For example, you can use a PC to run applications on mainframes, workstations, and other PCs.

■ **Performance**. A dedicated PC can respond quickly. Contention with other users and applications occurs only when there is substantive database activity.

■ **Extensibility**. Databases are more difficult to change than user interfaces. By separating the two, you can update a user interface without disrupting the database.

As with any technology, there are also drawbacks.

■ **Complexity**. You must apportion application logic between the two tiers. This splitting can be difficult if it is arbitrary and has no obvious basis.

■ **Dependencies**. Clients and servers are mutually dependent. Be careful in designing interfaces and coordinating updates that affect them.

 Consider a two-tier architecture for medium applications (less than twelve months of development effort).

Three Tiers

Client-server technology can support a more robust architecture—a ***three-tier architecture***—that cleanly separates data management, application logic, and the user interface. As Figure 3.4 shows, the data-management tier holds the database structure and data, and the application tier holds the application logic. The user-interface tier manages forms and reports.

Client-server computing is a good fit for the three-tier architecture. As the figure shows, the application tier is a client relative to the data-management tier. The user-interface tier is a client relative to the application tier.

The financial case study in [Blaha-98] illustrates the three-tier architecture. The software manages portfolios of stocks and bonds. The data-management tier holds the base data—primarily trades, dividends, and interest, as well as the value of stocks and bonds on various dates. The user interface presents data and computed results via forms and reports.

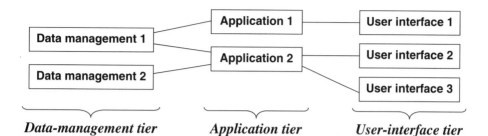

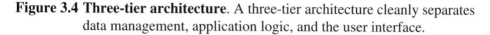

Figure 3.4 Three-tier architecture. A three-tier architecture cleanly separates data management, application logic, and the user interface.

The application tier contains the detailed logic. For example, the software can compute the composition of a portfolio on a given date by summing all the trades, dividends, and interest payments that have occurred as of the specified date. It can also compute the value of a portfolio on a date by summing the amount of each security times its price per share.

The exact boundaries between the tiers are somewhat subjective. For example, you can place application logic within the data-management tier with stored procedures. (See Chapter 7.) Similarly, some constraints on data (business rules) are difficult to represent with database structure; you can enforce them with the application and user-interface tiers. Despite this freedom, you should adhere to the three-tier ideal as much as possible to increase the flexibility and extensibility of your systems.

All three tiers should ensure data integrity. The user interface should check the data entered into forms and help users fix mistakes. The application tier should perform the most thorough checking. The data-management tier must maintain consistent data, despite access by multiple users and applications.

The three-tier architecture has several advantages.

■ **Economy**. You can use inexpensive machines for the user interface and more robust machines for application and database servers.

■ **Scalability**. Scalability is as good or better than that for two tiers.

■ **Familiarity**. You can choose familiar hardware for the user interface.

■ **Performance**. Again, a dedicated PC can quickly respond to a user. However, unlike a two-tier architecture, you can tune database machines without being encumbered by application logic.

■ **Extensibility**. Since application logic is separate, you have more flexibility than with two tiers to change the user interface or data manager.

■ **Protection**. Three tiers separate the database from application processing. Hence, there is reduced risk of an accidental or deliberate corruption of the database.

The three-tier architecture has some disadvantages.

■ **Complexity**. The communications software (see Chapter 18) for connecting the tiers can be difficult to master.

■ **Dependencies**. There is a mutual dependency between clients and servers.

 When possible, use a three (or more) tier architecture for your applications.

N-Tiers

Software need not be limited to three tiers. You can connect multiple applications, with each having a user-interface and data-management tier. For example, in Figure 3.5 an e-mail program invokes a calendar application. An e-mail message to schedule a meeting causes the calendar application to run.

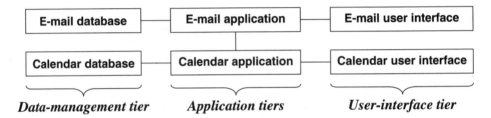

Figure 3.5 N-tier architecture. There may be multiple application tiers.

Comparison of Tiered Architectures

Table 3.1 compares the tiered architectures. A one-tier application lacks scalability, because it can handle only one user at a time. In contrast, two and three tiers support multiple users and typically let you add hardware as new users are brought on-line.

The performance of one tier suffices for small applications. More substantive applications require two and three-tier architectures that dedicate machines to specific tasks.

One-tier applications are simple to develop, but difficult to extend; this is a consequence of combining different kinds of computing. In contrast, two and three tiers take more effort to build, but result in more maintainable and extensible applications.

You should consider one tier only for throwaway and small applications (a few months of development effort). Consider two tiers for medium applications (as much as twelve months of development effort). For all other applications, you should try to use three tiers.

Criterion	One tier	Two tier	Three tier
Scalability	One user	Multiple users. Add hardware as users are brought online	
Performance	Adequate for small applications	Better. A dedicated PC for the user interface	Best. A dedicated PC for the user interface. Separate database and application machines
Extensibility	Poor. Combines everything into one file	Better. Can update user interface without disrupting the database	Best. Separates database, user interface, and application
Complexity	Simple to develop. Difficult to maintain	Developer must apportion application logic between the two tiers	Communications software for connecting the tiers can be difficult to master
Recommendation	Consider for small and throwaway applications	Consider for medium applications	When possible, use three (or more) tiers

Table 3.1 Comparison of tiered architectures

Transaction-Processing Monitors

A *__transaction__* is a group of commands that succeed or fail as an indivisible unit of work. For example, a transaction may transfer funds by debiting one bank account and crediting another. Both actions—the debit and the credit—must be performed as a single transaction, or the bank could find itself with a shortage or surplus of funds. Transactions are the essence of operational applications, which must perform numerous database updates quickly and without mistakes. Transaction-processing monitors are often used for operational applications.

__Transaction-processing (TP) monitors__ are systems whose express purpose is to process transactions reliably, efficiently, and economically. TP monitors use the underlying data managers for processing, but they add functionality for developing and managing application transactions. TP monitors have been widely used for mainframe computing, but are also important for computer networks. Commercial TP monitors include IBM's CICS, NCR's Top End, Transarc's Encina, BEA's Tuxedo, and Microsoft's MTS.

As Figure 3.6 shows, TP monitors use a three-tier architecture. The middle tier executes application procedures that perform transactions, the back tier has data management, and the front tier has user interfaces. The three-tier architecture lets TP monitors coordinate transactions across multiple databases. This architecture insulates applications from the database, but applications are dependent on a specific TP monitor.

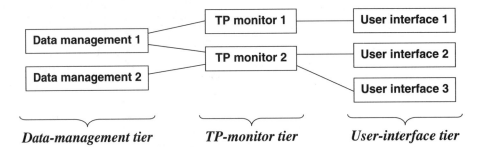

Data-management tier   *TP-monitor tier*   *User-interface tier*

Figure 3.6 TP monitor architecture. A TP monitor uses a three-tier architecture, but adds functionality for developing and managing transactions.

Many applications use TP monitors including bank ATMs, order fulfillment systems, and hotel reservation systems. TP monitors deliver the following benefits.

■ **Correctness**. A TP monitor guarantees that a transaction will execute *exactly* once. (In contrast, a database manager alone ensures that a transaction executes *at most* once.) A TP monitor can queue an application over the communications network and report back to the user within the scope of a transaction.

■ **Economy**. Some database managers are priced according to the number of connected users. An application with 500 on-line users would thus require 500 database connections, incurring a fee for each connection. A TP monitor implements special logic to combine several users into one connection. The savings in database fees can more than offset the cost of the TP monitor.

■ **Scalability**. A TP monitor makes it easy to add data managers and user interfaces incrementally as transaction volume grows.

■ **Performance**. Each database connection incurs an overhead of processing time and memory, so the database manager slows as the number of connections increases. TP monitors are designed to have a lower overhead per user.

■ **Protection**. Because it implements a three-tier architecture, a TP monitor separates the database from application processing. Hence, there is less risk of an accidental or deliberate corruption of the database.

TP monitors have the following drawbacks.

- **Complexity**. TP monitors are sophisticated software, and there is a learning curve for skilled use.

- **Vendor dependency**. A TP monitor separates applications from databases, but because TP monitor commands vary across vendors, a company can become dependent on a particular vendor.

 Consider a TP monitor for applications with a high transaction volume, many users, or operations that span databases.

Web-Based Architecture

Web applications use the Internet to connect client user interfaces (Web browsers) to servers. The Web-based architecture merits special mention, because of its ubiquity and potential for extremely high volume. Millions use the Internet, and potentially any number of people can access a single Web server. A client invokes a server by providing a Unified Resource Locator (URL)—a general-purpose name for an Internet resource. Web applications have two or more tiers. The user interface accesses the Web server and can't tell if it invokes other servers for further processing.

Web applications use the Hyper Text Transfer Protocol (HTTP) for conveying information over the Internet—establish the client-server connection, transmit data, and break the connection. HTTP is a stateless protocol; the server merely responds to each request that appears and has no memory of previous interactions. The client must maintain its own state—URL currently accessed, URLs previously accessed, past data, and any control parameters.

The information conveyed between the Web server and its clients is expressed as Hyper Text Markup Language (HTML) documents. HTML is essentially a simple language for presenting data and giving it a rough format. HTML documents may contain URLs, so that users can readily navigate from one document to another.

The simplest Web applications deal only with static HTML pages with fixed content. Each page is stored in a file, and the Web server retrieves a page when a client Web browser requests it. More sophisticated Web applications have dynamic HTML pages, where the content of a page is computed at run time. Such applications often query a database and retrieve content to populate a page.

Most often, the server does all the processing, and the client simply formats the data. However, a Web client can also provide application logic; it can perform processing with embedded Java and store local data in simple files or cookies. Java is a general-purpose programming language that is popular for Web applications. A *cookie* is a record in a special file that contains keywords and simple values. Typically, many Web applications share the same cookie file.

A Web-based architecture has several advantages.

- **Scalability**. The communications infrastructure for Web applications is well understood and widely available. Web applications have been deployed that support thousands of concurrent users.

- **Familiarity**. Virtually all computer users are familiar with the Internet and Web browsers.

- **Distribution**. The Web lets you readily handle users at many locations.

A Web-based architecture has the following disadvantages.

- **Security**. Security has always been a concern with the Web. Since the Web is prominent and accessible to the general public, it will always be the subject of some attacks.

- **Performance**. HTTP is simple and robust because it does not maintain the state of a client-server dialogue. However, the protocol can be inefficient, because the server must reestablish the context for each client contact.

    Consider using the Internet to host an application with multiple tiers.

Other Architectural Issues

Most database applications use one of the architectures just described. Still, miscellaneous issues do arise. An example is the financial case study described earlier [Blaha-98]. The software iteratively calculates return on investment—it guesses the rate of return and sums the discounted cash flow. Eventually, it guesses the correct rate for which the discounted cash flow equals the current value. The calculations are time consuming, so the book explores the architectural option of computing the rate of return upon user request or caching past values and keeping them consistent with changes to the underlying data.

You may also encounter issues that stretch the database paradigm. For example, [Blaha-90] describes an industrial application built on a relational database. The architecture extends relational database tables for use as decision tables.

When you must make these kinds of architectural decisions, I recommend a simple approach.

- **Think of candidate solutions**. This is essentially brainstorming, so try to be creative and defer judgment.

- **Choose decision criteria and assign weights**. Distinguish between criteria that absolutely must be met and qualities that are just desirable.

- **Evaluate candidate solutions**. Rate the solutions according to decision criteria, and reject those that do not satisfy mandatory criteria.

- **Perform sensitivity analysis**. Compare the scores of the candidate solutions. Determine if uncertainty in the decision criteria weights materially affects the final decision.

This approach helps you reach a deliberate decision and document the alternatives and reasons for assessments. It is also suitable for group decision making.

 Use a systematic approach in making architectural decisions, and document your reasons.

An application for real-time submarine data illustrates the importance of architecture. The developers built the application so that all communication messages occurred via a relational database. The intent was to manage the messages carefully. The problem was that the relational database performed much too slowly for real-time use.

The developers unsuccessfully tried to solve the problem by obtaining database manager source code and modifying it to run faster. A much better approach would have been to remove the database from the communications path and log messages on a deferred basis. Their mistake was that they did not think about their options and carefully examine them.

Business anecdote: Architecture can make or break an application

Chapter Summary

An architecture is the high-level plan or strategy for building an application. Many database applications have a straightforward architecture. The underlying database often has a rich and complex structure. Application logic (database queries and programming code) read from and write to the database. One or more user interfaces invoke application logic and display data.

There are several common architectures for database applications, which can be implemented with client-server technology. A two-tier architecture organizes an application into two layers. One layer focuses on the user interface and the other on data-management services. Application logic may be in either or both layers.

A three-tier architecture is more robust, because it separates application logic from data management and user interaction. A TP monitor is a specific kind of three-tier architecture. In essence, a TP monitor serves as a multiplexer that mediates the interaction of multiple users with multiple databases. Web applications use the Internet to connect clients to servers.

Beyond the choice of a basic architecture, other issues do arise. You can creatively resolve them by first thinking of candidate solutions and separately evaluating them.

✔ **State client-server queries precisely**. This way you avoid transmitting excess data.

✔ **Try to use a three (or more) tier architecture**. It provides a more robust architecture than two tiers.

✔ **Consider TP monitors**. These are helpful for applications with a high transaction volume, many users, or operations that span databases.

✔ **Consider the Internet**. The Internet is an option for connecting clients and servers.

✔ **Make deliberate architectural trade-offs**. Use a systematic approach to make important architectural decisions, and document your reasons.

Major recommendations for Chapter 3

Resource Notes

Some of the material in this chapter was taken from [Blaha-98]. [Bernstein-97] provides an excellent treatment of transaction-processing concepts and systems. [Orfali-96] is a very readable explanation of client-server and related technologies.

[Oliver-97] discusses systems engineering, which is a way to devise an architecture that can handle large, complex applications.

References

[Bernstein-97] Philip A. Bernstein and Eric Newcomer. *Principles of Transaction Processing*. San Francisco, California: Morgan Kaufmann, 1997.

[Blaha-90] MR Blaha, WJ Premerlani, AR Bender, RM Salemme, MM Kornfein, and CK Harkins. Bill-of-material configuration generation. *Sixth International Conference on Data Engineering*. February 5–9, 1990, Los Angeles, California, 237–244.

[Blaha-98] Michael Blaha and William Premerlani. *Object-Oriented Modeling and Design for Database Applications*. Upper Saddle River, New Jersey: Prentice Hall, 1998.

[Oliver-97] David W. Oliver, Timothy P. Kelliher, and James G. Keegan Jr. *Engineering Complex Systems*. New York, New York: McGraw-Hill, 1997.

[Orfali-96] Robert Orfali, Dan Harkey, and Jeri Edwards. *The Essential Client/Server Survival Guide, Second Edition*. New York, New York: Wiley, 1996.

4

Data Management Paradigms

Many applications have long-lived data and require a database. For other applications, files or groupware can provide an adequate and economical solution. All three data-management paradigms are used for operational and analytical applications.

Files

Applications can directly read from and write to sequential or random-access files.

- **Advantages**. Files are simple to use and have no purchase cost.
- **Disadvantages**. File complexity grows rapidly with the quantity and variety of data. Files have no intrinsic support for data-management features such as multiuser access, recovery from errors, transactions, and flexible queries. Large sequential files are inefficient for accessing small, random portions of data.

Figure 4.1 shows the kinds of data suitable for files.

- Data with high volume and low information density (such as archival files or historical records).
- Modest quantities of data with simple structure.
- Data that are accessed sequentially.
- Data that can be fully read into memory.

Figure 4.1 Data suitable for files. Files provide a low-tech solution to data management and should not be overlooked.

Consider files for a low-tech solution to data management.

One of my former clients had a severe business downturn. The client was desperate to cut costs; even the purchase of a $99 software package required managerial approval. The company was trying to reduce layoffs and preferred to develop software in-house, rather than purchase it, even if a purchase was much less expensive.

One cost the client was trying to forego was that of a DBMS. I suggested that the company either buy a DBMS or use files in a limited manner. Instead, the company tried to build its own DBMS. They finally scrapped the effort when the complexity and personnel demands became too much.

The moral is to use files simply and not waste time and money trying to replicate the functionality of a DBMS.

Business anecdote: Improper use of files

Groupware

Groupware is software that manages unstructured information for collaborating users. Groupware organizes data into documents that consist of items. Each item has an item name and one or more values.

The most prominent groupware product is Lotus Notes. Lotus Notes supports unstructured documents that can contain a variety of data types including voice, video, and multifont text. It stores related collections of documents in a file, which users can index and retrieve by document properties or by actual contents. A Notes application typically accesses many files. Developers relate information by creating hypertext links between documents in the same or different files.

■ **Advantages.** Developers need not define the groupware in advance, making it well suited for exploratory applications. It is also helpful for managing large and complex documents.

■ **Disadvantages.** Groupware incurs a substantial purchase cost. Because it is unstructured, it is prone to storing bad data. Groupware has limited support for data-management features such as multiuser access, recovery from errors, transactions, and flexible queries. There is only a de facto standard from a dominant product—Lotus Notes.

Figure 4.2 shows the kinds of data suitable for groupware.

> ■ Multimedia documents that must be shared.
>
> ■ Fluid data for which the structure is not known or understood.

Figure 4.2 Data suitable for groupware. Groupware provides a flexible approach, but is vulnerable to storing bad data.

 Be careful with groupware. It does not supplant rigorous data management.

Databases

A *__database__* is a permanent, self-descriptive store of data that is contained in one or more files. Self-description is what sets a database apart from ordinary files. A database contains the data structure, or *__schema__*—description of data—as well as the data. Unlike groupware, a database does not intersperse description with individual occurrences of data. Rather, many occurrences of data are stored against the same description. The premise of databases is that the data structure is expected to be relatively static, while the actual data may rapidly evolve.

A *__database manager__*, or *__database management system (DBMS__*) is the software for managing access to a database. Mature products that can handle large quantities of data are readily available.

■ **Advantages**. DBMSs provide general-purpose routines and protocols for managing large quantities of data and isolate applications from physical data-storage details. DBMSs facilitate sharing by multiple users and applications and can secure data against unauthorized access. They have sophisticated logic for protecting data against machine failures and errors. Finally, they support transactions and can ensure that a group of commands succeeds or fails as a single unit of work.

■ **Disadvantages**. DBMSs can incur a substantial purchase cost. Large databases require specially trained support staff to set policy, manage disc space, prepare backups, monitor performance, and deal with subtle problems that may arise. Databases are often complex to design.

Figure 4.3 shows the kinds of data suitable for databases.

- Data that require updates at fine levels of detail by multiple users.
- Data that must be accessed by multiple application programs.
- Data that require coordinated updates via transactions.
- Large quantities of data that must be handled efficiently.
- Data that are long-lived and highly valuable to an organization.
- Data that must be secured against unauthorized and malicious access.
- Data that are subject to sophisticated analysis for decision support.

Figure 4.3 Data suitable for databases. Databases provide heavyweight data management and are used for most important business applications.

 Favor databases for large collections of data.

Comparison of Paradigms

Table 4.1 compares data management paradigms.

Criterion	Files	Groupware	Databases
Purchase cost	None	Can be costly	Can be costly
Life-cycle cost	Variable	Variable	Variable
Data quality	Low	Low	High
Flexibility	High	High	Medium
Data management features	None	Low	High
Standards	None	None	Yes
Comment	Use for unimportant data or small amounts	Use for unstructured data	Use for most data-intensive applications

Table 4.1 Comparison of data management paradigms

Files have no purchase cost. Groupware and databases involve vendor software that can have a substantial purchase cost. The life-cycle cost is variable for all three paradigms and depends on purchase, development, deployment, and maintenance costs. Groupware and databases can increase development efficiencies for some applications.

Groupware combines description with each data occurrence. In contrast, a database defines description apart from data and stores many occurrences against the same structure; data must conform to the defined structure or it is not stored. Consequently, groupware is more flexible and less structured than a database, but groupware is more difficult to query and more vulnerable to data errors. Files have no built-in logic to assure data quality and also have high flexibility.

Databases offer many features for data management, including multiuser access, recovery from errors, security, transactions, and robust queries. Groupware has a lesser set of features namely multiuser access and simple queries.

There are several standards for databases, including the CODASYL standard for network databases and the SQL standard for relational databases. Chapters 5 and 6 discuss these standards

Hybrid Approaches

Occasionally, it is helpful to mix data-management approaches. For example, a graphics application might put detailed data in files and store just the file names in a database. A scientific application might put detailed, raw data in files and store only summary data in a database.

When I was at GE R&D, I studied product data managers (PDMs). A PDM manages mechanical parts and is often used in conjunction with computer aided design (CAD) software that draws parts. PDMs store the description of parts in a database—data such as the part number, weight, manufacturer, cost, and availability. At that time, PDMs stored the CAD picture data in individual files and embedded file names in the database. Past databases could not handle large data items, so this was an appropriate melding of files and databases.

Business anecdote: Combining files and databases

Chapter Summary

Developers can use three major data paradigms to manage data for applications: files, groupware, and databases.

Files are the simplest and most obvious approach. They have simple commands for reading and writing data and are occasionally sufficient.

Groupware builds on the basis of files and provides support for complex documents and unstructured applications. Groupware software has built-in functionality that speeds the development of document applications.

Databases provide rigorous data management and are used for most data-intensive applications. They provide many features including enforcement of data quality, multiuser access, recovery from errors, security, transactions, and robust queries.

✔ **Consider files**. Files provide a low-tech solution to data management and should not be overlooked.

✔ **Be careful with groupware**. Groupware is suitable for complex documents or applications whose structure is not known or well understood. However, groupware does not supplant rigorous data management.

✔ **Favor databases**. For large collections of data, use a DBMS to enforce quality and to manage the data cost effectively.

Major recommendations for Chapter 4

Resource Notes

Some of the material in this chapter was taken from [Blaha-98]. [NotesDesign-00] and Chapter 20 of [Orfali-96] have helpful information on groupware.

References

[Blaha-98] Michael Blaha and William Premerlani. *Object-Oriented Modeling and Design for Database Applications*. Upper Saddle River, New Jersey: Prentice Hall, 1998.

[NotesDesign-00] http://www.notesdesign.com.

[Orfali-96] Robert Orfali, Dan Harkey, and Jeri Edwards. *The Essential Client/Server Survival Guide, Second Edition*. New York, New York: John Wiley and Sons, 1996.

5

Database Paradigms

If your application stores data in a database, you must choose a database paradigm. The appropriate choices vary for operational and analytical applications.

Contemporary Database Paradigms

Most new applications use a relational database. Multidimensional databases are also important for some data warehouse applications.

Relational Databases

A ***relational database*** has data that are perceived as tables. Tables have a specific number of columns and an arbitrary number of rows, with a value stored at each row-column intersection. For example, in Figure 5.1 the *person* table has two columns and four rows. The basic features of relational DBMSs (RDBMSs) vary little from product to product. All RDBMSs support tables and implement a common core of SQL. Variations exist for data types, performance tuning, programming access, and system tables, although the SQL standard is gradually subsuming these areas. Chapter 6 discusses SQL in detail.

Figure 5.1 shows one possible design for stock ownership tables. The column names are listed at the top of each table and values in the rows underneath. Primary key columns are listed in bold font; the ***primary key*** is a minimal combination of columns that uniquely identifies each row in a table. Many designs are possible with relational databases. If you follow the guidelines in Part 3, you will have good designs.

Person table	
person ID	personName
1	Harry Eisenstat
2	William Bradford
3	Willis Hudlin
4	Bob Gibson

Company table	
company ID	company Name
1	IBM
2	Phillips
3	Sony

Ownership table		
person ID	**company ID**	stock Amount
1	1	100
1	2	200
2	3	512
3	1	350
3	3	300
4	3	400

Figure 5.1 A relational database. Relational databases provide a robust representation for data.

Relational databases are the dominant paradigm for new applications and have been used for most applications developed within the past decade. They are suitable for both operational and analytical applications.

Major commercial RDBMSs include Oracle, IBM's DB2, and Microsoft's SQL Server. Microsoft's Access is suitable for small-scale and non-critical use. For newly developed applications, you should use an RDBMS favored by your company. For purchased applications, most vendors offer a choice of several RDBMSs.

Because the core features of relational databases have been set by the SQL standard, a company should choose an RDBMS vendor according to pragmatic concerns.

- **Other applications**. You reduce administrative and license costs if you use the same vendor or a small number of vendors for your applications.

- **Market share**. Oracle, IBM, and Microsoft are major market players. The staying power of other vendors is less clear.

- **Price**. You may be able to negotiate a better price with one vendor than another.

RDBMS have various trade-offs.

- **Advantages**. The products are mature and reliable. They have a sound theoretical basis and much commonality as a result of the SQL standard. RDBMSs have features that facilitate changes to existing applications (see Chapter 6).

- **Disadvantages**. The notion of a table and the limited data types can be confining. RDBMSs combine awkwardly with programming languages. Occasionally, performance is too slow. (Although in practice, slow performance is usually a result of poor implementation, rather than an intrinsic RDBMS problem.) The

SQL standard is helpful, but it is easy to become dependent on vendor-specific features. RDBMSs are difficult to use as evidenced by the many errors I have found during reverse engineering. (See Chapter 19.)

Figure 5.2 characterizes the kinds of applications that should use an RDBMS.

- **Ordinary business applications**. Relational databases satisfy many business applications for which data naturally conform to the notion of tables.
- **Decision-support applications**. Relational databases also are a good fit for many applications that require a powerful query language.
- **Conservative applications**. Many developers prefer to use mature relational database technology with proven administration, error handling, and security features.

Figure 5.2 Relational database applications. Most modern data-intensive applications are built using relational databases.

 Choose relational databases for new applications unless there is a compelling reason to use another paradigm.

Multidimensional Databases

Two paradigms address analytical applications—relational and multidimensional databases. *__Multidimensional databases__* are organized about facts that relate to dimensions. (See Chapter 12.) A *__fact__* measures the performance of a business. Sample facts include sales, budget, profit, and inventory. A *__dimension__* specifies one of the bases for facts. Sample dimensions include date, product, customer, sales person, and store. Multidimensional DBMSs (MDBMSs) are specifically tailored for analytical applications.

The right side of Figure 5.3 shows a multidimensional database with a fact, sales, that depends on three dimensions—product (such as milk), store (such as Ballwin), and month. MDBMSs have operators for extracting subsets from large samples of data and operators for summarizing data and drilling down into detail. The left side of the figure shows relational database tables that could also be used to store the data.

■ **Advantages**. MDBMSs often run faster than RDBMSs for analytical applications. In particular, MDBMSs can quickly combine facts and dimensions.

product Name	store Name	month Name	sales Amount
milk	Wildwood	Jan	100
milk	Wildwood	Feb	90
milk	Wildwood	Mar	110
...	...	...	...
apples	Ballwin	Mar	25

	Jan	Feb	Mar
Wildwood	100	90	110
Chesterfield	150	160	180
Ballwin	80	85	85

Relational tables *Multidimensional cube*

Figure 5.3 A multidimensional database. Multidimensional databases are a viable option for analytical applications.

■ **Disadvantages**. There are no multidimensional database standards, and the products lack a theoretical basis. Because of their underlying design, MDBMSs don't scale up to large volumes of data. Multidimensional products vary widely in their capabilities and commands. Most firms already have an RDBMS. An MDBMS means they must support an additional platform.

Both relational and multidimensional databases are viable options for analytical applications. However, when performance is adequate, use a relational database.

New Database Paradigms

Object-oriented and object-relational databases are new database paradigms that are significant for specialty applications.

Object-Oriented Databases

Object-oriented databases are loosely based on concepts embodied in object-oriented (OO) programming languages. Commercial object-oriented DBMS (OO-DBMS) vendors include Versant, eXcelon (formerly Object Design), and Objectivity.

Figure 5.4 illustrates an OO database structure for the same stock ownership data shown in Figure 5.1. Relationships are represented with pointers.

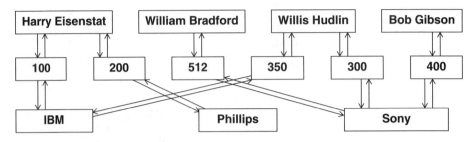

Figure 5.4 An object-oriented database. Object-oriented databases use pointers to maintain relationships.

OO-DBMSs are an option for operational applications, but they are poorly suited for analytical applications. It takes care and foresight to realize a three-tier architecture with an OO-DBMS. Low-level, highly reusable code should be placed with the OO-DBMS. Application code should be placed with the middle tier.

- **Advantages**. OO-DBMSs have been motivated by deficiencies in RDBMSs. OO-DBMSs can more quickly navigate data structures, support rich data types, and cleanly integrate with at least one programming language.

- **Disadvantages**. OO-DBMSs lack a theoretical basis and tend to have weak security. Many database operations must be programmed and cannot be expressed quickly using a query language. OO-DBMS query optimizers are inferior to those for RDBMSs. OO-DBMS products vary widely in their capabilities and commands. OO-DBMS vendors have small product sales and their financial stability is questionable.

Figure 5.5 characterizes the kinds of applications suitable for an OO-DBMS.

 Object-oriented databases are poorly suited for analytical applications. Use OO-DBMSs for operational applications only when an RDBMS lacks functionality or performance.

A vendor released a product built on an OO-DBMS. Later, this vendor ported the product to Oracle, an RDBMS, and was surprised when it ran ten times faster. The vendor, who was proficient with OO-DBMSs, had procured comparable expert assistance with Oracle.

The moral is that an OO-DBMS *may* run faster than an RDBMS. However, RDBMSs can be fast if used skillfully.

Business anecdote: An OO-DBMS is not necessarily faster

- **Engineering applications**. OO databases are a good fit for computer-aided design (CAD), computer-aided manufacturing (CAM), computer-integrated manufacturing (CIM), and computer-aided software engineering (CASE). These applications benefit from the rich data types and clean integration with programming languages.

- **Multimedia applications**. OO databases support complex graphics, audio, and video.

- **Knowledge bases**. Expert system rules are difficult to store in a relational database. When a rule is added, the entire rule base must be checked for inconsistencies and redundancies.

- **Applications with demanding distribution and multiuser-access requirements**. OO databases allow access to low-level services.

Figure 5.5 Object-oriented database applications. OO databases can be useful for niche applications that are ill served by relational databases.

Object-Relational Databases

The relational database vendors have noted the popularity of OO technology and are responding by adding OO features to their products. The combination is called an *object-relational database*. The OO features in the various products and the SQL standard are in a state of flux.

Some of the added OO features are worthwhile, use them carefully. Others are technically unsound and mar otherwise solid products. Chapter 6 explains further.

 Object-relational databases are a mixed benefit. Use with great care

Obsolete Database Paradigms

Database paradigms have evolved over the years. However, we still must consider old paradigms, because many legacy applications still use them.

Hierarchical Databases

A *hierarchical database* is organized as a collection of inverted trees of records (hence the term *hierarchy*). The inverted trees may be of arbitrary depth. The record at the top of the tree has zero or more child records; the child records, in turn, serve as parent records for their immediate descendants. The parent-child relationships continue down a tree. IBM's IMS is the most prominent hierarchical DBMS. It has been in use for several decades now and has accumulated many features. The market share of other hierarchical database products is fading.

Figure 5.6 shows two hierarchical databases with the stock ownership data. Harry Eisenstat owns 100 shares of IBM in both databases, for example. Both databases are two levels deep. The left side of the figure is organized about company records. The right side is organized about person records.

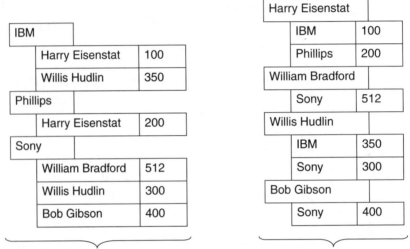

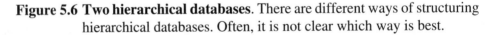

with Company as parent   *with Person as parent*

Figure 5.6 Two hierarchical databases. There are different ways of structuring hierarchical databases. Often, it is not clear which way is best.

Applications can navigate a hierarchy by starting at the top and successively navigating downward from parent to child until the desired record is found. Applications can interleave parent-child navigation with the traversal of pointers that may also be embedded in a record. Searching down a hierarchical tree is very fast, because parent and child records are in contiguous storage. Traversing pointers is only slightly slower. Other types of queries, in contrast, are slow and require sequential search.

Hierarchical DBMSs have weak languages for expressing queries and require programming code for most functionality. Consequently, they can be used only for operational applications, where you know the functionality in advance. Hierarchical DBMSs are not suitable for analytical applications, because they cannot readily express ad hoc queries.

- **Advantages**. IMS is fast, robust, and highly reliable.

- **Disadvantages**. IMS requires tedious design and programming. When data do not naturally occur as trees, which is true of most data, it is awkward to impose a parent and child. Pointers partially compensate for this forced dominance, but it is still difficult to devise a hierarchical structure for large models. Because of the arbitrary structure, hierarchical databases are difficult to maintain and extend.

 Hierarchical databases are obsolete. As a rule, avoid using them for new applications.

Network Databases

A ***network database*** is organized as a collection of records that are related with pointers. Network databases, which arose in response to the limitations of hierarchical databases, represent data in a symmetric manner. A network is more flexible than a hierarchy and still permits efficient navigation. Most network DBMSs adhere to the COmmittee for DAta SYstem Languages (CODASYL) standard. Do not confuse *network* databases with communication *networks*. These are different uses of the term "network."

Figure 5.7 shows a network database with the stock ownership data. The boxes denote records and the lines pointers. Note that while there are two possible hierarchical structures for stock ownership, there is a single network structure. In general, an application may have many possible designs for any database paradigm. However, network DBMSs provide a more flexible representation than hierarchical DBMSs, so network databases have fewer minor design differences.

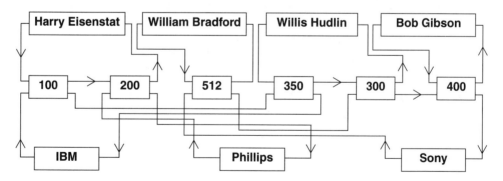

Figure 5.7 A network database. Network databases provide a natural representation for data, but the rigid structure complicates maintenance.

To find the stock owned by Harry Eisenstat, traverse the loop from the *Harry Eisenstat* record. He owns 100 shares of one stock and 200 shares of another. Traversing the loop from the *100* record (to *350* and then to *IBM*), we find that he owns 100 shares of IBM. Similarly, he owns 200 shares of Phillips.

Network DBMSs have weak query languages and require programming code for most functionality. Consequently they can be used for operational applications, but not for analytical applications.

- ■ **Advantages**. Network DBMS products are readily available. The products are efficient and typically observe the CODASYL standard.

- ■ **Disadvantages**. Rigidity is the main problem. Application code is directly tied to pointer chains. If developers change the network structure, they must revise all the affected application code. This makes network databases difficult to maintain and extend.

 Network databases are obsolete. As a rule, avoid using them for new applications.

In a consulting assignment, I encountered a financial application built on a network database. At first, I was appalled and wondered why the company had not converted to a relational database. However, I began to understand their situation as I learned more.

The application had a simple structure that had been stable for many years; the company just needed to keep it running. The volume of data was growing rapidly and the firm was hard pressed to process data within the allotted time. The network DBMS had been around a while, and the staff were adept at using its features. From the company's perspective, a relational database would only have introduced the risk of not processing data fast enough.

In this situation, it was perfectly acceptable to continue using a network database.

Business anecdote: When it's okay to use old database technology

Comparison of Database Paradigms

When performance is adequate, use a relational database rather than a multidimensional one. Relational databases have a standard. The products are robust and mature.

Use an OO-DBMS only when a relational database won't deliver the performance or features required for an application. Some people mistakenly believe they should use an OO-DBMS whenever they use an OO programming language. Relational databases work well with both conventional programming languages (such as Cobol, C, and Ada) and OO programming languages (such as Java and C++). OO-DBMSs vary widely in their commands and capabilities, so carefully evaluate a product before you commit to one. Also, the future viability of OO-DBMSs is questionable.

Do not use hierarchical and network DBMSs for new applications. Consider converting an existing application to a relational database when any of the following conditions applies.

■ **Performance is not an issue**. The application does not have strenuous performance demands. It takes time to wring out performance when shifting to another DBMS.

■ **Flexibility is needed**. The database structure may gradually change over time.

■ **Administration is too costly**. Few applications use the old DBMS, and it has become a maintenance burden.

Both OO and network databases represent relationships with pointers, but they differ in significant ways. A programmer accesses data from a network database by invoking special commands that traverse chains of pointers. In contrast, a programmer for an OO database writes ordinary programming code and the OO-DBMS automatically accesses the proper data.

Be careful with object-relational databases. Some features are sound, but have subtle trade-offs. Other features are ill considered and it is a shame they are in the products and the current SQL standard. The issues are complex, as Chapter 6 explains.

Table 5.1 summarizes the recommendations for the different kinds of DBMSs.

    Limit your applications to a few DBMSs. With many different DBMSs, it is difficult to exchange data and costly to administrate databases. You also lose purchasing leverage.

Hybrid Approaches

Sometimes it is helpful to use multiple DBMS paradigms within the same application. For example, an application might use an RDBMS as its primary data store, but use an OO-DBMS for a complex subsystem for which an RDBMS is too slow.

Database paradigm	Recommendation
Relational	The default choice. Use this for new applications, unless there is a compelling reason to use another paradigm.
Multidimensional	A viable option for analytical applications. Use when an RDBMS does not deliver adequate performance.
Object-oriented	Use for operational applications only when an RDBMS lacks functionality or performance.
Object-relational	They are a mixed benefit. Use with great care. (See Chapter 6.)
Hierarchical	Normally avoid these for new applications. Convert existing applications when there is a specific need.
Network	

Table 5.1 Summary of recommendations for database paradigms

Chapter Summary

There are several choices for a database paradigm.

Relational databases are the dominant paradigm for database management. The products are robust, fast, and theoretically sound. The only significant downside of relational databases is that they can be difficult to use, as Chapter 6 will explain. Multidimensional databases also are an option for analytical applications.

Object-oriented databases are occasionally helpful for niche applications that are poorly served by relational databases. Use the object-relational database paradigm carefully.

A hierarchical database is a collection of inverted trees of records. A network database is a collection of records that are related with pointers. Both paradigms are obsolete, and you should normally avoid them for new applications. You should gradually convert these applications to relational databases as the opportunity arises.

> ✔ **Limit the number of DBMSs**. Limit your applications to a few DBMSs. With many different DBMSs, it is difficult to exchange data and costly to administrate databases. You also lose purchasing leverage.

Major recommendations for Chapter 5

Resource Notes

Some of the material in this chapter is taken from [Blaha-98]. [Elmasri-00] has further detail on the various kinds of databases. [Chaudhri-98] describes industrial use of object-oriented databases.

References

[Blaha-98] Michael Blaha and William Premerlani. *Object-Oriented Modeling and Design for Database Applications.* Upper Saddle River, New Jersey: Prentice Hall, 1998.

[Chaudhri-98] Akmal B. Chaudhri and Mary Loomis. *Object Databases in Practice.* Upper Saddle River, New Jersey: Prentice Hall PTR, 1998.

[Elmasri-00] Ramez Elmasri and Shamkant B. Navathe. *Fundamentals of Database Systems, Third Edition.* Redwood City, California: Benjamin/Cummings, 2000.

6

Relational Databases

Because most new database applications use the relational paradigm, this chapter is devoted to relational database concepts and their use.

Overview

A relational database management system (RDBMS) has three major aspects. (See Chapter 5 for background on RDBMSs.)

- **Data that are presented as tables**. Tables have a specific number of columns and an arbitrary number of rows, with a value stored at each row-column intersection. RDBMSs use various devices to speed access, because literal tables are much too slow for practical needs. These tuning devices are usually transparent and not visible in the commands for reading and writing to tables.

- **Operators for manipulating tables**. SQL [Melton-93] is the standard language for accessing data. SQL commands operate on entire tables, as opposed to operating on individual rows. All data manipulation commands accept tables as input and yield a table as output. SQL commands can be used interactively, as well as within a program.

- **Constraints on tables**. An RDBMS refuses to store data that violate its constraints, returning an error to the user or requesting program. Constraints are enforced via the database structure.

The next three sections explain basic SQL commands for data definition, data manipulation, and data control. Then the last section revisits object-relational DBMSs, which Chapter 5 introduced.

Defining Database Structure

This section covers the most common SQL commands for defining a database's structure, or ***schema***.

Tables

The SQL commands in Figure 6.1 create empty tables. Even though the standard addresses them, data types vary widely across RDBMSs. Typical data types include number, character string, and date/time. This book uses Oracle examples. The upper-or-lower case distinction in the figure is unimportant to an RDBMS. I use all uppercase to highlight keywords.

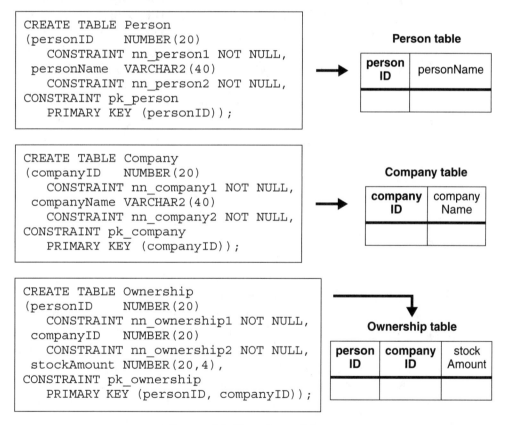

```
CREATE TABLE Person
(personID     NUMBER(20)
    CONSTRAINT nn_person1 NOT NULL,
 personName  VARCHAR2(40)
    CONSTRAINT nn_person2 NOT NULL,
CONSTRAINT pk_person
    PRIMARY KEY (personID));
```

Person table

person ID	personName

```
CREATE TABLE Company
(companyID    NUMBER(20)
    CONSTRAINT nn_company1 NOT NULL,
 companyName VARCHAR2(40)
    CONSTRAINT nn_company2 NOT NULL,
CONSTRAINT pk_company
    PRIMARY KEY (companyID));
```

Company table

company ID	company Name

```
CREATE TABLE Ownership
(personID     NUMBER(20)
    CONSTRAINT nn_ownership1 NOT NULL,
 companyID    NUMBER(20)
    CONSTRAINT nn_ownership2 NOT NULL,
 stockAmount NUMBER(20,4),
CONSTRAINT pk_ownership
    PRIMARY KEY (personID, companyID));
```

Ownership table

person ID	company ID	stock Amount

Figure 6.1 Creating tables

The *person* table has two columns, *personID* and *personName*. *PersonID* is a number used to identify persons and has a maximum length of 20 digits. *Person-*

Name is the name of a person and is a string with a maximum length of 40 characters. (*Varchar2* is the Oracle name for a character string.)

Neither *personID* nor *personName* can be null. **_Null_** means that a value is unknown or not applicable. The values for these columns must be filled in; that is, every person must be assigned a *personID* and *personName*. The not-null constraints are named *nn_person1* and *nn_person2*; the names are arbitrary as far as SQL is concerned, but as you can see, I favor stylistic names.

PersonID is the primary key of the *person* table—the minimal combination of columns that is unique and preferentially used to access each row. *PK_person* is the name of the primary key constraint.

Similarly, the *company* table has two columns, *companyID* and *companyName*. The *ownership* table has three columns, *personID*, *companyID*, and *stockAmount*. *StockAmount* is a fixed-point number with 4 fractional digits and 16 integral digits (20 digits total minus the 4 fractional digits). Note that *stockAmount* may be null; a person may own a stock and the amount may be unknown. The *ownership* table has a two-part primary key; both the person and the company must be specified to find an occurrence of ownership. Additional details may be specified in the *create table* command.

As you might expect, SQL can also destroy tables. Figure 6.2 shows the *drop table* command. This command destroys the table definition, any dependent definitions, and any data in the table.

```
DROP TABLE Ownership;
```

Figure 6.2 Dropping a table

Keys

Keys establish the identity of rows and connect tables to each other.

A **_candidate key_** is a combination of columns that uniquely identifies each row in a table. The combination must be minimal and not include any columns that are not needed for unique identification. No column in a candidate key can be null.

A **_primary key_** is a candidate key that is preferentially used to access the records in a table. A table can have at most one primary key; normally each table should have a primary key. A primary key can be an arbitrary number or a combination of columns with intrinsic meaning.

Figure 6.1 has three candidate keys, all of which are primary keys. The *person* table has a primary key of *personID*. The *company* table has a primary key of *companyID*. And the *ownership* table has a two-column primary key of *personID* and *companyID*.

A *foreign key* is a reference to a candidate key and is the glue that binds tables. A foreign key must have a value for all columns in a candidate key or it must be wholly null. The *ownership* table in Figure 6.1 has two foreign keys—*personID* refers to the *person* table and *companyID* refers to the *company* table.

Each foreign key should refer only to a table's primary key (and not some other candidate key). There are no disadvantages and several advantages to doing this. Multiple referents complicate the database structure, and it is good style to have consistency in an implementation. Searching and comparisons are also more difficult if there are multiple access routes to a record.

Figure 6.3 defines foreign keys for the *ownership* table. Given such definitions, an RDBMS keeps a foreign key consistent with its referent. For example, a user would not be allowed to enter an *ownership* record with a *personID* of 5, because that value is not found in the *person* table. (See Figure 5.1 on page 37.) Unfortunately, few developers understand foreign keys and, consequently, do not define them in applications. Frequently, this results in databases with inconsistent data and dangling references to data. Moreover, if foreign keys are not used, more programming is required.

```
ALTER TABLE Ownership ADD CONSTRAINT fk_ownership1
FOREIGN KEY (personID) REFERENCES Person;

ALTER TABLE Ownership ADD CONSTRAINT fk_ownership2
FOREIGN KEY (companyID) REFERENCES Company;
```

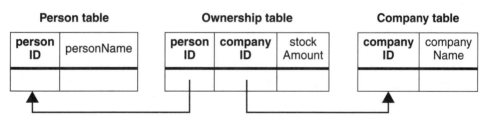

Figure 6.3 Creating foreign keys

The *alter table* command can add a specification to an existing table that may contain data. All existing data are checked against the new constraint; if the data do not satisfy the constraint, an RDBMS would refuse to add the constraint.

Define foreign keys in your applications. Each foreign key should refer to a primary key.

Sequences

Most RDBMSs (including Oracle) can generate sequences of integers. These are useful for arbitrary numbers that serve as primary keys (such as *personID* and *companyID*). Figure 6.4 defines sequences, and the section entitled "Inserting Data" later in this chapter generates values with them.

```
CREATE SEQUENCE personSequence;
CREATE SEQUENCE companySequence;
```

Figure 6.4 Creating sequences

Business Rules

Business rules are statements of business logic and often can be expressed in a database with SQL constraints. SQL constraints are an alternative to tedious programming code. Constraints are *declarative*—expressed as a statement, rather than as a series of programming steps. Furthermore, database constraints are more readable and visible than logic that is buried in programming code. A further benefit of constraints is that they are enforced across all applications that may access the database. In contrast, programming code may need to be repeated for the various applications and requires more maintenance effort.

Business rules are especially important for operational applications, where data must be updated frequently. Business rules are less important for analytical applications, because most updates are from periodic feeds that can be monitored and controlled.

Figure 6.1 illustrates two kinds of SQL constraints—the *not-null* and *primary-key* clauses. SQL also has constraints for candidate keys (not shown) and foreign keys (see Figure 6.3) as well as general constraints (see Figure 6.5). The amount of stock owned cannot be zero—otherwise, there is no need for an ownership record. I named the constraint *generalConstraint_ownership1*.

```
ALTER TABLE Ownership
ADD CONSTRAINT generalConstraint_ownership1
CHECK (stockAmount <> 0);
```

Figure 6.5 Adding a general constraint

 Use database constraints when possible, rather than writing programming code.

System Tables

RDBMSs have special system tables that contain the names and columns of tables, the data types of columns, who created the tables, and other information.

Users may read from, but not directly write to, system tables. An RDBMS updates the data in system tables as a side effect of commands. For example, if a user creates a new table, the table name is added to the system table that lists all tables.

Performance Tuning

Indexes provide the primary means for tuning a relational database. A database index is like a book index. An index consists of a list of items with subitems (and possibly finer subsubitems) that point to specific records in a table. Indexes are especially important for large tables with many records.

As Figure 6.6 shows, an index on *companyName* can directly find the *Sony* record, rather than search the *company* table one record at a time. The RDBMS starts with the first level of the index, finding the bracket (*R&B Falc–ZweigTl*) that includes *Sony*. It follows the reference to level 2, where it finds a smaller bracket (*R&B Falc–Systemax*) and then to level 3, which ultimately points to the *Sony* record. The example shows an index with three levels, but in general, an index can have any number of levels.

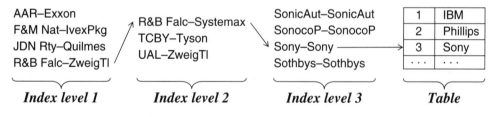

| Index level 1 | Index level 2 | Index level 3 | Table |

Figure 6.6 Searching via an index. Indexes greatly speed some queries. Index levels usually have more records than shown here.

Indexes let you not only find specific records quickly, but also enable rapid combination of tables. For example, a user might want to retrieve *personName*, *companyName*, and *stockAmount* by combining the *ownership*, *person*, and *company* tables—for each *ownership* record find the *personName* for the *personID* and the *companyName* for the *companyID*. (See the section entitled "Reading Data.")

Normally, designers should index every primary and candidate key. In fact, most RDBMSs create indexes automatically as a side effect of primary key and candidate key constraints. They should also index each foreign key not subsumed by a primary key or candidate key constraint.

Make sure every primary, candidate, and foreign key has an index.

In Figure 6.1, the *personID* foreign key of the *ownership* table is subsumed by the primary key (*personID* + *companyID*). In contrast the *companyID* foreign key is not subsumed, so an index should be defined on it. (See Figure 6.7.)

```
CREATE INDEX index_ownership1 ON Ownership (companyID);
```

Figure 6.7 Creating an index

To clarify the idea of subsumption, consider a phone book. The phone book has a three-part primary key—last name, first name, and address. Because the phone book is ordered primarily by last name, there is little benefit to having an index on last name. In contrast, first names are jumbled throughout. If someone wanted to search for phone numbers using first name alone, an index on first name would be helpful.

Once an application is running, the database administrator (DBA) can determine if it needs additional indexes and consider product-specific tuning mechanisms. Indexes consume disc space and slow some updates by about 20 percent, so they should not be added frivolously.

Some authors advise that developers defer indexes until the application is complete. This is not a good idea. If the keys are not indexed, combinations of tables will be slow—by as much as several orders of magnitude. Such sluggish performance will only confuse users. Instead developers should deliver all databases—even initial databases—with indexes on keys, so that they can see how fast the application will run and find any performance problems. It is easy to add these indexes from the start.

 Do not wait until an application is complete to create indexes on keys. Build them into an application from the start.

Views

A __view__ is a table that the RDBMS dynamically computes from a query stored in the database. A view does not physically exist, but is computed as needed. Views can be read as if they were an ordinary table. Some RDBMSs permit certain updates to views by automatically writing to the base tables. Views are often helpful for simplifying access to a database.

Views can sometimes make it easier to change a database. You can restructure the database tables and define views to accommodate applications that are based on the old structure.

Storage Space

I've found that most databases require about triple the storage space of the actual data to accommodate the system tables, indexes, page and record headers, logging, and room for future growth.

Manipulating Data

Users and applications manipulate the data in a relational database. SQL commands read, insert, delete, and update data. SQL is largely a nonprocedural language. An SQL command specifies properties of desired data, rather than how to access the data, which the RDBMS automatically determines.

Reading Data

The SQL *select* command reads data. Figure 6.8 finds the records with the specified values of *personID* and *companyID* and returns the values of *stockAmount* for these records. Since *personID* + *companyID* is the primary key and uniquely distinguishes the records, a single value of *stockAmount* is returned.

```
SELECT stockAmount
FROM Ownership
WHERE personID = 4 AND companyID = 3;
```

Figure 6.8 A simple *select* command

PersonID and *companyID* are artificial numbers with no intrinsic meaning, so a better query retrieves the amount for each *personName* and *companyName*. (See Figure 6.9.) The tables have artificial numbers, because it is a convenient way to design tables. (See Chapter 11.)

The query in Figure 6.9 joins the *ownership* table to the *person* and *company* tables. A *__join__* combines data from two tables on the basis of a comparison of values, in this case the equality of values. The query joins *personID* in *ownership* to *personID* in *person*. Similarly, the query joins *companyID* in *ownership* to *companyID* in *company*. The joins are efficient, because the joined columns all have indexes. Most joins combine foreign keys with primary keys—which is why I recommend indexing all primary and foreign keys.

```
SELECT personName, companyName, stockAmount
FROM Ownership, Person, Company
WHERE Ownership.personID = Person.personID AND
      Ownership.companyID = Company.companyID;
```

Figure 6.9 A *select* command that combines three tables

SQL queries do not directly invoke indexes. Rather RDBMSs have an optimizer that analyzes queries and automatically uses indexes when they are helpful.

Most SQL commands operate on entire tables, rather than individual rows. SQL also has a row-at-a-time interface for use with application programs. RDBMSs can deal with entire tables, but most programming languages cannot. SQL is not a complete language and so is often combined with a programming language. For example, it lacks iteration and has limited ability to test conditions.

SQL has additional notation for manipulating data. For example, data can be ordered and summarized in various ways. Set operations are available, such as table intersection, union, and subtraction. Nested queries can check certain conditions and ensure that there are no exceptions. These commands are beyond the scope of this book.

> A number of years ago, a colleague was able to receive New York Stock Exchange trades in real time and store them in a relational database. Today, the products are better and run faster.
>
> Another example is the bill-of-material (BOM) generator that we built at GE R&D [Blaha-90]. This application had 900 tables and several hundred queries with 20-way joins; the application had to find the many kinds of parts that composed a mechanical assembly. Each query with 20-way joins took no more than a few seconds to run.

Business anecdotes: Relational databases can be fast

Data Independence

A major objective of SQL is to provide ***data independence***. A person specifies the data that are desired and the RDBMS determines how to get them. This allows database administrators to tune performance more readily without disrupting application code.

With SQL, this goal is largely, but not fully, realized. The performance of a query can depend on how it is phrased, even though alternative phrasings may yield the same answer. Developers must consider performance tuning and likely optimization results when phrasing a query [Shasha-92].

Inserting Data

Figure 6.10 inserts several records into an empty database. The Oracle *nextVal* function increments a sequence and then returns the value. The *currVal* function returns the current value of the sequence.

```
INSERT INTO person (personID, personName)
VALUES (personSequence.nextVal, 'Harry Eisenstat');

INSERT INTO company (companyID, companyName)
VALUES (companySequence.nextVal, 'IBM');

INSERT INTO ownership (personID, companyID, stockAmount)
VALUES (personSequence.currVal, companySequence.currVal,
        100);
```

Person table

person ID	personName
1	Harry Eisenstat

Company table

company ID	company Name
1	IBM

Ownership table

person ID	company ID	stock Amount
1	1	100

Figure 6.10 Inserting data

Updating Data

Figure 6.11 reduces Bob Gibson's ownership of Sony from 400 shares to 200 shares. (See Figure 5.1 on page 37.)

```
UPDATE ownership SET stockAmount = 200
WHERE personID = 4 AND companyID = 3;
```

Figure 6.11 Updating data

Deleting Data

Figure 6.12 shows a command for deleting data. If Bob Gibson sold his Sony stock, the *ownership* record would be deleted.

```
DELETE FROM ownership WHERE personID = 4 AND companyID = 3;
```

Figure 6.12 Deleting data

Controlling Access

The third major aspect of SQL is controlling access to data. SQL has commands for authorizing users and granting and revoking privileges for accessing tables and views. Views are important in providing flexible data control. For example, a designer may define a view for employees that suppresses salaries. Authorized persons could then see the base table with salary information; others would see the employees but not their salaries.

Object-Relational Databases

Many RDBMSs have object-oriented (OO) features that are intended to increase their power and ease of use. These extensions are known as object-relational DBMSs (OR-DBMSs). They do not replace OO-DBMSs, because OR-DBMSs lack the functionality and programming simplicity of an OO-DBMS. The OO features of Oracle 8 are representative of recent OR-DBMSs.

- **Abstract data types (ADTs).** Conventional RDBMSs have limited data types, supporting numbers, strings, dates, and little else. ADTs let a database store any type of data, such as geographic coordinates, pictures, and audio clips. An ADT may also have operations bundled with it. For example, an audio clip may have an operation to go to a specified location. The vendors have given ADTs various names, such as Oracle cartridges and Informix data blades.

  On the downside, ADTs tie you to a vendor, because their details are beyond the SQL standard. Use ADTs only when their benefit is compelling.

- **Varying arrays.** Conventional RDBMSs limit the row-column intersection to a single value. With this extension, an RDBMS can store multiple values—an array of values of the same data type—at a row-column intersection.

  The disadvantage is again that you risk going beyond the SQL standard and becoming dependent on a vendor. Moreover, some RDBMS commands cannot access the data in an array. For example, a join cannot access an element in an array. Consider varying arrays only when you do not need to combine elements with other tables.

- **Nested tables**. A varying table extends an RDBMS by allowing it to store multiple values at a row-column intersection. The nested tables extension goes even further by allowing the row-column intersection to store an entire table. It has the same disadvantages as the varying arrays option, however, so use them only sparingly.

- **Binary large objects (BLOBs)**. The early RDBMSs limited values to a small size—typically 2,000 or 4,000 bytes. The BLOB feature lets a value of almost any size be stored.

  There are performance and functionality implications of using BLOBs. For example, you cannot index BLOB columns and you must use special functions to access part of a BLOB value. Occasionally, it is reasonable to use BLOBs when values are very large.

- **References**. Oracle 8 adds the notion of a pointer as a data type (*REF* data type). As an alternative to a foreign key reference, Oracle can store a pointer to a record. The intent is to support fast combinations of data and object orientation.

  It is an awful idea to add pointers to SQL. SQL pointers are theoretically unsound, add complexity, and do not add power [Date-98b]. I would not expect references to improve performance much beyond that of a skillful design. I strongly recommend that you completely avoid SQL references. Instead, just use foreign keys.

- **Object views**. Object views provide a layer that hides the relational database and makes it appear more like an OO-DBMS. You can superimpose object views on ordinary tables.

  Layers are a viable technology, as Chapter 7 explains. However, object views contravene the three-tier architecture. They place functionality in the data-management tier. Also, object views lock you into the particular programming language of a database vendor.

Thus, OR-DBMSs are a mixed benefit. They contain useful features (ADTs and BLOBs), as well as awful features (references). RDBMS vendors have a reasonable desire to incorporate OO features in their products. It is ironic that they have missed two important OO extensions. (See Chapter 22.)

Chapter Summary

This chapter gives a flavor of SQL. SQL has three kinds of commands: data definition, data manipulation, and data control. The data definition commands define database structures such as tables, business rules, and performance tuning. The data manipulation commands read, insert, delete, and update the actual data stored in the tables. The data control commands limit access to data. SQL strives to be a nonprocedural language; to a large extent, an SQL command describes the desired data, rather than the internal mechanisms by which it is retrieved.

An object-relational DBMS attempts to add object-oriented features to the infrastructure of a relational DBMS. This is a worthy goal. Unfortunately, the current object-oriented extensions add some questionable features to an otherwise sound relational DBMS core. Only some of the object-oriented extensions are worth using.

✔ **Enforce foreign keys**. Define foreign keys in your applications. Each foreign key should refer to a primary key.

✔ **Use database constraints**. Use database constraints when possible, rather than writing programming code.

✔ **Routinely tune databases**. Ensure that every primary, candidate, and foreign key has an index. Build these indexes into an application from the start.

✔ **Be careful with SQL extensions**. Be careful with the object-oriented extensions to SQL. Some extensions are unsound. Others make you more dependent on a vendor.

Major recommendations for Chapter 6

Resource Notes

[Melton-93] explains the SQL standard. [Koch-97] thoroughly describes the features of Oracle 8.

[Celko-95] is an excellent book for advanced SQL techniques. Few managers would want to read this book, but your staff should be aware of it. Similarly, [Shasha-92] has advanced techniques for tuning a relational database.

[Date-98a] is a thoughtful book about combining relational databases and object-oriented technology. It articulates a vision for how RDBMS products should evolve. In contrast, this book aims to help managers use the existing RDBMS products and applications that are available today.

References

[Blaha-90] MR Blaha, WJ Premerlani, AR Bender, RM Salemme, MM Kornfein, and CK Harkins. Bill-of-material configuration generation. *Sixth International Conference on Data Engineering*. February 5–9, 1990, Los Angeles, California, 237–244.

[Celko-95] Joe Celko. *SQL for Smarties: Advanced SQL Programming*. San Francisco, California: Morgan Kaufmann, 1995.

[Date-98a] CJ Date and Hugh Darwen. *Foundation for Object/Relational Databases: The Third Manifesto*. Reading, Massachusetts: Addison-Wesley, 1998.

[Date-98b] CJ Date. Don't mix pointers and relations. *Third Annual Object/Relational Summit*. Washington DC, September 1998.

[Koch-97] George Koch and Kevin Loney. *Oracle 8: The Complete Reference*. Berkeley, California: Osborne McGraw-Hill, 1997.

[Melton-93] Jim Melton and Alan R. Simon. *Understanding the New SQL: A Complete Guide*. San Francisco, California: Morgan Kaufmann, 1993.

[Shasha-92] Dennis E. Shasha. *Database Tuning: A Principled Approach*. Upper Saddle River, New Jersey: Prentice Hall, 1992.

7

Data Processing

This chapter discusses common data-processing issues that arise for operational and analytical applications. The chapter is intended mostly for in-house and outsourced development. The section on converting legacy data is also relevant for purchased applications. The emphasis is on relational databases.

Combining Databases with Programming

Relational databases and conventional programming languages have divergent styles that make them difficult to combine. Relational databases are declarative; developers describe the data they want instead of how to get it. In contrast, most programming languages require that logic be reduced to a sequence of steps.

Many techniques are available for combining databases and programming languages. Too often I see practitioners blunder into the first technique that comes to mind. It is important to consider all the options.

Preprocessor and Postprocessor

Preprocessors and postprocessors are often helpful for batch applications (Figure 7.1). The basic idea is simple: Query the database and create an input file, run the application, and then analyze the output and store the results in the database.

However, database interaction via intermediate files can be awkward. The preprocessor must request all database information before executing the application, and output files with complex formats can be difficult to process. This technique is useful for old software or certified software that cannot be altered.

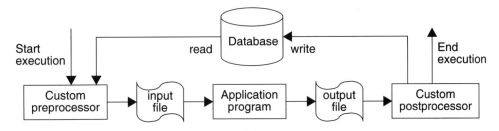

Figure 7.1 Preprocessor and postprocessor. Consider this option for old batch software or certified software that cannot be altered.

Script Files

Sometimes all you need is a file of DBMS commands (Figure 7.2). For example, typing *@filename* into interactive SQL (SQL Plus) of the Oracle DBMS causes the commands in *filename* to execute. Developers can use an operating system shell language to execute multiple script files and to control their execution.

Script files are helpful for simple database interaction, such as creating database structures. They are also useful for prototyping.

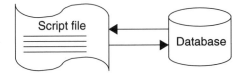

Figure 7.2 Script files. Consider this option for simple database interaction and prototyping.

Embedded DBMS Commands

Another technique is to intersperse SQL commands with application code (Figure 7.3).

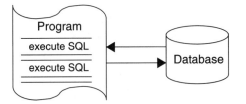

Figure 7.3 Embedded DBMS commands. Use this option only when necessary, because it is difficult to maintain.

Some languages, such as Cobol, require that you embed SQL code in application programs. Unfortunately, such programs can be difficult to read and maintain. The essential problem is that the conceptual basis for an RDBMS is different than that for most programming languages.

Custom Application Programming Interface

A better alternative to embedded DBMS commands is to encapsulate database read and write requests within dedicated procedures that collectively provide an interface to the database (Figure 7.4).

A custom application programming interface (API) isolates database access from the rest of the application. An API can help you partition the tasks of data management, application logic, and user interface according to a three-tier architecture. (See Chapter 3.)

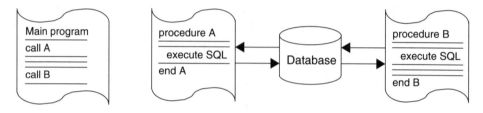

Figure 7.4 Custom application interface. This technique isolates database access from the rest of the application.

Stored Procedures

A *stored procedure* is programming code that is stored in a database (Figure 7.5).

Some RDBMSs require stored procedures for maximum efficiency. Stored procedures also let applications share general functionality. On the downside, they can put application logic in the database and compromise a three-tier architecture. They also vary widely across products. Developers should use stored procedures with care.

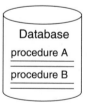

Figure 7.5 Stored procedures. Be careful with stored procedures, because they can compromise a three-tier architecture.

Fourth Generation Language

A *fourth-generation language (4GL)* is a framework for straightforward database applications that provides screen layout, simple calculations, and reports (Figure 7.6).

4GLs are widely available and can greatly reduce application development time. They are best for straightforward applications and are not suitable for applications with complex programming.

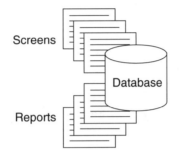

Figure 7.6 Fourth-Generation language (4GL). Consider this option for straightforward applications.

Generic Layer

A generic layer hides the DBMS and provides simple data access commands (such as *getRecordGivenKey* and *writeRecord*) [Blaha-98]. Developers can write application code in terms of the layer and largely ignore the underlying DBMS (Figure 7.7).

A well-conceived generic layer can simplify application programming. However, it can also impede performance and restrict access to database functionality.

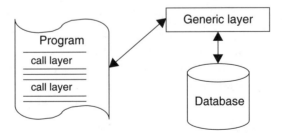

Figure 7.7 Generic layer. Consider this option when performance is not demanding and simple database functionality is needed.

Metadata-Driven System

The application indirectly accesses data by first accessing the data's description (the metadata) and then formulating the query to access the data (Figure 7.8) [Blaha-98]. For example, an RDBMS processes commands by accessing the system tables first and then the actual data.

Metadata-driven applications can be quite complex. This technique is suitable for applications that learn and other specialized situations.

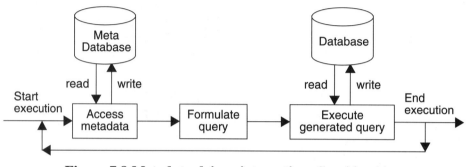

Figure 7.8 Metadata-driven interaction. Consider this option for advanced applications.

Combining Options

Sometimes it is helpful to mix techniques. For example, a developer could use a 4GL and implement some functionality with stored procedures. Table 7.1 summarizes the techniques for combining databases and programming languages.

> Here is a sad story. A company had outsourced development of an application for a new customer service. The application came back and was found to run much more slowly than needed. It could not keep up with the volume of calls and threatened to become a business disaster.
>
> A colleague inspected the software and found the problem—the vendor had improperly coupled programming code to SQL. Each SQL command retrieved an entire table. Programming code then checked the records, one at a time, until the desired record was found. The heavy communications traffic and automatic access locks on entire tables caused the poor performance. When he rewrote the SQL code to include *where* clauses to filter the data, performance increased by several orders of magnitude.

Business anecdote: It matters how you couple programming code to a database

Data interaction technique	Recommendation
Preprocessor and postprocessor	Consider for old batch software or certified software that cannot be altered.
Script files	Consider for simple database interaction and prototyping.
Embedded DBMS commands	Use only when necessary. An API provides a better approach.
Custom API	Often a good choice.
Stored procedures	Use them for general-purpose logic. Place application logic in a separate middle tier whenever possible.
4GL	Consider for straightforward applications.
Generic layer	Consider when performance is not demanding and simple database functionality is needed.
Metadata driven	Consider for specialized situations.

Table 7.1 Data interaction techniques. Consider all your options for combining databases and programming languages.

Trading Programming for Database Code

It is important to properly balance the roles of the DBMS and the programming language. Some programmers regard a DBMS as just a low-level store-and-retrieve mechanism analogous to files, and end up writing programming code for all their logic. This is short sighted. Logic can often be off-loaded to RDBMS queries, improving performance, increasing extensibility, reducing development time, and decreasing bugs. The improved performance of queries is due to reduced communication traffic and robust RDBMS algorithms.

Data Security

Security concerns the physical and logical protection of data.

Physical protection mitigates the effects of media failure and hardware and software crashes. DBMSs protect against media failure with backup copies of the database and logs of interim activity. Transactions guard against hardware and software

We successfully completed the bill-of-material (BOM) application mentioned in the previous chapter and deployed it for production use. We then found that we needed an additional output for coupling it to another application. Our application was a BOM generator and GE had other software for managing BOMs on the shop floor. We needed to generate a BOM hierarchy in depth-first order.

Our first inclination was to write programming code to generate the desired format. But programming code would entail lots of pointer traversals, take 1-2 months of tedious work, and be error prone. Instead I devised a database query to generate the output. The query took about 2 days to write, was self documenting, was straightforward to test, and ran plenty fast for our needs.

Business anecdote: Off-loading functionality to database queries

crashes. DBMSs guarantee that database files will reflect only transactions that have successfully completed.

Logical protection helps an organization control who can read and write various kinds of data. Organizations must guard against password compromises, penetrations of communications networks, and personnel turnover. Users should be able to access only the data for which they are authorized. Most DBMSs maintain audit trails so that database administrators can reconstruct past database activity.

Views are also helpful for controlling access to data. (See Chapter 6.) For example, a designer may define a view for employees that suppresses salaries.

It is often helpful to define privileges for categories of users. For example, an organization may define privileges for a clerk, a salesperson, a manager, a secretary, and a database administrator. As new users are authorized, they are assigned the privileges of the appropriate category. This use of categories is more convenient and less error prone than assigning permissions directly to users.

Improving Performance

Most database applications are I/O bound or communication bound (distributed databases). However, other factors, such as CPU use, disc contention, and delays from frequent screen displays, can also affect response time. Several techniques can improve the performance of RDBMS applications.

- **Create indexes**. Indexes are the primary means for tuning performance. Chapter 6 presents guidelines for defining indexes.

■ **Carefully phrase queries**. In principle, RDBMSs are intended to be nonprocedural; developers state what is desired, and the RDBMS efficiently accesses the data. However, in practice, RDBMS optimizers are imperfect, and how a query is phrased can influence the choice of algorithm. The next three bullets elaborate.

■ **Use joins rather than nesting**. Most RDBMSs optimize joins better than nested queries. Figure 7.9 shows equivalent queries for the stock example from Chapters 5 and 6. The recommended query uses joins to find Bob Gibson's stocks. The nested query also finds the stock, but often performs more slowly. Nesting is occasionally needed for complex queries, but generally you should avoid using it.

Recommended query with joins:

```
SELECT companyID, stockAmount
FROM Ownership, Person
WHERE Ownership.personID = Person.personID AND
      personName = 'Bob Gibson';
```

Discouraged query with nested queries:

```
SELECT companyID, stockAmount FROM Ownership
WHERE personID IN
  (SELECT personID FROM Person
   WHERE personName = 'Bob Gibson');
```

Person table

person ID	personName
1	Harry Eisenstat
2	William Bradford
3	Willis Hudlin
4	Bob Gibson

Company table

company ID	company Name
1	IBM
2	Phillips
3	Sony

Ownership table

person ID	company ID	stock Amount
1	1	100
1	2	200
2	3	512
3	1	350
3	3	300
4	3	400

Figure 7.9 Use joins rather than nesting. Use joins instead of nested queries where possible.

■ **Define intermediate tables**. Normally, a developer should pass a query to the RDBMS in its entirety and give the RDBMS freedom to optimize. *Sometimes, it is helpful to use multiple queries with intermediate tables.* When an RDBMS processes joins, it spawns intermediate tables without indexes. By subdividing a query, a developer can index the intermediate tables and possibly speed execution. Intermediate tables add clutter and complicate multiuser access, however, so use them sparingly.

■ **Use precomputation**. Developers can sometimes increase efficiency by precomputing a common portion of several queries.

■ **Check the RDBMS query optimizer**. Many RDBMSs will show their decisions for evaluating SQL expressions. The RDBMS query plan shows the effect of query formulation on the optimizer's choice of algorithms.

■ **Update statistics**. Many RDBMSs maintain statistics, such as table size and data distribution, that influence the optimizer's choice of algorithms. A database administrator (DBA) should periodically update these statistics during routine maintenance.

■ **Avoid insert contention**. An application may experience lock contention if records are frequently inserted and the RDBMS writes to the same disc page. A *lock* seizes control of a resource for a period of time to preclude conflicting use. For example, Oracle's default behavior is to write records to the last page for a table. Developers can use row-level locking or spread inserts across multiple pages to reduce contention.

■ **Use functions carefully**. Be careful with functions because they can preempt the use of indexes during query optimization. Most RDBMSs will forgo the use of indexes for columns that are subject to a function in a *where* clause.

   For example, a user may be looking for stock ownership data and be uncertain whether it is stored under *Robert Gibson* or *Bob Gibson*. A substring function could retrieve all *personName* records ending with *Gibson*. However, the substring function would frustrate use of an index, if one were defined for *personName*. In such a situation, it would be best to split *personName* into two columns, *lastName* and *firstName*.

■ **Physically tune the RDBMS**. A DBA can manipulate various RDBMS parameters that affect efficiency. Furthermore, adding physical memory or communications bandwidth can often improve database performance. Tuning mechanisms vary greatly and are outside the scope of this book.

Converting Legacy Data

Legacy data processing is important both for operational applications (seeding new applications and exchanging data) and for analytical applications (loading data from operational systems into data warehouses). Many applications are poorly conceived, so it can be challenging and time consuming to rework their data. Developers must be proficient with both modeling and databases. There are several key issues.

- **Cleansing data**. Developers must repair errors in source data. Errors arise from user mistakes, flaws in database structure, and errors in application programs. For example, an application program may have missed some invalid part names. A combination of fields might be intended to be unique, but the data may have errors if the database structure does not enforce uniqueness.

- **Handling missing data**. You must decide how to handle missing data. Can you find it elsewhere? Do you want to estimate it, or can you use null values? You might want to require manual entry by users.

- **Merging data**. Data sources may overlap. For example, one system may contain engineering data for mechanical parts; another may have manufacturing data. A new application may need both. For complex sources, it is best to model them first and then decide how to merge them.

- **Changing structure**. Typically, source structures differ from target structures, so the data must be adjusted. For example, one application may store a phone number in a single field; another may split country code, area code, and local phone number into separate fields. Corresponding fields often have different names, data types, and lengths. There may be different data encodings; for example, sex can be encoded as male or female, M or F, 1 or 2, and so on.

Developers should begin data processing by loading the data into staging tables. The staging tables should mirror the original structure. For example, if the old application uses files and the new application uses a relational database, create one staging table for each file. Each column in a file maps to one column in a table with the same data type and length. Most RDBMSs have commands that readily perform this kind of loading.

The staging tables get the data into the database, so that they can be operated upon with SQL commands. It is better (less work, fewer errors, easier to modify) to use SQL commands than to write a lot of programming code. Staging tables enable the full power of database queries to convert data from the old to the new format.

Often, you can find alternative sources of the data to be loaded. Customer data may be available from sales records, customer service records, and an external marketing firm, for example. To resolve overlap, load the most accurate source first and then load the next most accurate and so on. Before loading each source, place it in a staging table, so that SQL can automatically subtract any overlap with the current database. If you do not do this, you could load the same customer twice, for example. This approach is a simple way to resolve conflicts in data, and it biases the database towards the best sources.

Chapter 12 provides additional detail on data conversion.

> I often begin data conversion by reverse engineering existing databases so that I can understand them. One of the oddest databases I have seen was intended to simplify legacy data processing. It had many mistakes, because the developers tried to distort the database of the new application to match that of the old application.
>
> A better approach is to model the application without worrying about data conversion. Essentially, you can choose to complicate the structure of the new application or the conversion code. It is much better to complicate the one-shot conversion code than the long-lived structure of the new application.
>
> Reference: Michael Blaha. An industrial example of database reverse engineering. *Sixth Working Conference on Reverse Engineering*, October 1999, Atlanta, Georgia.

Business anecdote: The wrong way to handle legacy data

Chapter Summary

Operational and analytical applications have many similar data-processing issues.

One tricky issue is combining relational databases with programming languages. Relational databases are powerful and profound, but their declarative style clashes with conventional programming languages. It is important to consider all the options when you combine the two.

Relational databases can yield excellent performance. Indexes are the primary structural means for tuning a database, but you can also improve database queries. This chapter lists several techniques for boosting query performance.

Finally, there are several key issues in legacy data conversion. It is important to load data into staging tables that reflect the original structure. You can then operate on these with SQL commands. A good way to begin any data conversion is to reverse engineer the existing databases.

> ✔ **Consider all options for combining databases and programming languages**. Don't simply use the first approach that comes to mind.
>
> ✔ **Consider substituting database queries for programming code**. In select situations, database queries can be written with 10-100 times less development time and fewer bugs.
>
> ✔ **Try to off-load legacy data conversion effort to SQL**. Use programming code only where necessary.

Major recommendations for Chapter 7

Resource Notes

Some of the material in this chapter was taken from [Blaha-98].

References

[Blaha-98] Michael Blaha and William Premerlani. *Object-Oriented Modeling and Design for Database Applications*. Upper Saddle River, New Jersey: Prentice Hall, 1998.

Part 3

Database Design Technology

Part 2 described some of the many issues involved in dealing with database management systems, particularly RDBMSs. As the previous chapters have illustrated, relational databases are powerful. They are also much more difficult to use than many vendors would have you believe. Individual tables are straightforward and intuitive, but applications with hundreds of tables—and this is common—are difficult to fathom. Organizations frequently buy products with only a hint of how they work or build software that fails spectacularly, because no one really understood the problem being addressed.

In Part 3, I describe how you can understand these applications through models, whether you build applications yourself, contract their development, or buy them. Modeling is useful, because it lets you think deeply and coherently about a problem and the way the software should or does address it. Organizations that excel at modeling have a competitive advantage, because they buy products they understand and develop products that do what they are supposed to do. Models let you build the superstructure of a problem and then realize it with lower level building blocks of programming and database code. Many tools can apply design rules and generate a database structure. With a sound model at the foundation of database design, application performance is predictable and often optimal.

Part 3 begins with the principles of modeling. Chapter 8 describes modeling's many benefits, as well as the difficulties it poses. It also surveys the types of models available. Chapter 9 covers modeling notations—Entity-Relationship (ER) and IDEF1X—and how to use them to best advantage. Chapter 10 describes key issues that arise with assimilating models by an organization.

A big part of modeling is understanding the kind of application you are buying or developing. Chapters 11 and 12 detail the characteristics of the two main classes of database applications—operational and analytical—and present some rules for designing sound applications. The focus is on relational databases, because of their market prominence, but the principles transcend individual products. Chapter 13 summarizes the design rules introduced in Chapters 11 and 12 and contrasts the two kinds of applications.

Part 3 is foundational for the discussion that follows on software engineering and advanced aspects of technology for database applications.

8

Modeling Principles

Models provide the linchpin for both developed and purchased software. You must understand what you want before you can obtain it. Models can help you develop better software at lower cost. Also, you can make wiser decisions when choosing between competing vendor products. This chapter explores the substance of models and motivations for building them.

What is a Model?

A _**model**_ is an abstraction of something that lets you thoroughly understand it. A model provides a roadmap for a database, similar to a blueprint for a building, that is studied and revised many times before it is built. Figure 8.1 summarizes the purpose of models. Models make it easier to develop software, because they let you separate deep conceptual issues from distracting and relatively straightforward implementation details.

Figure 8.1 Purpose of modeling. Models make it easier to develop software and purchase products.

Models also make it easier to purchase software. A model of requirements promotes consensus within your organization and helps you tell the vendors precisely what you want. Models of products help you understand what the vendors are offering. Models have several specific qualities.

- **Abstraction**. A model suppresses implementation details and focuses on deep aspects of a problem.

- **Basis in reality**. A model helps you organize your software in correspondence to the real world.

- **Simplification**. A model lets you focus on particular aspects of an application instead of having to deal with the entire application at once.

- **Abridgement**. Because it abstracts and simplifies an application, a model also reduces the size of a problem.

Why Build Models?

The most compelling reason for building models is that you obtain software that works—and works well. The model that has been verified with both business needs and technological capabilities becomes the core of an application. Thinking in terms of models provides several important benefits.

- **Better quality**. Your application can be no better than the underlying thought. If you understand an application, you are likely to succeed. Other things could still go wrong (such as funding, market timing, and project management), but your chance of success is high. In contrast, if you poorly understand an application, your chance of success is slim to none. A newly developed application will be confusing to users, will lack a clarity of purpose to program against, and will be difficult to maintain. For a purchased application, you will not understand vendor products deeply and will be relying on blind luck.

    Modeling is first, and foremost, a means for achieving clear thinking and coherence. Frederick Brooks [Brooks-95, page 42] contends "that conceptual integrity is *the* most important consideration in system design." (The italics are his.)

- **Reduced cost**. Models let you select a better product and thereby get more business benefit per dollar. A better product is often easier and thus less expensive to deploy. For a newly developed application, you can shift your activities toward the relatively inexpensive front end of software development and away from costly debugging and maintenance. More than 60 percent of a software budget is consumed by maintenance [Pressman-97, page 762], so such a shift is well worthwhile.

Models also make it easier to convert data from old applications to populate a new one.

■ **Faster time to market**. Skilled developers can build applications more quickly. It is faster to deal with difficulties at the conceptual stage than when software has been cast into programming and database code.

■ **Better performance**. The clarity of a sound model and its database embodiment enable good performance. Because the model is understandable and grounded in reality, it is straightforward to pose business queries. Given the correspondence between the model and the database, business queries readily translate into database code. This predictability means that you can thoroughly tune the application to get the fastest response.

■ **Greater maintainability**. Models document intent. If you build software via models, your software will have a coherent organization that can be extended more readily.

■ **Communication**. Models reduce misunderstandings and promote consensus among developers and customers. Important names, definitions, decisions, and assumptions become visible for everyone. Stakeholders can ask important questions early on, and it is easier to coordinate the work of multiple developers.

With all these advantages, it makes sense to develop software routinely via models. The cost of constructing models is far outweighed by improved quality, reduced debugging cost, quicker time to market, and simpler maintenance. Similarly, models of requirements and package finalists can help you make better purchase decisions. (See Chapter 16.)

 Use models to help you develop software. Use models to help you make better decisions for software purchases.

One last point about model building: Conceive the model *first* and use it to drive application development. Too many developers construct models as an afterthought to comply superficially with an edict to use models. The ability to internalize a model's content and drive it through application development sets apart excellent developers from mediocre ones.

 Conceive your models first and then develop the application. Do not construct models as an afterthought.

About ten years ago, my colleague, Bill Premerlani of the GE R&D Center, wrote a compiler that generated SQL code from a picture of a model. The software consisted of several passes: recognize the grammar of the input file, determine graphical connectivity, translate graphic figures to model constructs, and emit SQL code for the model constructs. Our application was unusual, and we could not use the modeling tools available at that time.

Premerlani wrote the software, from start to finish, in six weeks flat. The software had few bugs, was extensible, and performed well. Admittedly, Premerlani is a super programmer but modeling facilitated his excellence.

Business anecdote: Building software through models

Difficulties with Models

The benefits of using models to guide software development and purchase are compelling, but I don't want to give the impression that it is easy. Modeling requires discipline and effort, more than most people realize, and there are several difficulties.

- **Intellectual rigor**. Modeling requires that you deliberate about an application, instead of just writing code or selecting a product empirically. This paradigm shift can be difficult. If developers do not learn to think abstractly, models may not lead to better and less costly software.

   It will take a substantial commitment from your organization for modeling to be successful. Your firm will have to allot funds for training and mentoring. Your staff will have to spend time taking courses, reading the literature, practicing modeling, and doing exercises. I've found that most people underestimate the effort required and some developers cannot do modeling at all.

 Budget funds for training and mentoring your staff. Critically monitor their progress.

- **Difficulty of measuring progress**. Model-driven development also requires different management techniques. There is much up-front work during which little code is written, so managers cannot weigh code to assess progress.

   You can mitigate this problem by decomposing applications into lesser pieces that are coherent and can be accomplished within a limited time (such as a few months). Progress is more apparent for these small pieces than if the application was handled as a monolith. Some organizations favor a rapid prototyping approach in which developers quickly build the nucleus of an application and then successively elaborate it. Chapter 15 discusses the software-development life cycle.

 Try to break large projects into smaller and more manageable pieces so that you can better assess progress.

■ **Complexity**. Models can lead to excessive complexity. Models simplify a problem, but there is always the temptation to include fine details that increase the size of an application, but don't necessarily contribute to satisfying requirements.

   When models become large (defined in Chapter 9), it is time to step back and reconsider. Do you really need details in all parts of the model, or can you simplify incidental portions? Sometimes large models are justified, but more often not. This complexity evaluation is not for novice modelers. Only highly experienced modelers have the skill to do this type of reassessment.

> When I look back on my projects over the years, I can see that I have sometimes been guilty of excessive complexity. The models were sound, but some applications were more trouble and work than I expected. Looking back, I would have tried harder to simplify the models to reduce development effort. It is easy to fall into the trap of building software that is more complex than needed.

Business anecdote: Excessive complexity

Kinds of Models

Software developers use a wide variety of models in practice, including:

■ **Structural models**—models of data structures and relationships.

■ **State-transition models**—models of stimuli that occur and a system's response to them (time-related behavior).

■ **Functional models**—models of the computation to be performed.

Of the various kinds of models, structural models are the most helpful for database applications and hence the only kind of model I discuss. From now on, the term *model* will denote a structural model.

I have seen some people model the functionality of an application and then try to devise a database. A functional approach can be helpful for programming applications, but is poorly suited for designing databases. You cannot discover deep issues of structure and relationships by merely thinking about process. A database application revolves about a database and so too should your model. Once you have a structural model in place, it is of course helpful and appropriate to test the model by thinking about functionality.

Use a structural model to drive the development of a database application. A functional or process model is not suitable.

Structural Models

A ***structural model*** defines the data that can be stored and retrieved for a database. It provides:

- **Structure**. A model specifies the structure of a database. The structure lists the data elements and the relationships among groups of them.

- **Constraints (business rules)**. A model constrains the data that can be stored. For example, a frequent flyer account normally pertains to one customer; a model can note this and a database can enforce it. The constraints in a model become constraints in a database. Constraints enforce many of the rules of a business, thereby reducing errors and simplifying implementation. Modeling provides a way to understand critical business rules, capture them, and drive them into the finished application.

- **Potential for computation**. A model is a blueprint for the questions that can be asked and how they can be formulated. Much application logic consists of traversals of a model and the corresponding database structure to read or modify the data elements.

When reviewing models, actively consider their suitability for enforcing constraints and resolving business questions.

Naming Conventions

Models with crisp and unambiguous names are easier to understand.

When constructing names, use approved keywords and abbreviations. Naming conventions improve the readability of models and the consistency of data across applications. [Schuldt-93] and [Kismet-99] are two good references on naming conventions, and you can find more by searching for "metadata" on the Web. Choose a convention, and build a list of keywords and abbreviations that fit your business.

A common convention is to use a three-part name—a mandatory prime word + an optional modifier word + a mandatory data type word. Table 8.1 shows several examples from a model for airline frequent flyer data.

Field name	Prime word	Modifier word	Data type word
accountNumber	account		number
accountStartDate	account	start	date
mileageActualAmount	mileage	actual	amount
otherActivityType	otherActivity		type

Table 8.1 Sample names. Naming conventions improve the readability of models and the consistency of applications.

 Use a naming convention and approved keywords to improve model readability and consistency.

Chapter Summary

A model is an abstraction of something that lets you thoroughly understand it. A model captures important business relationships and enables superior applications. With models, you can deliver software of high quality with predictable cost, schedule, and performance.

It is not easy to think in terms of models. The biggest impediment is the paradigm shift—the deliberation about an application, rather than just writing code or empirically selecting a product. Aggressive training and mentoring is a partial solution. Chapter 10 has further advice.

Software developers use many models in practice, but structural models are best for database applications. A structural model serves several purposes. First, it describes the structure of a database. Second, it constrains the data that can be stored; database managers reject any data that violate constraints. Third, it provides a blueprint for questions that the database can answer.

Any model should follow an established naming convention.

✔ **Use models**. Skillful modeling has many benefits for purchasing and developing applications, including better quality, reduced cost, faster time to market, and better performance.

✔ **Build applications via models**. Conceive your models first, and then develop the application. Do not construct models as an afterthought.

✔ **Use a structural model**. Functional and process models are useful for scoping an application, but are not suitable for designing a database.

✔ **Standardize names**. Use a naming convention and approved keywords to improve model readability and application consistency.

Major recommendations for Chapter 8

Resource Notes

This book emphasizes structural models which are dominant for database applications. The Zachman Framework [Zachman-87] [Inmon-97] provides a more expansive treatment of models.

References

[Brooks-95] Frederick P. Brooks, Jr. *The Mythical Man-Month, Anniversary Edition*. Reading, Massachusetts: Addison-Wesley, 1995.

[Inmon-97] WH Inmon, John A Zachman, and Jonathan G Geiger. *Data Stores, Data Warehousing, and the Zachman Framework*. New York, New York: McGraw-Hill, 1997.

[Kismet-99] http://www.kismeta.com

[Pressman-97] Roger S Pressman. *Software Engineering: A Practitioner's Approach, Fourth Edition*. New York, New York: McGraw-Hill, 1997.

[Schuldt-93] Ronald L. Schuldt and Barbara A. Barman. Implementing a national data element standardization and registration strategy. *CALS Expo 1993*. Found on the Internet via //http:www.dama.org.

[Zachman-87] John A Zachman. A framework for information systems architecture. *IBM Systems Journal 26*, 3 (1987).

9

Modeling Notations

This chapter explores some popular notations for modeling databases: Entity-Relationship (UML and Chen) and IDEF1X. The notations have the same basic concepts, but vary in their terminology, graphical symbols, and support for advanced concepts. I use the UML and IDEF1X notations in several subsequent chapters.

The chapter is designed to give a flavor of several notations, so that you can efficiently review models and understand their capabilities. I present the same example throughout this chapter so that you can compare the notations.

Entity-Relationship Notations

The ***Entity-Relationship (ER)*** approach [Chen-76] is the most popular approach to modeling databases. There are many ER dialects, none of which is dominant, so the term *ER* actually refers to a family of notations. The purpose of ER models is to develop an understanding of requirements so that they can be expressed with a database in a complete and efficient manner. Commercial tools are readily available for constructing ER models and generating a corresponding database structure. ER models have the following trade-offs.

- **Advantages**. ER models are succinct and cause you to think deeply before getting encumbered with implementation details. ER models are straightforward to understand, yet powerful enough to model real problems.

- **Disadvantages**. ER has *many* dialects. All support the core concepts (entities, relationships, and attributes), but they differ in notation and degree of support for advanced concepts.

Two of the most popular dialects are the Unified Modeling Language (UML) and Chen.

Unified Modeling Language Dialect

Figure 9.1 summarizes the UML dialect [Booch-99] [Rumbaugh-99]. Figure 9.2 shows a sample UML model for an operational application. (Chapter 12 shows a UML model for an analytical application.) The model concerns frequent flyer account data for airlines and is admittedly incomplete. The model would support business processes such as posting customer credits and generating monthly statements.

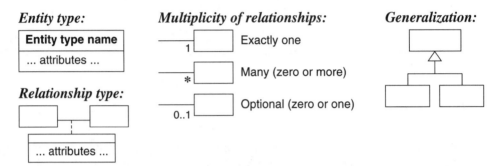
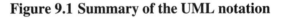

Figure 9.1 Summary of the UML notation

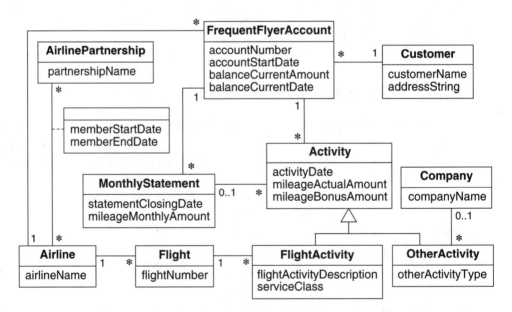

Figure 9.2 An ER model using the UML notation. ER models provide a powerful means for thinking about the essence of a database.

The model reflects requirements. Airlines offer frequent flyer accounts. A customer can have multiple frequent flyer accounts. Each frequent flyer account is for one airline and one customer. Multiple activities can be posted to a frequent flyer account, such as airline flight activities and other activities (credit card purchases, car rentals, and hotel stays). The activities are eventually reported to the customer in a monthly statement. There are many such statements for a frequent flyer account.

Airlines can belong to many partnerships; each partnership can have multiple airlines. For example, the Star Alliance has member airlines United Airlines, Lufthansa, SAS, and others. United participates in additional partnerships, such as one with TransWorld Express. The model records the dates an airline starts and ends partner membership.

Each box in Figure 9.2 with a bold font name denotes an entity type. There are ten entity types, including *FrequentFlyerAccount*, *Customer*, and *Activity*. An ***entity*** is a concept, abstraction, or thing that can be individually identified and is relevant to an application. An ***entity type*** is a description of a group of entities with similar properties, meaning, and relationships to other entities. Models intrinsically involve entity types because models describe the possible occurrences. A model is ultimately implemented as database structures, which are then populated to hold the actual entities.

The diagram has 20 attributes which are shown in the lower portion of the boxes. Attributes for the entity type *Customer*, for example, are *customerName* and *addressString*. An ***attribute*** describes values that can be stored in the eventual database. Thus the database could store a name and an address for each customer.

The diagram has nine relationship types, each of which is indicated by a series of one or more lines between entity types. (The lines connected to the triangle are another construct to be discussed shortly.) Relationship types can be given names (written next to one of the lines) but they are not required for the UML. The line between *FrequentFlyerAccount* and *Customer* is one of the relationship types. A ***relationship*** is a physical or conceptual connection between entities. A ***relationship type*** is a description of a group of relationships with similar properties and meaning. Relationship types are the "glue" that connect the entity types in a model. The precise choice of entity types and relationship types to include depends on the application and the modeler's judgment.

Attributes *memberStartDate* and *memberEndDate* describe the relationship type between *Airline* and *AirlinePartnership*. These attributes clearly belong to the relationship type and not to the related entity types. They are connected to the relationship type with a dotted line. The airlines in a partnership may start and end their membership on different dates. All other attributes in Figure 9.2 describe entity types.

Multiplicity can be indicated at each end of a relationship type—the "*," "1," and "0..1" annotations in the diagram. **_Multiplicity_** is the number of occurrences of an entity type that may connect to a single occurrence of a related entity type. In the diagram, the relationship type between *Customer* and *FrequentFlyerAccount* has one-to-many multiplicity. That is, each frequent flyer account pertains to one customer, but a customer may have many (zero or more) frequent flyer accounts. The "*" is UML notation for "many." The "0..1" illustrates at-most-one multiplicity. The "0..1" to the right of the *MonthlyStatement* box means that an activity appears in at most one monthly statement, but may not be in a monthly statement if it has not been reported yet. In the literature, *multiplicity* is sometimes called *cardinality* or *connectivity*.

Generalization is the final concept in the diagram and is shown with a triangle. **_Generalization_** organizes entity types by their similarities and differences. The triangle under the *Activity* box means that an activity can be a flight activity or some other activity. The attributes and relationships for the *Activity* entity type pertain to all activities. In contrast, only a *FlightActivity* may have a description, service class, and a relationship to a flight. Only an *OtherActivity* has a relationship to a company and an *otherActivityType* attribute to indicate whether the occurrence is a credit card purchase, car rental, or hotel stay. The apex of the triangle connects to the entity type with the general information. Lines connect the base of the triangle to the other entity types with specific information.

Chen Dialect

Figure 9.3 summarizes Chen's dialect. Figure 9.4 shows the airline model using Chen's dialect. A box denotes an entity type, and ovals denote attributes. A diamond indicates a relationship type with lines connecting the related entity types. There are several kinds of generalization, and the figure shows the form appropriate for the airline example (the lines, the encircled "d", and the horseshoes shown below *Activity*). Despite its much different appearance, the model with Chen's notation has the same meaning as the UML model.

IDEF1X Notation

The IDEF1X notation [Bruce-92] is often used to design relational databases. Unlike the ER approach, there is a single IDEF1X notation. Commercial tools are readily available for constructing IDEF1X diagrams and generating database structure. IDEF1X has the following trade-offs.

■ **Advantages**. It is a standard notation, and many developers are familiar with it. It is an excellent notation for expressing details of relational database designs.

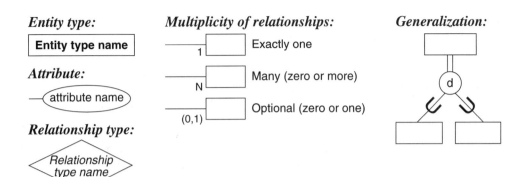

Figure 9.3 Summary of Chen's notation

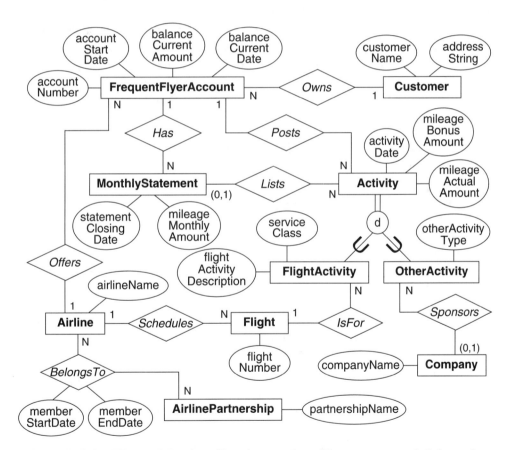

Figure 9.4 An ER model using Chen's notation. There are several dialects for ER modeling, but their basic concepts have the same meaning.

In this regard, it is superior to ER. For example, IDEF1X crisply displays primary and foreign keys (to be explained shortly).

■ **Disadvantages**. Unfortunately, the strength of IDEF1X is also its weakness. IDEF1X is a poor notation for modeling, because it prematurely injects design details. It forces you to deal with relational database details at the very time you are trying to understand an application. Abstract thinking is already difficult without such an unnecessary complication.

Consequently, I strongly discourage the use of IDEF1X for modeling. It is, however, appropriate to prepare an ER model and then switch to IDEF1X for relational database design.

Figure 9.5 summarizes the IDEF1X notation and Figure 9.6 restates the airline example. IDEF1X distinguishes between independent (square box) and dependent entity types (rounded box). *__Independent entities__*, as the name suggests, can exist on their own. In contrast, a *__dependent entity__* can exist only if some other entity also exists; the primary key of a dependent entity incorporates the primary key of another entity. Independent and dependent entities are sometimes called *__strong__* and *__weak__* entities, respectively. The combined square and rounded boxes in Figure 9.5 denote either kind of box. Thus, for example, independent and dependent entity types may both participate in nonidentifying relationships.

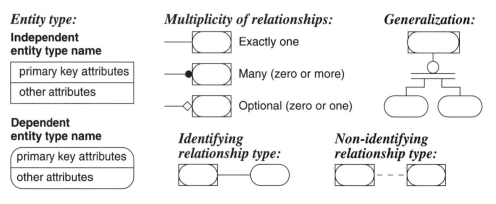

Figure 9.5 Summary of the IDEF1X notation

IDEF1X lists the name of the entity type above the box. The top portion of the box contains primary key attributes, and the lower portion contains the remaining attributes. The notation "FK" denotes a foreign key, and "AK" followed by a number denotes an alternate key (a candidate key).

IDEF1X requires that many-to-many relationships be promoted to entity types. It shows the remaining relationship types redundantly with both lines and foreign

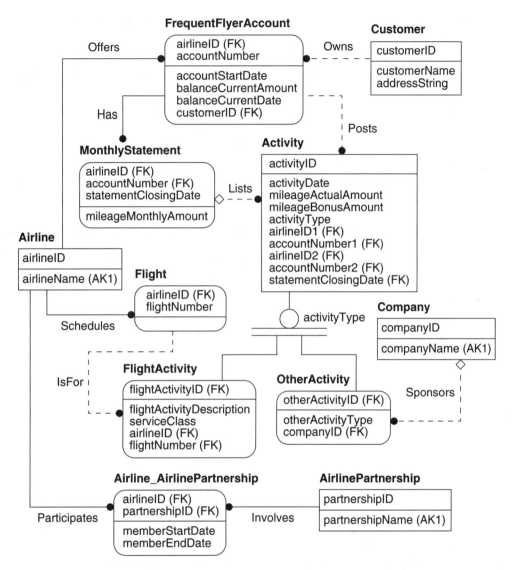

Figure 9.6 A model using the IDEF1X notation. IDEF1X is a poor notation for modeling, but excellent for relational database design.

keys. The lines are labeled with relationship type names. A line is solid for an identifying relationship type. (The foreign key is in the top portion of the entity type box.)
A line is dashed for a non-identifying relationship type. (The foreign key is in the
lower portion of the entity type box.) For example, *FrequentFlyerAccount* has a solid
line to *Airline*, because *airlineID* is in the top portion of the *FrequentFlyerAccount*

box. In contrast, the line from *FrequentFlyerAccount* to *Customer* is dashed, because *customerID* is in the lower portion of the box.

The solid ball denotes many multiplicity (zero or more). A diamond denotes at-most-one multiplicity (zero or one). The lack of a symbol indicates a multiplicity of exactly one.

The large circle with a line underneath denotes generalization. The double line indicates that the generalization is exhaustive; each occurrence of activity must be either a flight activity or an other activity. The attribute *activityType* next to the circle is called a ***discriminator*** and indicates whether each activity record is elaborated by flight activity or other activity. The ER models did not explicitly state this attribute, although they implied it.

Compare Figure 9.6 to Figure 9.2. Note how the UML model is simpler and more concise. The IDEF1X model shows an implementation with a relational database. There are many other possible implementations. For example, different decisions could be made for identifying entities and would affect the corresponding foreign keys. Figure 9.7 shows an alternate IDEF1X model restating most entity types as independent. Both Figure 9.6 and Figure 9.7 are correct and have the same information content; the choice depends on the designer's style. In contrast, an ER notation (such as the UML) lets you think completely in the conceptual realm and defer design details until your model is complete.

Do not use IDEF1X for conceptual modeling. You can, however, prepare an ER model and switch to IDEF1X for relational database design.

Comparison of Modeling Notations

Table 9.1 compares the notations. The UML is the most readable notation, as you can tell by looking at the figures in this chapter. Precision refers to the rigor of a notation and its ability to express fine constraints. The UML has a formal constraint modeling language [Warmer-99] that can handle a wide variety of situations.

The UML and IDEF1X notations have been standardized. I am not aware of any standards for the other ER dialects. The UML is a new notation that has been well received by database professionals. All the notations have mature tools. The IDEF1X notation poorly supports conceptual modeling, and this hobbles IDEF1X modeling tools. UML tools currently have weak support for database design. (Chapter 17 describes modeling tools in more detail.)

My personal preference is the UML notation, because it is concise and programmers also accept it. Furthermore, the UML is a standard notation, as Chapter 22 ex-

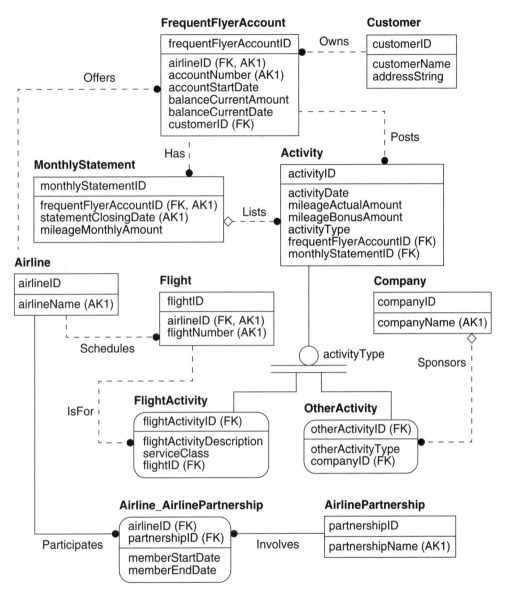

Figure 9.7 An alternate IDEF1X model. IDEF1X models depend
on both the underlying content and design decisions.

plains. The UML also includes several additional kinds of models that are
occasionally helpful for database applications.

It is important not to obsess over the precise choice of notation. What is critical
is that your staff use models and learn to think abstractly.

Criterion	UML	Chen	IDEF1X
Readability	High	Medium	Medium
Precision	High	Medium	Medium
Is standard?	Yes	No	Yes
Popularity for database applications	Medium	High	High
Quality of tools for modeling	Good	Good	Poor
Quality of tools for database design	Weak	Good	Good
Other comments	Also addresses programming		

Table 9.1   Comparison of modeling notations

 Do not be overly concerned about the choice of a modeling notation. The important thing is to use models and learn to think abstractly.

Judging the Quality of Models

Managers seldom construct models, but they should participate in reviews. Here are some general criteria for judging models. ([Blaha-98] presents additional technical criteria.)

- **Simplicity** A model should not be needlessly complex. Many applications can be modeled with no more than 50 entity types. Few applications require more than 250.

- **Names**. The names in a model should be crisp and meaningful. If the names confuse business experts, change the names. It is difficult to devise good names, so don't be surprised if you encounter lengthy discussions.

- **Scope**. A model must fully address the requirements, but not greatly exceed them. At least 80 percent of a model should pertain to immediate needs. As much as 20 percent can anticipate future needs.

- **Extensibility**. A model should be readily extended. New requirements should cause additions, but little alteration. If you add 20 percent new entity types to a model, you should not need to revise more than 20 percent of the original model.

- **Visual display**. The visual layout should make a model easier to understand.

- **Documentation**. A model should have a thorough written explanation. The explanation should define important application terms, explain the rationale for subtle decisions, and walk the reader through the model. Typically every five entity types should require one page of explanation.

- **Review**. A model is more likely to be of high quality if it has been subjected to vigorous review. Chapter 17 has more to say about reviews.

Bear in mind that it may take 5-10 revisions before a model converges and satisfies these criteria and essential business needs.

Chapter Summary

Two families of notations are often used for structural models. Entity-Relationship (ER) modeling is the most popular and the one I recommend, because it helps developers think abstractly. The ER approach has many dialects of which the UML is the cleanest and most concise. Another ER dialect is also a reasonable choice.

The IDEF1X notation is also popular, but I strongly urge that you do not use it for modeling. Modeling is already difficult without adding the impediment of an unsuitable notation. IDEF1X models force you to deal with relational database design details at the time you are conceiving a model. A much better approach is to construct a model first, and then address relational databases (possibly using IDEF1X). I elaborate on this in Chapter 15.

✔ **Do not obsess with choosing a notation**. The choice of a notation is a secondary decision. The most important issue is that you use models, and learn to use them well.

✔ **Do not use IDEF1X for conceptual modeling**. It is better to prepare an ER model and switch to IDEF1X notation for relational database design.

Major recommendations for Chapter 9

Resource Notes

[Booch-99] explains UML modeling and is written from a programming perspective. [Rumbaugh-99] is a reference manual for the UML. [Warmer-99] explains the object constraint language (OCL) that is part of the UML. [Blaha-98] shows how to apply UML models to database applications; it is a good complement to this book, but is more technical. Also, [Blaha-98] is focused on operational applications, while this book takes a broader look across operational and analytical applications.

[Chen-76] is the seminal paper for ER modeling. [Teorey-99] is a well-written book that articulates the details of using ER models for database applications.

[Elmasri-00] also explains ER models and shows how to use them in designing relational databases. This book provides a thorough explanation of databases and the underlying theory. Appendix A of [Elmasri-00] has a nice summary of many ER notation variants.

[Bruce-92] presents a clear exposition of the IDEF1X approach to relational database design. Bruce also presents many useful design techniques.

References

[Blaha-98] Michael Blaha and William Premerlani. *Object-Oriented Modeling and Design for Database Applications*. Upper Saddle River, New Jersey: Prentice Hall, 1998.

[Booch-99] Grady Booch, James Rumbaugh, and Ivar Jacobson. *The Unified Modeling Language User Guide*. Reading, Massachusetts: Addison-Wesley, 1999.

[Bruce-92] Thomas A. Bruce. *Designing Quality Databases with IDEF1X Information Models*. New York, New York: Dorset House, 1992.

[Chen-76] PPS Chen. The Entity-Relationship model—Toward a Unified View of Data. *ACM Transactions on Database Systems 1*, 1 (March 1976).

[Elmasri-00] Ramez Elmasri and Shamkant Navathe. *Fundamentals of Database Systems, Third Edition*. Redwood City, California: Benjamin Cummings, 2000.

[Rumbaugh-99] James Rumbaugh, Ivar Jacobson, and Grady Booch. *The Unified Modeling Language Reference Manual*. Reading, Massachusetts: Addison-Wesley, 1999.

[Teorey-99] TJ Teorey. *Database Modeling and Design, Third Edition*. San Francisco, California: Morgan-Kaufman, 1999.

[Warmer-99] Jos Warmer and Anneke Kleppe. *The Object Constraint Language*. Reading, Massachusetts: Addison-Wesley, 1999.

10

Managing Models

In preceding chapters, I've described how modeling is key to developing and acquiring a sound database application. For developed applications, modeling increases product quality and performance, while reducing development cost and product time to market. For acquired applications, models give you a deeper understanding of what you want and how the prospective product meets those requirements.

I've also mentioned that the mind-set associated with modeling is not intuitive. Managers must take specific actions to root modeling firmly in their organizations. This chapter describes those actions.

The Importance of Skilled Staff

If you want developers to learn modeling, you must look for personnel with traits that fit with modeling requirements. Look for personnel with:

- **Intellect**. Bright people can help you realize the full benefits of modeling. "Study after study shows that the very best designers produce structures that are faster, smaller, simpler, cleaner, and produced with less effort. The differences between the great and the average approach an order of magnitude." [Brooks-95, page 202]

- **Abstract thinking**. A person must be willing to think abstractly and work indirectly. They must resolve abstract concepts before dealing with code. This technique of working indirectly is difficult to master.

- **Work ethic**. A desire to achieve is essential and cannot be presumed.

■ **Experience**. Experience with software (various languages, databases, and kinds of applications) aids the ability to model. Modeling also becomes easier as a person performs more of it; modelers build a mental library of modeling patterns— situations they have seen before and know how to address.

■ **Sociability**. A modeler must be able to interact with various interests—business experts, database designers, programmers, and managers.

Many organizations try to staff a project with whoever is available at the time—often with people who are between projects. Some of this is reasonable, but you need to make sure that project personnel have the proper skills. You will not be a hero if you provide employment but fail to complete your project.

Once you have personnel with these qualities, I suggest the following techniques for helping them learn to model.

■ **Training and mentoring**. Invest in training that involves hands-on practice and exercises. A person learns to model only by doing it, not by talking about it. Provide training shortly before (ideally a few weeks ahead of) an actual project. It is not a good idea to provide training too far in advance, or the attendees will forget too much.

Reinforce training with mentoring. Your staff will need active help as they seek to apply the training material. It will not suffice to bring in outside resources to service a project. There must be a transition of knowledge from the outside resources to your staff.

■ **Teaming**. Application models should be constructed by small teams that initially consist of application developers, business experts, and external consultants. After several applications, you should no longer need the external consultants and your best in-house modelers can provide special expertise. The purpose of teaming is to disseminate information within your firm, knowledge about both computing technology and the business.

■ **Seminars**. Periodic seminars provide cost-effective education. Encourage your staff to present technical seminars. The presenter often learns as much by presenting as the audience does by listening. Seminars get people talking and exchanging ideas across an organization. Everyone learns about the various projects and can leverage related efforts. Seminars provide encouragement for dealing with the difficulties of modeling.

■ **Continual learning**. Your staff should strive to find new ideas and adopt the best practices of the larger software community. Periodic attendance at technical conferences, professional meetings, and university courses are all helpful. Books and magazines can provide useful ideas.

Generally speaking, a beginner can learn to model in about six months, given suitable training and mentoring. However, some people never learn to model. They might be able to draw diagrams and recite some of the formalisms, but they never obtain the knack for abstract thinking. Assign these people to other tasks.

 Recognize that modeling is difficult. Be proactive, and help your staff learn to model.

A colleague had an extended consulting assignment, and the client accepted his offer to present a weekly technical seminar. The seminars were a great success and raised the technology level throughout the organization. They also contributed to the cohesion of the project team.

Business anecdote: The value of seminars

Estimating Modeling Effort

Modeling is just one of many project tasks, but it is unfamiliar to many managers. The following factors affect modeling effort.

- **Purpose of the model**. You need a more thorough model to build an application than to assess a vendor.

- **Application complexity**. Tangible applications are simpler; highly abstract applications take longer. For example, it is easier to build software for handling customer calls, than to build a system for all kinds of customer interaction.

- **Modeling skill**. A skilled modeler can work an order of magnitude faster than an inexperienced one.

- **Tools**. It helps if the technologist has access to a powerful modeling tool and is proficient with it. However, not all tools are beneficial. In one consulting engagement, I used an old modeling tool imposed by my client. The tool reduced my productivity several fold.

- **Model size**. The time to construct a model is not linear with its size. Modeling time is roughly proportional to the number of entity types and relationship types to the 1.5th power. Thus, a model with 500 entity and relationship types takes about 30 times longer than a model with 50.

■ **Quality of review**. Thorough review reduces the number of iterations needed for a model.

Given all these factors, most models require from one to six months of effort.

Modeling Sessions

Direct discussion with users is one of the most important sources of requirements, because it provides insights into the expectations of those who will ultimately decide whether the product is successful. There are several techniques for engaging users and obtaining their input: back-room, round-robin, and live modeling.

   Consider different ways of interacting with users.

Back-Room Modeling

The most popular way to build a model is to talk to business experts, record their comments, and then go off-line and model—***back-room modeling***. Many analysts prefer this approach, because they can focus on what the user is saying and wrestle with the model later when they are alone. Over a series of meetings, users answer questions and volunteer information that they think may be helpful. After each meeting, the analyst incorporates their comments and the model gradually improves. Typically, the model stays in the background and is not shown to users.

It is better to meet with several users than have one-on-one meetings. A multi-user meeting has a better chemistry, because users stimulate each other's memory. There is a risk of intimidation in a one-on-one session, which is less likely with multiple users. Most analysts prefer to meet with a group of users who share an interest. For example, an analyst might meet separately with salespersons and engineers.

Back-room modeling has the following trade-offs.

■ **Advantages**. It requires the least modeling skill and is appropriate for analysts who are tentative with modeling.

■ **Disadvantages**. The painstaking cycle of interaction with users is cumbersome for skilled modelers. The slow interaction can also be troublesome for users, because multiple interviews are required. Analysts must carefully transcribe information or it will be forgotten.

Round-Robin Modeling

Round-robin modeling is more complex than back-room modeling, but more efficient at gathering requirements. The analyst still meets with small groups of users, segmented by interest or functional area, but in round-robin modeling, the users see the model. As users express requirements, the analyst traverses the model and tries to resolve them. An analyst can resolve simple issues during a meeting and complex issues afterwards.

I call this approach *__round-robin modeling__*, because an analyst parades the model from group to group until all concerns are addressed. Several iterations are required, because one group might surface an issue that an analyst needs to confirm with a previous group. Back-room modeling also parades from group to group, but the model is suppressed in the sessions.

I initiate round-robin modeling with a seed model that is based on existing materials such as written documentation and reverse-engineering artifacts. I don't like to start with a blank sheet of paper, because it wastes time and tries the patience of users. In contrast, a seed model stimulates discussion. Users see the analyst as well prepared and can focus on deeper issues.

In the meetings, I tell the users that they are the business experts and that I need their help in capturing requirements; I am the computer expert, and they should let me handle the details. Generally, users heave a sigh of relief. I don't dwell on formalisms and explain notation as I go. Participants don't have a problem, because I continually explain the model.

Round-robin modeling has the following trade-offs.

- **Advantages**. It requires fewer meetings than back-room modeling. Because the model is prominent, an analyst can resolve some issues during meetings. In contrast, with back-room modeling, the analyst just takes notes and may overlook needed details.

- **Disadvantages**. It still requires several iterations, and it is inefficient to shuttle ideas across the user groups. If there is contention, it can be difficult to reach agreement. The analyst is in the uncomfortable position of being an intermediary among conflicting user groups.

Live Modeling

Expert modelers can use the technique of *__live modeling__*. I arrange a meeting of 10-20 persons with a range of interests—developers, managers, and various kinds of business experts. During the meeting, I build a model live on the fly, listening to suggestions, volunteering comments, resolving names, and agreeing on scope. Usually, I can keep pace with the dialogue. A projector displays the model that I draw with a modeling tool. A typical session lasts about two hours, and three sessions can usually elicit 80 percent of the structure for a model with 50 entity types. Large and complex models take additional sessions.

As of this writing, I have conducted live modeling sessions for about 25 projects, and all have gone well. The project gets off to a quick and productive start. The participants get a flavor of the give and take of modeling, as well as the model's content. Live modeling deflates any notion of modeling being a tedious, wasteful activity.

The size and variety of the group is constructive; reluctant participants see the reaction of others and want to get involved to air their point of view. Comments from one person tend to trigger comments from another. I have had special success with skeptics.

It is acceptable to start live modeling with a clean sheet of paper, but the analyst should prepare and learn about the application in advance. The ideas will come quickly, and the analyst must be ready. Sometimes I prepare a seed model if I have prior information (requirements documents, manuals, important legacy databases to reverse-engineer). Normally, I request a written problem statement to stimulate discussion if there are any lulls.

I am an active facilitator, not just a passive recorder; I ask questions and probe the attendees when answers seem unsatisfactory. I make suggestions on the basis of my experience with related problems. Ultimately, business experts make the final decisions. Occasionally, I encounter a deep modeling issue that I defer until the next meeting.

Often there are animated discussions over names. These can be helpful. Good names avoid misunderstandings. Also the discussions stimulate related information. I press business experts to devise good names—names that are brief, crisp, and not subject to confounding interpretations.

Live modeling has the following trade-offs.

■ **Advantages**. This is clearly the best way to obtain user input for proficient modelers. With a small amount of time, the analyst can acquire a great deal of information. The participants have different areas of knowledge and different perceptions; by placing them in the same meeting, they can reconcile their views.

A major side benefit is that the meetings induce the participants to talk to each other. This has business benefit aside from the modeling. Persons from different backgrounds who usually don't have the time or inclination are brought together and converse.

■ **Disadvantages**. An analyst has to be highly confident of modeling, able to run a meeting, and adept with a modeling tool. Live modeling is good at eliciting structure—entity and relationship types. It is less effective at finding attributes, because it is difficult to coordinate a large group for fine detail. Other input sources (see Chapter 15) can provide the missing detail.

Comparison of Interviewing Techniques

Table 10.1 summarizes the different techniques for organizing modeling sessions.

	Back-room modeling	Round-robin modeling	Live modeling
Explanation	Record comments from user groups and build the model offline	Show model to user groups, but still build it offline	Meet with users all at once and build the model during the meeting
Required modeling skill	Low	Medium	Very high
Number of meetings for model with 50 entity types	About 15 meetings, each 2 hours long	About 12 meetings, each 2 hours long	About 3 meetings, each 2 hours long
Other comments	Tedious approach for a skilled modeler	It is awkward for a modeler to be an intermediary and shuttle ideas across user groups	Rapid modeling is satisfying for users; dialogue has business benefit

Table 10.1 Techniques for modeling sessions. An adept modeler can conduct user interviews more efficiently.

Modeling Pitfalls

In my consulting work I have observed several pitfalls with modeling of which you should be aware.

■ **Analysis paralysis**. Some managers fear (with justification) that modeling can become an end in itself. Some persons become so focused on modeling that they lose sight of its purpose. This situation is most likely to arise with analysts who have not written much database or programming code. It can also arise with beginning modelers who are inefficient and unsure when modeling is complete.

　　A project plan can help you avoid analysis paralysis by allotting time to tasks. The plan should specify the effort for modeling and the intended deliverables.

■ **Parallel modeling**. On several occasions, I have seen organizations construct redundant models with different paradigms. I often find object-oriented (OO)

Carefully plan your projects to reduce the likelihood of analysis paralysis.

and database modeling occurring in parallel. OO teams tend to be dominated by programmers who do not understand databases. Similarly, database professionals have their accustomed techniques and are often unfamiliar with OO technology. This chasm in practice mirrors the chasm in the literature. The OO and database communities have their own style and jargon, and few persons operate in both camps. The current limitations of tools exacerbate the divide.

Oddly enough, the schism is more a matter of terminology and style, rather than substance. Your best course of action is to be aware of culture gaps. Let your staff construct parallel models for programming and databases if they find it helpful. This is one way to cope with the limitations of current tools. In short, tolerate almost anything to get the staff to model, but insist that the models be frequently reconciled.

 Permit parallel modeling efforts, but insist that the models be reconciled.

In one assignment, I encountered a company that was constructing OO, ER, and IDEF1X models for the same application. Three teams were proceeding in parallel and with little dialog, even though they were all trying to model the same thing. The root of the problem was that each team only understood their favored technology and could not speak the other "languages." They seemed surprised when I began cross checking the models.

The moral is that it is tolerable to construct parallel models, but your staff must reconcile the content.

Business anecdote: Monitor parallel modeling

- **Failure to think abstractly**. Many persons cannot think abstractly and fail to learn the skill of modeling. With models you indirectly realize an application, rather than just directly dealing with code.

    About the only cure is a lot of practice. Inexperienced modelers should practice solving exercises. They should work on actual applications under the guidance of a mentor. Those who are still not able to model should be assigned other tasks.

Realize that modeling is difficult and may be assimilated by only some of your staff.

■ **Excessive scope**. The purpose of modeling is to model the real world, but only the portion relevant to your business objectives. Some people lose focus and model extraneous information.

You can mitigate this pitfall with a project plan and regular reviews.

 Be careful with the scope of models, and check them for business relevance.

■ **Rigid conception**. Developers should conceive applications broadly and flexibly and be expansive in formulating a database. You can make the user interface more restrictive and not tap the full database power. In this way, you suppress the additional flexibility from the user until it is needed.

For example, a personnel database may have a many-to-many relationship between employee and company, even if no company is shown on screens and the subject company is assumed. Such a database would allow for restructuring and business mergers and would be more flexible than a database for which a person may only have a single employer.

This advice has a special urgency for database applications, because it is awkward to restructure a populated database. Databases can be distributed to multiple locations, and it can be difficult to restructure a database without disrupting routine operation. In contrast, a user interface has no "memory" of past data and is much easier to change; you can install a new interface in parallel to an existing interface and remove the old interface when it is no longer needed. The purpose of database applications is to enable business decisions, not encumber them.

 Carefully organize a database, because databases are difficult to restructure.

■ **Lack of documentation**. Much too often I encounter undocumented models. Diagrams alone are not sufficient; they need an explanation. The reader must be led through each diagram, and terminology must be defined. A narrative should explain subtleties and the rationale for any controversial decisions. It should also include examples to illustrate fine points.

 Thoroughly document your models.

Chapter Summary

There are many issues for managing models. The difference in productivity between expert and average developers can be an order of magnitude. You can increase the expertise of your staff by inducing them to learn modeling. You should invest in training, mentoring, in-house seminars, and continuing education.

There are several techniques for engaging users and obtaining their input: back-room, round-robin, and live modeling. Which technique is appropriate depends on the nature of a project and the talent of your staff.

I enumerated several modeling pitfalls you should try to avoid. Plan your projects so modeling is not practiced in excess of its benefits. Tolerate several modeling paradigms and notations in your organization, but insist that redundant models be reconciled.

✔ **Recognize that modeling is difficult**. Be proactive and help your staff learn to model.

✔ **Carefully structure discussions with users**. Actively consider different interaction techniques.

Major recommendations for Chapter 10

References

[Brooks-95] Frederick P. Brooks, Jr. *The Mythical Man-Month, Anniversary Edition*. Reading, Massachusetts: Addison-Wesley, 1995.

11

Operational Applications

This chapter shows how to design operational applications with a relational database. Developers can get excellent results by doing the following.

- **Devise an architecture**. An architecture is the high-level plan or strategy for building an application. (Chapter 3)

- **Model the application**. A high-quality model facilitates maintenance and improves the quality of data that is stored. (Chapters 8–10)

- **Design structure**. There are systematic rules for converting a model into a database structure. Model constraints become database constraints. (This chapter)

- **Design functionality**. The model serves as a blueprint for writing SQL code. Indexes ensure that the RDBMS traverses relationships quickly. (This chapter)

What is an Operational Application?

Operational applications involve the routine and critical operations of a business and are concerned with rapid transaction processing. A *transaction* is a group of commands that succeeds or fails as an indivisible unit of work; an entire transaction is written to a database, or nothing is written. Transactions can fail for a variety of reasons, such as application errors, computer crashes, and disc and communication failures. Examples of operational applications include payroll processing, order entry, financial trading, and flight reservations.

Many operational applications are performed on-line, while the user waits, and are thus referred to as *on-line transaction processing (OLTP)*. OLTP applications tend to be simple, access few records, and must respond within seconds; they often service forms on a screen for inquiries and data entry.

Other operational applications are performed off-line in batch mode. Because these applications are long, users often run them at odd hours (overnight and on weekends), so that they do not lock data and contend with interactive users. One purpose of batch applications is to load data warehouses and enable analytical processing. Batch applications also result from routine business activities, such as balancing the books at the end of a month.

Designing Structure

Developers should use basic design rules to ensure a consistent database structure, good performance, and ready maintenance. Many tools support these rules, and you should use them to generate database designs.

 Use a tool to generate database designs. Check the quality of the resulting code until you are confident of the accuracy of the tool.

I have designed many relational databases over the years. Whenever I build a relational database, I first model it and then map it to tables. The performance has always met my expectations. I use the techniques described here and only occasionally have had to finesse a problem.

Business anecdote: The merits of a uniform design strategy

In Chapter 9, I advocated that developers construct UML models to help them understand an application and then switch to the IDEF1X notation for designing a relational database. There are several reasons for this recommendation. Most persons find it difficult to build models; the use of a clean notation without design distractions (the UML) facilitates an already difficult task. UML tools are weak at database design, and it is too time consuming and error prone to design databases by hand. The IDEF1X notation is well supported by tools, and many UML tools can export their models to IDEF1X tools.

Identity

The first step in designing a relational database is to deal with identity. Developers should normally define a primary key for each table, although there are occasional exceptions. All foreign keys should refer only to primary keys, not to other candidate keys. (See Chapter 6.)

There are two basic approaches to defining primary keys.

- **Existence-based identity**. An artificial number attribute is added to each entity type table and made the primary key. The primary key for each relationship table consists of identifiers from the related entity types.

   Existence-based identifiers have the advantage of being a single attribute, small, and uniform in size. Most RDBMSs provide sequence numbers so that they can allocate identifiers efficiently. Existence-based identifiers can make a database more difficult to read during debugging and maintenance. IDs also complicate merging of databases; sometimes ID values contend and must be re-assigned. Artificial numbers should only be used internally in applications and not be displayed to users.

- **Value-based identity**. Some combination of real-world attributes identifies each entity. The primary key for each relationship table consists of primary keys from the related entity types.

   Value-based identity has different trade-offs. Primary keys have intrinsic meaning, making it easier to debug the database. On the downside, value-based primary keys can be difficult to change. One change may propagate to many foreign keys. Some entity types do not have natural real-world identifiers.

Figure 11.1 shows an awkward aspect of value-based identity. The top model (an excerpt from Figure 9.6) uses value-based identity and the *Activity* table has two copies of *airlineID* and *accountNumber*. One copy comes from the reference to *Frequent-FlyerAccount* and the other from *MonthlyStatement*. With value-based identity, there is no way to eliminate this duplication and still maintain referential integrity in the database. The bottom model (an excerpt from Figure 9.7) uses existence-based identity and avoids this situation.

I recommend that developers use existence-based identity for RDBMS applications with more than 30 entity types. The uniformity and simplicity of existence-based identity outweighs any additional debugging effort. Both existence-based and value-based identity are viable options for small applications. All examples in this chapter use existence-based identity.

Most IDEF1X models that I have seen in industry mix existence-based and value-based identity, often haphazardly. During training and mentoring (see Chapter 10), your developers should learn to be deliberate in dealing with identity.

 Deliberately choose an approach for identity. Use existence-based identity for most RDBMS applications.

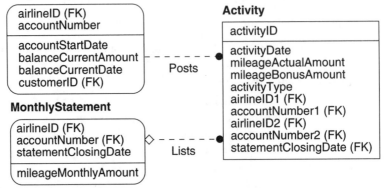

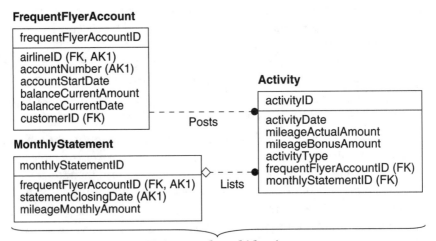

Figure 11.1 IDEF1X models with value-based and existence-based identity.
Use existence-based identity for most RDBMS applications.

Entity Types

Normally you should map each entity type to a table and each attribute to a column. You can add columns for an existence-based identifier, buried relationships, and generalization discriminators.

RDBMSs support the notion of **_null_** for a value that is unknown or not applicable. You can specify that a column be mandatory and must have a value (not null) or that it is optional and may be empty (null allowed). Nulls are a controversial topic

[Date-95, Chapter 9]. Although nulls complicate databases and often confuse users, missing data does occur, and given the popularity of SQL, there is little choice but to use them.

You should define all primary-key and candidate-key columns as not null. Discriminator columns and columns that arise from mandatory relationships are also not null. For the remaining columns, you should usually allow nulls to simplify usage. For example, you may not know the customer's address when entering a customer record in the database.

Figure 11.2 shows a conceptual model (UML notation) and the corresponding relational database design (IDEF1X notation).

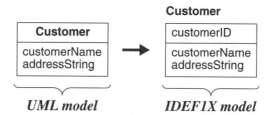

Figure 11.2 Designing entity types. Make each entity type a table.

Relationship Types

The design rules for relationship types depend on the multiplicity. Figure 11.3 shows the rule for many-to-many relationships. The relationship type is promoted to a table, and the primary key is the combination of the primary keys for the related entity types. The *FK* is IDEF1X notation for a foreign key.

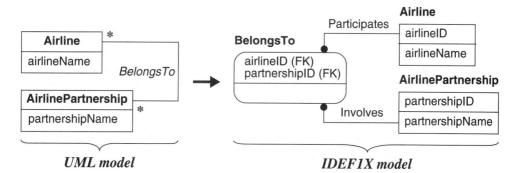

Figure 11.3 Designing many-to-many relationship types.
Promote each one to a table.

Figure 11.4 shows the recommended rule for one-to-many relationships. The relationship type becomes a foreign key buried in the table for the "many" entity type. I added the candidate key on *airlineID* and *flightNumber* because the combination must be unique for airline flights. The *AK1* is IDEF1X notation for an alternate key (a candidate key).

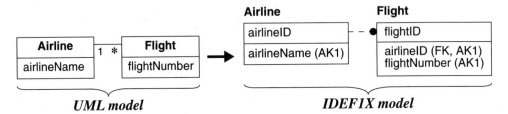

Figure 11.4 Designing one-to-many relationship types. Bury a one-to-many relationship type as a foreign key in the "many" entity type table.

One-to-one relationships seldom occur. Developers can handle these by burying a foreign key in either entity type table.

Generalizations

The simplest approach is to map the general entity type and each specific entity type to a table as Figure 11.5 shows. The primary key names may vary but an entity should have the same primary key value throughout a generalization. The ***discriminator*** (*activityType*) is an attribute that indicates the appropriate specific record for each general record. Applications must enforce the partition between specific entities because an RDBMS will not. For example, an RDBMS would let an *Activity* record have both a *FlightActivity* record and an *OtherActivity* record. An RDBMS will not stop such a multiple reference. (See Chapter 22.)

Indexes

The final structural design step is to tune the database by adding indexes. Most RDBMSs create indexes as a side effect of SQL primary-key and candidate-key constraints. You should also create an index for each foreign key that is not subsumed by a primary-key or candidate-key constraint. (Chapter 6 explains subsumption.)

These indexes are important. Indexes on foreign keys and primary keys let you combine tables quickly. Without these indexes, users will become frustrated. Indexes should be an integral part of a database design because they are straightforward to include and there is no good reason to defer them.

Some authors advise that you analyze how an application accesses data and define indexes only for the traversed foreign keys. This is usually not a good idea. It is

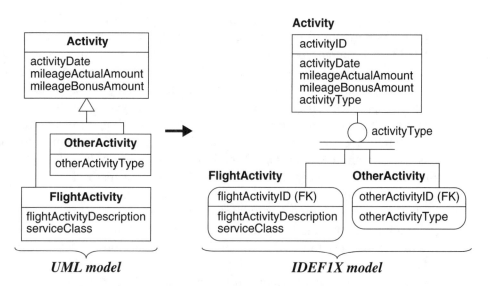

Figure 11.5 Designing generalization. Create separate tables for the
general entity type and each specific entity type.

difficult to anticipate all traversals. If you miss one, database performance can slip
by several orders of magnitude. The overhead of defining an index for every foreign
key is modest (typically slows updates by about 25%) and much better than the risk
of being surprised by an unexpected traversal.

The database administrator (DBA) may define additional indexes for frequent
queries. The DBA may also use product-specific tuning mechanisms.

 *Define an index for every foreign key that is not subsumed by a pri-
mary key or candidate key constraint.*

Normal Forms

A ***normal form*** is a guideline for relational database design that increases data consistency. As tables satisfy higher levels of normal forms, they are less likely to store
redundant data and contradictory data. Normal forms are not fiat rules. Developers
can violate them for good cause, such as to increase performance for a bottleneck or
for a database that is read and seldom updated. Such a relaxation is called ***denormalization***. The important issue with normal forms is to violate them deliberately and
only when necessary.

Normal forms were first used in the 1970s and 1980s. At that time, developers designed databases by creating a list of desired fields, which they then had to organize

into meaningful groups before storing them in a database. That was the purpose of normal forms. Normal forms organize fields into groups according to dependencies between fields. For example, both the airline and account number are needed to determine the current balance of frequent flyer points. Unfortunately, it is easy to overlook such dependencies. If any are missed, the resulting database structure may be flawed.

The ER approach [Chen-76] provides a better way to prepare databases. Instead of focusing on the fine granularity of fields, developers think in terms of entity types, which naturally organize fields into meaningful groups. The UML notation, which I favor, is one of many ER dialects. ER models do not diminish the validity of normal forms—normal forms apply regardless of the development approach.

However, ER modeling does eliminate the need to check normal forms. If developers build a sound ER model, it will intrinsically satisfy normal forms. (See Chapter 9 for advice on judging the quality of models.) The converse also holds—a poor ER model is unlikely to satisfy normal forms. Furthermore, if developers cannot build a sound model, they will probably be unable to find all the dependencies that are required for checking normal forms. It is less difficult to build models than to find all the dependencies.

The bottom line is that developers can still check normal forms if they want after ER modeling, but such a check is unnecessary.

 It is certainly acceptable to check normal forms, but it is unnecessary if developers prepare a sound model.

Summary of Design Rules

Table 11.1 summarizes the basic structural design rules for RDBMSs.

Concept	ER construct	Basic design rule
Entity type	Entity type	Map each entity type to a table and each attribute to a column in the table
Relationship type	Many to many	Use distinct table
	One to many	Use buried foreign key
	One to one	
Generalization	Generalization	Create separate tables for the general entity type and each specific entity type

Table 11.1 Summary of structural design rules for operational applications.
These rules are prominent for most database generation tools.

An Example

An example illustrates use of the design rules. Figure 11.6 shows an excerpt of the airline model in Chapter 9. Figure 11.7 shows an IDEF1X design model for the excerpt using existence-based identity.

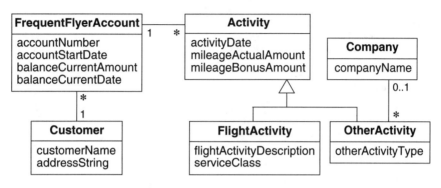

Figure 11.6 ER model for excerpt of airline example

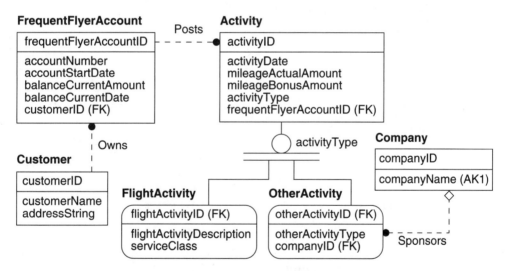

Figure 11.7 An IDEF1X design model for airline excerpt

Figure 11.8 shows Oracle SQL code that I wrote according to the IDEF1X model. This code is typical of what you should expect to receive from a tool. The uppercase-lowercase distinction is not significant for SQL but is intended to increase readability; uppercase denotes keywords, and lowercase denotes names of constructs. The *unique* clause is the SQL notation for enforcing a candidate key.

```
CREATE TABLE FrequentFlyerAccount
(frequentFlyerAccountID NUMBER(30)
   CONSTRAINT nn_ffa1 NOT NULL,
 accountNumber       VARCHAR2(20)  CONSTRAINT nn_ffa2 NOT NULL,
 accountStartDate    DATE          CONSTRAINT nn_ffa3 NOT NULL,
 balanceCurrentAmount NUMBER(12),
 balanceCurrentDate DATE,
 customerID          NUMBER(30)    CONSTRAINT nn_ffa4 NOT NULL,
CONSTRAINT pk_ffa PRIMARY KEY (frequentFlyerAccountID));

CREATE INDEX index_ffa1 ON FrequentFlyerAccount
   (customerID);

ALTER TABLE FrequentFlyerAccount ADD CONSTRAINT fk_ffa1
   FOREIGN KEY (customerID)
   REFERENCES Customer ON DELETE NO ACTION;


CREATE TABLE Customer
(customerID          NUMBER(30)
   CONSTRAINT nn_customer1 NOT NULL,
 customerName        VARCHAR2(255)
   CONSTRAINT nn_customer2 NOT NULL,
 addressString       VARCHAR2(255),
 CONSTRAINT pk_customer PRIMARY KEY (customerID));


CREATE TABLE Activity
(activityID          NUMBER(30)    CONSTRAINT nn_act1 NOT NULL,
 activityDate        DATE          CONSTRAINT nn_act2 NOT NULL,
 mileageActualAmount NUMBER(12),
 mileageBonusAmount NUMBER(12),
 activityType        VARCHAR2(20)  CONSTRAINT nn_act3 NOT NULL,
 frequentFlyerAccountID NUMBER(30)
   CONSTRAINT nn_act4 NOT NULL,
CONSTRAINT pk_act PRIMARY KEY (activityID));

ALTER TABLE Activity ADD CONSTRAINT enum_act1
   CHECK (activityType IN
   ('FlightActivity', 'OtherActivity'));

CREATE INDEX index_act1 ON Activity
   (frequentFlyerAccountID);

ALTER TABLE Activity ADD CONSTRAINT fk_act1
   FOREIGN KEY (frequentFlyerAccountID)
   REFERENCES FrequentFlyerAccount
   ON DELETE CASCADE;
```

Figure 11.8 SQL code for airline excerpt

```
CREATE TABLE Company
(companyID          NUMBER(30)
    CONSTRAINT nn_company1 NOT NULL,
 companyName         VARCHAR2(30)
    CONSTRAINT nn_company2 NOT NULL,
 CONSTRAINT pk_company PRIMARY KEY (companyID),
 CONSTRAINT uq_company1 UNIQUE (companyName));


CREATE TABLE FlightActivity
(flightActivityID  NUMBER(30)
    CONSTRAINT nn_flightAct1 NOT NULL,
 flightActivityDescription VARCHAR2(255),
 serviceClass       VARCHAR2(5),
 CONSTRAINT pk_flightAct PRIMARY KEY (flightActivityID));

ALTER TABLE FlightActivity ADD CONSTRAINT fk_flightAct1
    FOREIGN KEY (flightActivityID)
    REFERENCES Activity ON DELETE CASCADE;


CREATE TABLE OtherActivity
(otherActivityID    NUMBER(30)
    CONSTRAINT nn_otherAct1 NOT NULL,
 otherActivityType VARCHAR2(20),
 companyID          NUMBER(30),
 CONSTRAINT pk_otherAct PRIMARY KEY (otherActivityID));

CREATE INDEX index_otherAct1 ON OtherActivity
    (companyID);

ALTER TABLE OtherActivity ADD CONSTRAINT fk_otherAct1
    FOREIGN KEY (otherActivityID)
    REFERENCES Activity ON DELETE CASCADE;

ALTER TABLE OtherActivity ADD CONSTRAINT fk_otherAct2
    FOREIGN KEY (companyID)
    REFERENCES Company ON DELETE NO ACTION;
```

Figure 11.8 (continued) **SQL code for airline excerpt**

The *FrequentFlyerAccount* table has an implicit index created by the primary key constraint. The data types and lengths are arbitrary; for example, I assumed that 20 characters would be sufficient for the account number. I also assumed the account number might contain characters and consequently I used the Oracle string data type (*varchar2*). *FrequentFlyerAccountID* is not null because it is the primary key; I assumed *accountNumber* and *accountStartDate* were also required. The table has a foreign key of *customerID*, which is indexed to ensure fast traversal upon a join to

Customer. This field is not null because the model shows that a *FrequentFlyer-Account* has a mandatory *Customer*.

The *Customer* table has no foreign keys and indexes besides the implicit primary key index.

The *Activity* table has a foreign key of *frequentFlyerAccountID* that is not null. The discriminator *activityType* is also not null and the check constraint ensures that it is one of two possible values: *FlightActivity* or *OtherActivity*. The *on delete cascade* clause is an advanced SQL feature; on deletion of a *FrequentFlyerAccount* record, all corresponding *Activity* records are automatically deleted.

The unique constraint for the *Company* table enforces the candidate key on name.

The *FlightActivity* and *OtherActivity* tables reference the primary key of *Activity*. If an *Activity* record that is a flight activity is deleted, the corresponding *FlightActivity* record is automatically deleted. Similarly, if an *Activity* record that is an other activity is deleted, the corresponding *OtherActivity* record is automatically deleted. *OtherActivity* also has a foreign key reference to *Company*. The *no action* clause prevents the deletion of a *Company* that is referenced by an *OtherActivity*. (Actually, Oracle deviates from the SQL standard and does not support the *no action* clause, but omitting the clause still provides the same behavior.)

You can use the airline example to check the quality of code generated by your database design tools. Make sure that the tools generate the proper indexes and foreign-key commands. In my applications I have seen little (if any) performance degradation from an RDBMS enforcing foreign-key statements.

Designing Functionality

There are several ways to design functionality for relational database applications. Chapter 7 elaborates the first three techniques listed below.

■ **Programming code**. The most common technique for realizing application functionality is to write programming code that interacts with the database.

■ **SQL code**. Application functionality can often be off-loaded to SQL code. Models provide a blueprint for writing SQL code. (See upcoming examples.)

■ **Stored procedures**. A stored procedure is programming code that is stored in a database.

■ **Tables**. Sometimes it is helpful to store functionality in tables. For example, tables can store values for mathematical functions. I have also used relational database tables to store decision tables.

Developers should try to avoid embedding start, commit, and abort transaction commands in low-level procedures. Such commands may keep you from reusing logic in higher level procedures, which have their own needs for transaction scope. It is good style to limit start, commit, and abort commands to procedures that accomplish meaningful business functionality.

Furthermore, applications should generally avoid user interaction during transactions. Many DBMSs place locks on data for the duration of a transaction. Locks prevent other users from accessing the data and reduce database availability. If an application has an open transaction and is waiting for a user, there could be a problem if the user decides to take a coffee break. If user interaction must occur during a transaction, an application should use a time-out to bound response time.

Examples

Models are not merely passive data structures, but they can help you think about functionality. Figure 11.9 and Figure 11.10 each show a sample traversal for the airline model excerpt and the corresponding SQL code. SQL programming variables are italicized. The examples are meant to give a flavor of how models can lead to SQL code for manipulating data. *Substr* and *to_char* are Oracle functions.

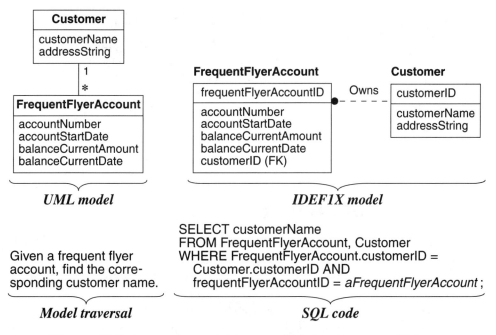

Figure 11.9 A sample model traversal. A developer can think in terms of a model for writing SQL data access code.

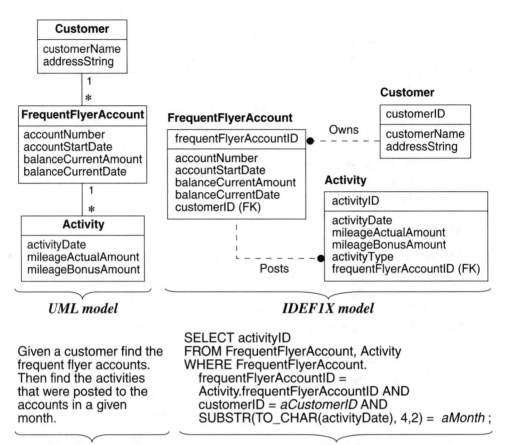

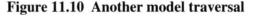

Figure 11.10 Another model traversal

Chapter Summary

Operational applications execute the routine and critical operations of a business. There are four primary steps for designing these applications with a relational database: devise an architecture, model the application, design structure, and design functionality.

There are systematic rules for converting models into tables. The major tasks are choosing an approach for identity and designing entity types, relationship types, and generalizations.

There are several ways to design functionality. The most common approaches are to use programming or SQL code. Programming code may be stored in executable files or as stored procedures that the RDBMS manages. Sometimes it is helpful to represent functionality as tables in addition to the tables that store data.

✔ **Generate database designs**. Use a tool to generate database designs. Check the quality of the resulting code until you are confident of the accuracy of the tool.

✔ **Deliberately choose an approach for identity**. Use existence-based identity for most RDBMS applications.

✔ **Thoroughly tune a database**. Define an index for every foreign key that is not subsumed by a primary-key or candidate-key constraint.

✔ **Address normal forms**. You will automatically satisfy normal forms (aside from deliberate violations) by preparing a sound model.

Major recommendations for Chapter 11

Resource Notes

[Blaha-98] covers additional details of designing databases. [Muller-99] also shows how to use the UML to develop operational applications. [Kent-83] has a thorough explanation of normal forms.

References

[Blaha-98] Michael Blaha and William Premerlani. *Object-Oriented Modeling and Design for Database Applications*. Upper Saddle River, New Jersey: Prentice Hall, 1998.

[Chen-76] PPS Chen. The Entity-Relationship model—toward a unified view of data. *ACM Transactions on Database Systems 1*, 1 (March 1976).

[Date-95] CJ Date. *Relational Database Writings 1991-1994*. Reading, Massachusetts: Addison-Wesley, 1995.

[Kent-83] William Kent. A simple guide to five normal forms in relational database theory. *Communications of the ACM 26*, 2 (February 1983).

[Muller-99] Robert J. Muller. *Database Design for Smarties: Using UML for Data Modeling*. San Francisco, California: Morgan Kaufmann, 1999.

12

Analytical Applications

This chapter describes analytical applications and shows how to develop them. Analytical applications can use either relational or multidimensional databases, but as the introduction to Part 3 noted, the emphasis is on relational databases because of their market dominance. Developers must address the following.

- **Model the data warehouse**. A data warehouse has additional modeling issues beyond those discussed in Chapters 8–10.

- **Devise an architecture**. The explanation from Chapter 3 applies, but there is a variation (the bus architecture) relevant to data warehouses.

- **Design the data warehouse**. There are systematic rules for converting a model into a data warehouse.

- **Populate the data warehouse**. This chapter elaborates the discussion of legacy data conversion from Chapter 7.

- **Analyze data**. Data warehouse queries go beyond the needs of operational applications.

What is an Analytical Application?

Analytical applications emphasize complex queries that read large quantities of data and enable organizations to make strategic decisions. Analytical applications execute against a *data warehouse*, which combines disparate data sources, providing one location for decision-support data. The data are placed on a common basis—for the same period, same geographical area, and same currency. Examples of analytical applications include sales analysis, casualty studies, inventory management, and fraud detection.

Users seldom update the data in a data warehouse; instead, it receives periodic extracts from multiple operational databases and external sources. A data warehouse may store historical data for as long as 5 to 10 years. Data accumulates from repeated extracts, and data warehouses typically grow to gigabyte and terabyte sizes.

Normally a data warehouse is implemented apart from operational systems, so that analysts exploring the warehouse do not contend with day-to-day activities. There are other reasons for this separation. Decision support requires that data be reconciled and integrated across applications, as well as a history of data. The data warehouse is not intended for passing data between operational applications and is dedicated to decision support.

As Figure 12.1 shows, a data warehouse receives input from operational databases and external sources. An example of an external source is Dun and Bradstreet (D&B) data about companies. D&B tracks companies worldwide and maintains data about them, such as revenue, business addresses, and corporate officers. Output data are provided in response to queries and for data mining. The warehouse discards old data by summarizing them, and then offloading the detail to archival storage.

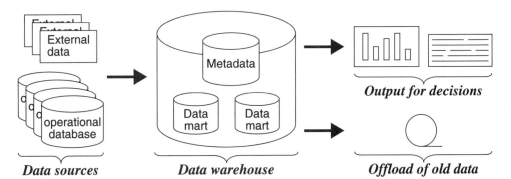

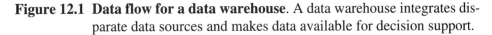

Figure 12.1 Data flow for a data warehouse. A data warehouse integrates disparate data sources and makes data available for decision support.

A data warehouse can be divided into ***data marts***. Since a data mart has a smaller scope, it can be built more quickly and yields quicker payback. Often a data mart is built to satisfy the needs of a department. All the data marts must combine into a data warehouse, so developers must make sure that no data marts conflict.

A data warehouse must also manage metadata that change over time, including the data warehouse's physical structure, a description of the source data, mappings from the source data to the data warehouse, and a history of refreshes and offloads.

Many data warehouse applications are interactive and referred to by the term ***online analytical processing (OLAP)***. Data warehouses must be carefully structured so OLAP applications can quickly respond to users.

Modeling a Data Warehouse

Data warehouses revolve around facts that are bound to dimensions. A *__fact__* measures the performance of a business. Sample facts include sales, budget, revenue, profit, inventory, and return on investment. As much as possible, facts should be numeric values (and not strings), so that a user can summarize them. A *__dimension__* specifies one of the bases for facts. Sample dimensions include date, location, product, customer, sales person, and store.

Modeling is different for analytical than for operational applications. Operational applications concern atomic entities that are bound together with relationships, often forming a complex web. In contrast, analytical applications have a simpler and more predictable structure; facts are surrounded by dimensions. Dimensions may have further structure, but the elaboration of dimensions should not be extensive.

Figure 12.2 shows a sample data warehouse model for grocery sales. A *Sale* is a fact that depends on six dimensions: *PaymentType*, *Date*, *Customer*, *Product*, *Cashier*, and *Store*. An industry has many categories; a category has many products. Hence, product sales data can be rolled up into categories and industries. Similarly, a region has many districts, and a district has many stores. A payment type can be cash, check, or credit card. Credit card types include Discover, Visa, Mastercard, and American Express. *SaleAmount, salePrice*, and *time* are attributes of *Sale*.

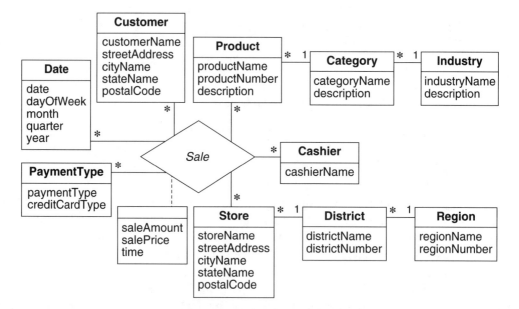

Figure 12.2 A model for store sales. ER models for data warehouses should be focused on facts and dimensions.

Note that the data warehouse model includes only data that are useful for decision support. It does not include purely operational data, such as the credit card number and expiration date. Thus, a data warehouse contains only some of the data found in operational applications.

A data warehouse for a large organization will consist of roughly 10–25 fact tables. Each fact table will have 5–15 dimensions [Kimball-98, page 147]. If there are too few dimensions, you probably need to think more deeply about possible queries and different aspects of data. If there are too many dimensions, some of the dimensions are probably not independent, and you should combine them.

> *Reconsider a data warehouse model if facts have fewer than 5 or more than 15 dimensions.*

Each dimension can have many attributes—some are merely descriptive; others enable roll-up. For example, *Store* has two descriptive attributes (*storeName* and *streetAddress*) and three attributes that enable roll-up (*cityName, stateName*, and *postalCode*). Thus, a data warehouse can process individual sales and find the total sale amount for individual stores, cities, states, and postal codes.

When modeling a data warehouse, you should avoid prematurely summarizing facts and subsequently limiting queries. Instead, start by modeling the finest grained facts and add summaries only when the model is intact. The model in Figure 12.2, for example, captures only detailed sales data—individual sales of products to customers.

The Bus Architecture

It is good practice to build data warehouses with a ***bus architecture*** and define dimensions consistently across fact tables. A bus architecture lets an organization obtain early financial payback before the warehouse is complete. There is a small amount of planning to determine dimensions and facts. You can then build and populate tables incrementally as you bring a data warehouse on-line. Business analysts use the warehouse and influence its evolution. Fact tables will share many dimensions for a correctly modeled data warehouse.

Figure 12.3 illustrates the bus architecture by extending the grocery sales model. A *Purchase* is a fact that depends on six dimensions: *Product, Supplier, Date, Store, ShippingMethod*, and *LotSize*. In principle, a store should determine inventory from purchases and sales of product, but mistakes do occur and products are sometimes stolen from store shelves. The *Inventory* fact records the measurement of *Product* for a *Store* on some *Date*. A full-fledged data warehouse should normally have 5–15 dimensions per fact—more than this simple example shows.

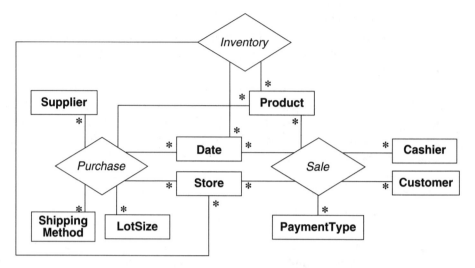

Figure 12.3 A bus architecture for store sales. The bus architecture defines dimensions consistently across fact tables.

 Use the bus architecture and incrementally build a data warehouse one data mart at a time.

Designing a Data Warehouse

Star Structure

Most data warehouses have a ***star structure***. Fact tables are the focus; each fact table stores data for some combination of dimension tables. For operational applications, developers can cope with a complex structure and they build queries. In contrast, business users pose many analytical queries; the star structure is a simple structure conducive to finding data.

Figure 12.4 shows a star structure corresponding to Figure 12.2. The example correlates facts about grocery store sales with six dimensions (*Customer*, *Date*, *Product*, *PaymentType*, *Cashier*, and *Store*). Note the use of artificial numbers (IDs) to identify the various dimensions. (See Chapter 11.) Fact tables can have millions of records and small dimension references reduce fact size.

The star structure simplifies a database by denormalizing data structure. (Chapter 11 explains denormalization.) Users can then more readily write queries that

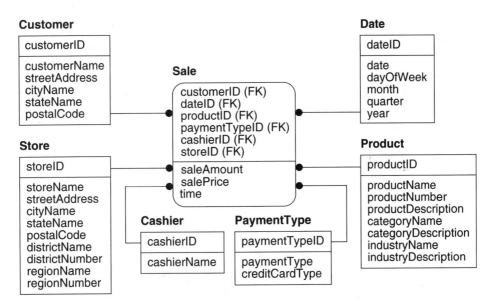

Figure 12.4 A star structure for store sales using IDEF1X. A star structure has a fact table that is bound to several dimension tables.

combine and summarize dimensions. (In contrast, because developers build operational queries, they can mitigate any drawbacks of a complex data structure.) A simple structure also lets the database evolve more flexibly. There is little downside to
denormalizing dimensions, because end users seldom update a data warehouse.

Normally use a star structure to build a data warehouse.

Other Structures

A *snowflake* structure results when dimensions are split into multiple tables. For example, there could be separate tables for store, district, and region. Snowflakes complicate a data warehouse and are usually unnecessary. Most dimension tables are
small compared with fact tables, and repeated attributes do not consume that much
disc space. Consider snowflakes only for monster dimensions with many records
that occupy 10 percent or more of the overall disc space.

Fact constellations are fact tables that share dimensional tables, which is often
desirable. With careful modeling and the use of the bus architecture, many dimensions can be shared.

Design Rules

Most large data marts (greater than a few gigabytes) are implemented with relational databases. The rules for designing analytical applications differ from those for operational applications, because analytical applications have few user updates, but many broad, complex queries. Table 12.1 lists the analytical design rules.

Concept	ER construct	Basic design rule
Entity type	Entity type	Combine the entity types for a dimension
Relationship type	Many to many	Use distinct table
	One to many	Subsume by combining the entity types for a dimension
	One to one	
Generalization	Generalization	Fold specific data into the table for the general entity type

Table 12.1 Summary of structural design rules for analytical applications. The preferred design rules yield a simple data structure.

- **Entity type**. The star structure described earlier implies one table for each dimension. The *Store* dimension table, for example, combines the *Store*, *District*, and *Region* entity types. This combination denormalizes the database structure, which is appropriate, given that a data warehouse is used to build complex queries and is seldom updated by a user.

- **Relationship type**. The facts in a data warehouse are many-to-many relationships on multiple dimensions. A fact table may store multiple attributes when they are at the same level of granularity. For example, the *Sale* fact table stores *saleAmount*, *salePrice*, and *time*. Incidental one-to-many and one-to-one relationships occur with describing dimensions and are folded into a dimension (except for monster dimensions).

   Developers should normally define foreign keys as part of the database structure. Foreign-key enforcement can help catch loading errors. The downside is that enforcement may slow data loading.

- **Generalization**. Developers can handle generalization by folding specific data into the table for the general entity type. Generalization seldom occurs with data warehouse models, however, because there is little need to store fine detail about different kinds of data. Figure 12.5 shows an operational model for payment data. A data warehouse would not need data such as *checkNumber* and *approvalNumber* because they are not important to decision support.

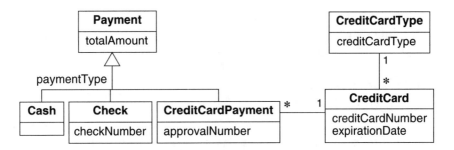

Figure 12.5 An operational model of payment data. Operational models
have detail that is not needed for decision support.

A general rule of thumb is that the entire data warehouse takes three or four times as
much space as the data for base facts [Kimball-98, page 585].

Summarizing Data

Summarization is the single most effective way to boost performance in a large data
warehouse and can make certain queries 100 to 1,000 times faster. In effect, summaries are preemptive queries. Summarization anticipates the kinds of queries that users will often ask and precomputes the results.

Ideally, you should store summaries as well as base data. That way no information is lost, and the base data is still available for other queries. The disadvantage of
redundant summaries is that they slow loading and consume more disc space. It is
best to store summaries in their own fact tables, apart from base data and to store
data at different summarization levels separately [Kimball-98, page 556].

Summaries are difficult to build, because it is hard to anticipate what users will
ask. In practice, developers forecast query activity and build summaries accordingly.
Administrators then monitor database activity and adjust summaries to tune performance. Ultimately, user feedback and warehouse experience is needed to arrive at
the best summaries.

How many summaries are appropriate? [Kimball-98] suggests that summaries
consume 25 to 100 percent of the disc space of the base data. If summaries occupy
less than 25 percent, then query response would probably substantially improve with
more summaries. If summaries occupy more than 100 percent, you could probably
discard some summaries with little effect on query performance. You can compute
disc space for a table by multiplying the estimated number of records by the average
size per record (add the size of each field).

Some warehouses would be too large if all base data was stored. In that case, you
must either reduce the time period of the data or discard some base data and replace
it with summary data. Such discarding is problematic, however, because it restricts

the possible queries. A common technique is to summarize data more coarsely as it ages—for example, to summarize recent data by day, older data by week, and oldest data by month. Eventually, after several years, you can move the data off-line.

Partitioning Data

Many RDBMSs support the partitioning of tables— allocating records to different storage areas according to the value of a partition field. With data warehouses, it is often helpful to partition tables by date to make refresh, rolling summarization, and archiving easier.

Partitions can make some queries faster. For example, the system can more quickly search a date partition for a particular month than an entire table. Partitions also ease maintenance because you can add or drop individual partitions from a table. Just about the only downside of partitions is that they can increase storage space, because disc pages may be less completely filled with records. Even this disadvantage is insignificant if you use a partition to divide tables coarsely, say, a partition for each month or quarter.

Indexes

As with operational applications, you should create an index on each foreign key, so that the system can quickly traverse from a foreign key to the referenced key. Occasionally, it is helpful to add indexes on other frequently accessed columns.

Populating a Data Warehouse

Data conversion is a complex, time-consuming, and tedious task that consumes, on average, about 60 percent of warehouse development time [Kimball-98]. Commercial tools can automate much of the routine data processing. However, you will still need to write custom code for special situations.

Choosing Data Sources

The first step is to identify the various sources and the data they can provide. Data may be available from both operational and external sources. You should prioritize multiple sources for the same data with the following criteria.

- **Accuracy**. Sources vary in the quantity of errors and difficulty of repair.

- **Completeness**. Can the data source populate entire fact or dimension records? For example, it would be helpful if a source of product data included its category and industry, as in Figure 12.4.

■ **Timeliness**. How quickly does a source reflect operational activity? For example, a source that is updated on-line would be more timely than a source that is updated via periodic batch update.

■ **Closeness to source of entry**. Data are often passed along from program to program. Usually, it is better to be close to the origination of the data than be subject to alteration along the way.

■ **Closeness to data warehouse model**. A source with structure closer to the data warehouse model has simpler conversion code.

The next step is to prepare a detailed mapping of source columns to data warehouse columns. Consider only data that are relevant for decision support. For example, a data warehouse may retain the area code, but discard the actual phone number. You will need the advice of business experts to understand data intricacies. Table 12.2 shows some mappings for populating the store sales example.

The table shows two sources of customer data. First, customers are loaded from the internal order delivery table (current customers), and then people are added from the external mailing list (prospective customers). It would take some sophistication to automate the comparison of names, because of all the possible misspellings and abbreviations (such as Chas. for Charles). Some commercial firms can provide this kind of processing for large quantities of data. For small quantities, you could rely on string matching followed by human inspection.

Many old applications store names and addresses in uppercase. Converting strings to mixed case improves their readability. Many tools can provide this kind of cleansing, and it is also straightforward to program.

The order delivery table stores an entire address as a string. The strings must first be parsed into separate fields before they can be loaded into the data warehouse. Furthermore, state names and two-character codes are mixed and must be converted to state names. Such parsing enables business users to write queries to roll-up sales to cities, states, and postal codes.

Source data are often not available. It can be especially difficult to get data from poorly designed legacy applications. Sometimes it is helpful to reverse engineer a data source to understand its structure better.

Extracting Data

The next step is to obtain the source data and transmit them to the data-processing machine. Simply reading source data can be a problem. Some formats are poorly documented, and vendors may not make it easy to read their databases.

Source table	Source column	Target table	Target column	Comment
... General comments...				First, load order delivery data; then, load external mailing list. Process all strings to mixed case.
Order delivery database	customer	Customer	customerName	
	address		streetAddress	Parse address to separate fields. Source mixes state names and abbreviations. Remove dashes from postal codes.
			cityName	
			stateName	
			postalCode	
External mailing list	name	Customer	customerName	
	address1		streetAddress	Concatenate source strings.
	address2			
	city		cityName	
	stateCode		stateName	Convert two-character code to string.
	zipCode		postalCode	Remove any dashes.
Store dimension		Store		A dimension is available from a previous data mart.

Table 12.2 A sample source-to-target mapping. Mappings provide the foundation for populating the data warehouse.

After the initial population, the data warehouse must be refreshed with operational updates. It can be difficult to determine what data has changed from the last time the source was read. There are several techniques for detecting changes.

■ **Snapshot driven**. Compare the source data with a prior copy.

■ **Trigger driven**. Use triggers to catch operational updates as they occur and write to a revision table. A _**trigger**_ is a database command that executes on some specified occurrence.

■ **Transaction driven**. Inspect the DBMS transaction log and propagate the transactions to the data warehouse.

■ **Full refresh**. Process a complete copy of source data.

Cleansing Data

Clean data is required to maximize the benefit of a data warehouse. Operational applications have their own purposes (invoice customers, deliver products, manage manufacturing) apart from a data warehouse. For example, multiple customer names can be tolerable for an operational application if paperwork and materials still get to the right person. In contrast, such flaws compromise a data warehouse and the ability to analyze data broadly. There are many issues to resolve.

- **Inconsistent field lengths**. One application may have company names with a length of 30; another may have 50 characters. The data warehouse must have a single length.

- **Inconsistent data types**. Applications can store U.S. postal codes as numbers or strings. They must store international postal codes as strings.

- **Different encodings**. For example, applications can encode sex as male or female, M or F, 1 or 2, and so on. You must choose one encoding for the data warehouse.

- **Inconsistent units of measure**. One application may list weight in pounds; another in kilograms. The data warehouse listing must be consistent.

- **Missing data**. Developers may be able to find another source or estimate the missing data. The data warehouse can define special dimension records for "don't know," "hasn't happened yet," "not applicable," and other situations.

- **Duplicates**. As much as possible, cleansing must consolidate duplicates, such as variations on customer names.

- **Illegal values**. Many applications have restricted fields that users choose from a list of values. For example, payment type might have the options of cash, check, or credit card. Cleansing must reject illegal values.

- **Foreign key errors**. If the warehouse database defines foreign keys, it will not store dangling references. However, the cleansing process might still need to report violations in the source data so that they can be repaired.

- **Identity errors**. A candidate key might logically apply even if the source data violates it.

- **Overloaded fields**. Cleansing must separate overloaded fields into their constituents.

- **Misspellings**. Cleansing should correct any misspellings when found.

- **Capitalization**. Processing to mixed case can make upper case data more readable.

- **Unwanted effects**. The cleansing process might correct data for a confounding effect. For example, removing the effect of a coupon promotion might determine base grocery store sales.

Even this long list of flaws is not complete. Many developers become frustrated by source errors and want to repair them. Usually, that is a mistake because many source errors are not a business issue. Instead data warehouse developers should accept operational applications as is and cope with the errors. A data warehouse effort must not become sidetracked by operational repair.

When cleansing data, try to avoid writing a lot of programming code, which is time-consuming to write, costly, and difficult to maintain. Instead, use tools to process errors as much as possible and supplement them with custom-written SQL code. Only when you exhaust both these options, should you resort to programming.

 Accept operational applications as is. Don't sidetrack a data warehouse project by trying to fix operational flaws. Clean-up of operational databases is a separate issue to be justified on its own merits.

In one project a developer had written Visual Basic programming code to convert data. After three months, the code was only partially complete and took an hour to process a 1 MB legacy file. The sponsors became frustrated and ended his work.

I became involved in the project when the sponsors asked me to write the conversion logic. In two weeks, I wrote an MS-Access SQL script that converted 1 MB of data in 30 seconds. Why did my work succeed where the earlier effort failed? One reason is that a skilled developer can write SQL much faster than programming code. Another reason is that Visual Basic is a slow, interpreted language, while MS-Access SQL is compiled and runs fast.

Business anecdote: Using SQL code to process data

Reconciling Data

Once data are cleansed, data sources with overlapping structure and content must be reconciled or the data warehouse will be fragmented and unable to answer some queries.

Developers can resolve overlapping structure by reverse engineering, modeling, and learning about source applications. This work is necessary because most operational applications are built with little thought to coordination. The study of structure should be confined to the data relevant to the data warehouse. Chapter 21 covers the related topic of integrating operational applications for data exchange.

Developers must also reconcile content. Sources may have overlapping data, such as an order delivery database and external mailing list referring to the same person. Often it is difficult to determine identity—whether two records describe the same thing. A name may not uniquely identify a person. For example, there are many Jim Smiths. Social security number only applies to people in the United States. In practice, persons are identified with a combination of fields. Some vendors have advanced tools that use artificial intelligence techniques to determine when two records refer to the same person.

When data sources have overlapping, but conflicting data, you must decide what to load. Often it is too tedious to decide record by record. A simple approach is to load sources in declining order of accuracy. Before loading each source, place it in a staging table and subtract any overlap with the current database. (You can use SQL commands to perform the subtraction.) This approach biases the database towards the best sources.

> One of my clients had multiple sources of company information to reconcile. They used Dun and Bradstreet (D&B) numbers for the headquarters office to identify each company. Some records already had D&B numbers. They used in-house software to assign D&B numbers to most remaining records by matching their names to the names in a D&B master file. For the records that still remained, they made manual decisions.
>
> They loaded several record sources in declining order of accuracy, using D&B numbers to determine records that overlapped. The whole process worked well.

Business anecdote: Using D&B numbers to identify companies

Loading and Refreshing Data

After cleansing and reconciling multiple sources, you are ready to load the data. It is best to load dimensional data first to establish keys and then load fact data and reference the dimensional keys.

Typically, loading is done a data mart at a time, usually during off hours, when data need not be on-line. If data must be on-line, you can make a copy of the data mart available for queries. Updates are triggered by new operational data, as well as the consolidation and purging of data that has aged in the data warehouse.

Most RDBMSs have a bulk load facility that efficiently loads tables. This facility is more efficient than loading records individually with the SQL insert command.

You should enable referential integrity during bulk loading to ensure that all facts refer to dimensions that truly exist.

As you load data, they must be sorted, summarized, and indexed. Often it is most efficient to drop indexes, load the data, and then rebuild indexes—do this if you are loading more than 10–15 percent of the total rows. If you have multiple storage areas, you must partition the data. Finally, you must purge or archive old data when they are no longer worth the storage space and query overhead.

An important issue is the lag time between changes to operational data and propagation to the data warehouse. As a rule, you should refresh warehouse data no more than every 24 hours [Inmon-93]. There are two reasons for delay. First, it is more convenient to load warehouse data during off hours. Second, the warehouse is not intended for operational purposes. A 24-hour lag time helps ensure that the organization uses it for decision support.

Analyzing Data

Business users must be able to explore the database to acquire an understanding of the data. Special client software coupled to the data warehouse can make it easier to build queries.

Queries

Data warehouses involve many ad hoc queries that perform numerous scans, combinations, and summaries. Power users can use tools to build queries, but most users need prepackaged queries. Common analytical operations include:

- **Roll up**. Summarize data and decrease detail along one or more dimensions.
- **Drill down**. Increase detail along one or more dimensions.
- **Selection**. Filter the rows that are displayed. Most selection comes from restrictions on dimension attributes.
- **Projection**. Choose the attributes that are displayed.
- **Slice and dice**. Reduce the dimensionality of the data by choosing rows and columns.
- **Pivot**. Reorient the view of data by changing the dimensions used to summarize facts. The idea of a pivot is taken from a spreadsheet.
- **Sorting**. Order the data in a different way.

Some tools are smart enough to automatically use summaries that let a query execute more quickly. Such tools also simplify maintenance, because administrators can add and remove summaries while the data warehouse is on-line.

A helpful technique for speeding response is to experiment with random data samples (say, every 1,000th record) to detect trends. You can then validate the hypotheses against the full database.

Another useful technique is to materialize intermediate tables rather than try to build one large, complex query. This can greatly simplify SQL code, but you must manage additional tables.

Data Mining

Not every question can be readily stated. ***Data mining*** discovers subtle trends and patterns by using artificial-intelligence techniques. For example, you could analyze grocery sales to determine the products that have synergistic effects when located close together in a store. Data mining can take hours, so it is often scheduled for off hours to avoid degrading the interactive response. Data mining can be especially helpful with very large data sets.

Chapter Summary

Analytical applications let organizations make strategic decisions. These applications execute against data warehouses—specially prepared databases that reconcile data from multiple sources. Data warehouses revolve about facts bound to dimensions. A fact measures the performance of a business. A dimension specifies one basis for a fact.

It is a good practice to organize a data warehouse into data marts that serve the needs of specific departments. The data marts must have dimensions that are consistent across fact tables. The bus architecture lets you develop data marts one at a time, eventually leading to an entire data warehouse.

Most data warehouses have a star structure that stores the data for each dimension in a single table. In practice, most large data warehouses are implemented with relational databases. The design rules for analytical tables differ from those for operational tables. A general rule of thumb is that the entire data warehouse takes three to four times as much space as the data for base facts. Summarization is the single most effective way to boost the performance of a large data warehouse. Partitioning and indexing are also important.

Data conversion is a complex, time-consuming, and tedious task that consumes, on average about 60 percent of warehouse development time. Most of the effort is spent on cleansing data and reconciling overlapping sources. Commercial tools can automate much of the routine processing. However, when you need to write custom code for special situations, write it in SQL; use a programming language only as a last resort.

You should prepackage common queries for ordinary business users. Power users can use tools to build queries and advanced techniques like data mining to detect subtle trends and patterns.

✔ **Carefully choose dimensions**. Reconsider a data warehouse model if facts have fewer than 5 or more than 15 dimensions.

✔ **Incrementally build a data warehouse**. Use the bus architecture and build one data mart at a time.

✔ **Normally use the star structure**. Use another structure only when there is a compelling reason.

✔ **Don't rewrite operational applications for a data warehouse**. Repair of operational databases should be a separate issue justified on its own merits.

Major recommendations for Chapter 12

Resource Notes

Larry Greenfield [Greenfield-99] has a Web site with helpful information about data warehouses. [Chaudhuri-97] thoroughly explains data warehousing within the confines of a paper. [Inmon-93] is a concise explanation of data warehouse concepts and rationale. Ralph Kimball is also a leader in data warehouse technology; Chapters 5 and 6 of [Kimball-98] are especially good.

References

[Chaudhuri-97] Surajit Chaudhuri and Umeshwar Dayal. An overview of data warehousing and OLAP technology. *SIGMOD Record 26*, 1 (March 1997), 65–74.

[Greenfield-99] http://pwp.starnetinc.com/larryg

[Inmon-93] WH Inmon. *Building the Data Warehouse*. New York, New York: Wiley-QED, 1993.

[Kimball-98] Ralph Kimball, Laura Reeves, Margy Ross, and Warren Thornthwaite. *The Data Warehouse Lifecycle Toolkit*. New York, New York: Wiley, 1998.

13

Design Summary

This chapter compares design aspects of operational and analytical applications and provides a list of items that can help you produce a quality database design.

Two Kinds of Applications

__Operational__ applications involve the routine and critical operations of a business and are concerned with rapid transaction processing. The queries tend to be highly focused and access a small number of records. Most queries are predictable and provided by developers. Because operational applications are important to day-to-day business, they must be highly available and seldom interrupted by computer down time. Many operational applications are stovepipes that have little coordination with other applications. Most operational applications perform on-line, while the user waits—they are called on-line transaction processing (OLTP).

In contrast, *__analytical__* applications emphasize complex queries that read large quantities of data. The main function of these applications is decision support. They execute against a data warehouse that combines disparate data sources and provides one location for decision-support data. Users seldom update a data warehouse; instead, updates are done with periodic extracts from operational databases and external sources. A data warehouse may store data for as long as 5 to 10 years. Many analytical applications perform on-line, while the user waits—they are called on-line analytical processing (OLAP).

Structural Design Rules

Table 13.1 restates the database design rules from Chapters 11 and 12.

Concept	ER construct	Operational design rule	Analytical design rule
Entity type	Entity type	Map each entity type to a table and each attribute to a column in the table	Combine the entity types for a dimension
Relationship type	Many to many	Use distinct table	
	One to many	Use buried foreign key	Subsume by combining the entity types for a dimension
	One to one		
Generalization	Generalization	Create separate tables for the general entity type and each specific entity type	Fold specific data into the table for the general entity type

Table 13.1 Comparison of design rules. The different purposes of operational and analytical applications affect the choice of design rules.

Note the divergence between the two kinds of applications. The fundamental principles of database theory do not vary—the different design rules reflect their distinct purposes, as well as different expectations for query and update traffic.

Operational applications have relatively simple queries and many user updates, so the database must be carefully designed to enforce data quality. A complex design can be tolerated, since developers usually prepare the queries.

In contrast, analytical applications have complex queries and few user updates. Since the queries are sophisticated and often built by users, the database structure must be kept simple. Analytical applications can pay less attention to data quality, but must be able to read data quickly.

Design List

Table 13.2 shows important issues that a thorough database design must address.

All database designs must specify the structure of tables and the attributes within the tables. Attributes have a name and a data type. For each attribute, you can

Topic	Subtopic	Operational applications	Analytical applications
Attributes	Names	*	*
	Data types	*	*
	Mandatory or optional (nulls)	*	*
Table structure	Names	*	*
	Primary keys	*	*
	Candidate keys	*	*
	Foreign keys	*	*
	Other constraints	*	
	Normal forms	*	
Performance tuning	Indexes	*	*
	Summarization		*
	Data partitioning		*
Data conversion		*	*

Table 13.2 Database design list. These issues are critical to a
thorough database design.

specify whether the value is optional and can be omitted (null allowed) or is manda-tory and must have a value (not null).

Tables also have a name and are subject to a variety of constraints. A candidate key is a combination of columns that uniquely identifies each row in a table. The combination must be minimal and not include any columns that are not needed for unique identification. A primary key is a candidate key that is preferentially used to access the records in a table. A foreign key is a reference to a candidate key (normal-ly a reference to a primary key) and is the glue that binds tables. Relational databases can also enforce many simple constraints; Figure 11.8, for example, shows a con-straint that limits *activityType* to one of two possible values.

Normal forms are principles for database design that remove redundancy and re-duce the likelihood of update errors. Operational databases should normally observe normal forms. In contrast, analytical databases are usually denormalized in an effort to simplify queries and speed response. Update errors are not as much of an issue for analytical databases, because end users seldom update them.

Indexes are the most important tuning technique for operational applications. They are also important for analytical applications, but not as important as summarization. Summarization consists of preemptive queries that reduce the data to be processed by several orders of magnitude. Partitioning data can also be helpful for analytical applications. Neither summarization nor data partitioning is needed for operational applications, because the typical query accesses only a few records.

Data conversion is important for both kinds of applications. Analytical data conversion tends to be more difficult because there are more data to cleanse, reconcile, and load. Furthermore, analytical conversion is ongoing, while operational conversion is often just a one-shot effort.

This book covers the most critical aspects of database design, but there are issues outside its scope. I have only touched on the topic of security, for example. Organizations must assign ownership of data: who maintains an application's data and ensures its veracity. Storage space must be assigned for database data; excessive space is wasteful, and insufficient space encumbers operation. I have also not covered the myriad details that database administrators must handle, such as monitoring performance and ensuring database integrity.

Chapter Summary

The same fundamental database theory underlies both operational and analytical applications, but each has different motivations and access behavior. Operational applications have many simple queries and updates. In contrast, analytical applications have few user updates, but the queries are often complex.

The requirements for operational applications lead to spider webs of atomic tables that aim to ensure data quality. The requirements for analytical applications lead to simple database designs—multiple fact tables each of which is surrounded by dimensions. Operational applications usually observe normal forms. In contrast, analytical applications have different goals that make normal forms inapplicable.

Part 4

Software Engineering Technology

In its Software Engineering Standard (IEEE 610.12-1990), the Institute of Electrical and Electronics Engineers (IEEE) defines *software engineering* as "a systematic, disciplined, quantifiable approach to the development, operation, and maintenance of software." Software engineering is critical to the success of database applications. A firm that can proficiently and predictably handle software has a clear business edge. Proficiency is important so that you can quickly turn your business desires into software. Predictability is important so that you can accurately assess software cost and make sound investment decisions.

Chapter 14 discusses the importance of using a methodology—a specific systematic approach to the development, operation, and maintenance of software, whether it be purchased or developed. A methodology has two major aspects—concepts (discussed in Part 3, Chapters 8 and 9) and process (this part).

Chapter 15 addresses the development process—the sequence of steps for building models and using them to develop software. It is important to preserve your degrees of freedom during development. Do not make coding decisions when you are still trying to understand a problem. There is no advantage of making premature decisions, and you run the risk of an inferior result.

Chapter 16 is the counterpart to Chapter 15 and presents a process for acquiring software. As you would expect, the process for purchasing software is simpler than that for developing it.

Part 4 concludes with Chapter 17 in which I discuss project management issues for database applications. Expert developers lead to a leaner and more effective organization. The chapter presents specific actions you can take to leverage the efforts of your staff.

14

Methodology

Regardless of who develops it, a vendor or your organization, software must be engineered. A methodology provides the means for carrying out this task.

What is a Methodology?

A *methodology* is a specific systematic approach to the development, operation, and maintenance of software. It is, in essence, a particular approach to software engineering. Because different authors have different recommendations as to the best way to engineer software, there are multiple methodologies.

A methodology has two major aspects: *process* and *concepts*. A process guides the practitioner through system development. The process is supported by underlying concepts and a notation for expressing the concepts.

Why Use a Methodology?

The reasons for using a methodology stem from the IEEE definition for software engineering—"a systematic, disciplined, and quantifiable approach" (see Part 4's introduction).

- **Systematic**. A systematic approach is necessary if you wish to achieve repeated, predictable success. A sound methodology is inherently systematic.

- **Disciplined**. The rigor in a methodology partially compensates for differing skill levels among the members of a development team. A methodology establishes definitive tasks to perform and makes intermediate work products available for review.

- **Quantifiable**. Both producers and consumers of database applications need accurate estimates of manpower, elapsed time, and development cost. To estimate accurately, you must have quantitative data from past projects and techniques for extending the numbers to new projects. A methodology provides the means for acquiring these data.

Even if you purchase software, a methodology is still relevant. You can build models to help you understand precisely what you need and what the vendor is offering. You can also assess a vendor's methodology and their likelihood of delivering reliable software.

 Use a methodology. Your organization should have a disciplined and reproducible approach to obtaining software.

How Software Is Often Built

Many organizations build software haphazardly. The following themes characterize their practices.

- **Weak management**. Managers give developers a functional specification for their portion of an application and let them build it however they want.

- **Poor planning**. Management and developers are overoptimistic and overreach. They have trouble distinguishing between the long-range vision for software and intermediate deliverables.

- **Stovepipe applications**. Applications proceed with only partial rationalization against other projects. This results in disjointed databases that are difficult to exploit for decision support.

- **Excessive programming**. Developers resort to brute-force programming. They lack imagination in framing problems in terms of SQL. They lack confidence in meshing programming and databases.

- **Technology fads**. Developers fixate on products, technologies, and tools apart from their merits.

With each of these, ultimately, everyone wastes much time and effort, as many applications fail.

How Software Should Be Built

Other organizations build software in a forthright manner and learn from their successes and failures. The following themes characterize advanced organizations.

- **Strong management**. Managers require that software be built through models that have been reviewed with business leaders and other developers.

- **Sound planning**. There is still the long-term vision for an application, but it is tempered with intermediate deliverables that are quickly delivered to customers and yield business value.

- **Reconciled applications**. Reviews lead to exchanges of ideas and synchronize application models. Sometimes organizations can reuse selected subsystems and code.

- **Thoughtful programming**. Developers are skilled at programming, but use it judiciously in conjunction with SQL and software purchase.

- **Technology edge**. Developers monitor new products, technologies, and tools and use them to extend their abilities.

The discipline of a methodology brings a solid, coherent core to an application that reflects the business knowledge and business needs.

Specific Methodologies

This book advocates modeling and development rigor, but just sketches out a methodology. These references provide more detail for database applications.

- **Information engineering**. James Martin was one of the first authors to address the specific needs of database applications. The IE approach combines an ER model with models for programming code [Martin-89].

- **Batini, Ceri, and Navathe**. [Batini-92] explains the fundamentals of ER modeling and proposes a joint data and process driven database design methodology.

- **Object-oriented approaches**. OO methodologies are the newest software development approach and are the culmination of several influences: OO programming languages, ER data models, and software engineering. [Blaha-98], [Martin-97], and [Muller-99] are OO approaches to database applications.

Regardless of your preference, make sure that you choose a methodology specific to database applications. Database applications are distinctive, because they are dominated by large amounts of data that must be maintained for a long time. You will be less likely to succeed if you choose a general-purpose approach, such as functional decomposition, which is used for many programming applications.

 Use a tailored methodology. You will have greater success if you use a methodology specific to database applications, rather than a general-purpose one.

Chapter Summary

A methodology is a specific systematic approach to the development, operation, and maintenance of software. It is thus an approach to accomplishing software engineering. A methodology can help you realize the thoughtful, repeatable, and predictable development of software. An awareness of methodology is still relevant if you buy software.

✔ **Use a methodology**. Your organization should have a disciplined and reproducible approach to obtaining software.

✔ **Use a tailored methodology**. You will have greater success if you use a methodology specific to database applications, rather than a general-purpose one.

Major recommendations for Chapter 14

References

[Batini-92] C. Batini, S. Ceri, and S. Navathe, *Conceptual Database Design*. Reading, Massachusetts: Benjamin/Cummings, 1992.

[Blaha-98] Michael Blaha and William Premerlani. *Object-Oriented Modeling and Design for Database Applications*. Upper Saddle River, New Jersey: Prentice Hall, 1998.

[Martin-89] James Martin. *Information Engineering Book I: Introduction*. Upper Saddle River, New Jersey: Prentice Hall, 1989.

[Martin-97] James Martin and James Odell. *Object-Oriented Methods: A Foundation, Second Edition*. Upper Saddle River, New Jersey: Prentice Hall, 1997.

[Muller-99] Robert J. Muller. *Database Design for Smarties: Using UML for Data Modeling*. San Francisco, California: Morgan Kaufmann, 1999.

15

Development Process

The models in Part 3 provide the means for software engineering. This chapter shows how to use models to develop operational and analytical applications. (Chapter 16 presents a corresponding process for software purchases.) As a manager, you will probably not build models yourself, but you should be aware of what your staff is doing. Furthermore, you should be actively reviewing models and monitoring their quality.

This chapter starts with a summary of the outputs and inputs for database application development. The outputs can be produced from the inputs by proceeding through several well-defined stages. The presentation of the stages is linear, but the actual process need not be linear.

Outputs from Development

The outputs from database application development include:

- **Architecture**. An *architecture* is the high-level plan or strategy for building an application. For example, you may want to deliver an application with distributed computing or a distributed database. You may partition a large application into smaller components.

- **Models**. A model can help you think clearly about a problem and focus your attention on the difficult issues. As development proceeds, the model becomes the basis for design and implementation.

- **Data dictionary**. A *data dictionary* complements a model by defining important concepts, as well as giving examples and rationale.

- **Narrative**. A model is a form of documentation, but a model alone is not sufficient. Modelers should also provide a data dictionary and a written narrative. (They can fold the data dictionary into the narrative if they prefer.) The narrative should walk the reader through the model and explain subtleties and major decisions.

Always supplement a model with an explanation, such as a data dictionary and a narrative.

- **Database structure**. By applying a small number of straightforward rules (see Chapters 11–13), a developer can prepare a database structure (the initial empty database) from a model. The resulting performance is not only fast, but highly predictable. Important concepts in the model carry forward directly to the database structure.

- **Converted data**. Users often want new applications prepopulated with basic data. They should not have to enter part names, customer names, addresses, phone numbers, and the like that are already known from other applications and standard sources of data. Data warehouses must receive periodic refreshes from operational databases.

- **Programming code**. Most application logic is straightforward and deals with database traversal. Nevertheless, some applications have algorithms that must be programmed. For example, you may have a complex formula for computing product price or an expert system that predicts future orders.

- **User interfaces**. Database applications have some interface between the database and the user. User-interface technology is outside the scope of this book, but a sound model and database structure will enable ready access to data, making it easier to develop a quality user interface.

The ultimate output of development is, of course, the finished system. Table 15.1 shows the pertinent outputs for in-house and outsourced development. With outsourcing, you relinquish only two tasks—preparing programming code and the user interface—but they are the most time-consuming tasks.

As a rule, you should prepare your own model and not outsource this task. A model is the crown jewel of your intellectual thought, and it is too risky to depend on another organization.

Prepare your own models, even when you outsource development. It is too risky to depend on someone else.

Output	Build an application in-house	Outsource application development
Architecture	*	*
Model	*	*
Data dictionary	*	*
Narrative	*	*
Database structure	*	*
Converted data	*	*
Programming code	*	
User interface	*	

Table 15.1 Output list. The appropriate development outputs depend on the procurement option.

In addition, I recommend that your staff, not an external organization, prepare the database structure. Many people do not know how to design a database, so you want to ensure that it is done right. An application cannot recover from a bad database design. The database is the foundation for an application and must be solid. If your staff is skilled, they can quickly design the database and off-load much of the work to tools. Roughly speaking, they should be able to design a database in about 10 percent of the time that it takes to build a model.

 Have your staff prepare the database structure, even when you outsource development.

Inputs to Development

It is important to consider all input sources. A skilled developer should be adaptable and able to glean requirements from whatever is available. Common inputs include:

- **Business documentation**. Business experts provide the inspiration, justification, and rough scope for most applications. They often provide a statement of motives and intent, screen mock-ups, scenarios, and sample reports. The business may impose some design decisions (such as the choice of a database manager or hardware platform) and implementation decisions (such as software engineering standards). The business must clearly define criteria for success.

One of my clients commissioned contract programmers to build an application. The contractors had full control, as long as they met requirements. The resulting application had adequate performance and a reasonable user interface, but the database design was a mess. The application was prone to errors in data and was difficult to extend.

My client decided that it was less work to redo the application than live with the problems. My client modeled the application and properly designed the database; the contract programmers reworked the code. The resulting application ran faster, had better data quality, and could be maintained.

The moral is that a properly designed database will save you both time (faster development) and money (reduced maintenance).

Business anecdote: Controlling the database

■ **User interviews**. An obvious technique for obtaining requirements is to interview business experts. Developers can question users for missing information and clarification. Oftentimes, user comments are obtained during a modeling session, as Chapter 10 explains.

■ **Technical reviews**. In user interviews, developers interact with business experts. Technical reviews are complementary and leverage the ideas of technologists and line managers.

■ **Related applications**. These provide grist for modeling (see Chapter 19) as well as data for populating the database. You should consider systems that are to be replaced, as well as systems that will remain, but overlap the new system.

■ **Prior experience**. You are fortunate if developers are familiar with the application's subject matter. Such experience will accelerate work. Sometimes it is helpful to visit the environment where users work and observe their activities.

■ **Enterprise models**. (See Chapter 21.) An ***enterprise model*** describes an entire organization or some major aspect of an organization. An enterprise model is helpful to the extent that it covers your application.

■ **Standard models**. You should consider any relevant models that are available from standards organizations.

 Don't dwell exclusively on user interviews. Take advantage of all available input sources.

Table 15.2 summarizes the strengths and weaknesses of the various input sources.

Input source	Strengths	Weaknesses
Business documentation	Directly expresses business sentiments. Often available.	Often has inconsistencies, omissions, and errors.
User interviews	Developers pose the questions.	Users may not have much time for interaction. There is little time to reflect during interviews.
Technical reviews	Educate developers. Help the organization reconcile applications.	Many developers are reluctant to air their work publicly.
Related applications	Ensure developers will not overlook past requirements. Often have useful data.	Yield some obsolete requirements. Involve reverse engineering, which is a difficult skill.
Prior experience	Highly desirable if you are so fortunate.	Developers may rely on it to the exclusion of input from business experts.
Enterprise models	Rich information source.	Quality is highly variable.
Standard models	They are free. It is desirable to conform to standards.	Quality is highly variable.

Table 15.2 Sources of requirements. There are multiple sources of requirements with different trade-offs.

Stages of Development

Software development has a sequence of well-defined stages. I elaborate on each stage in the following subsections.

- **Analysis**. Model the application from the perspective of the real world.
- **Design**. Decide how to build the application from the analysis model.
- **Implementation**. Write the actual database and programming code.
- **Data conversion**. Populate the application database with available data.
- **Testing**. Ensure that the application is suitable for actual use.
- **Training**. Help users master the new application.
- **Maintenance**. Preserve the soundness of the application over the long term.

The key aspect of this process is the distinction between analysis and design. First, you determine *what* you want. Only then do you decide *how* to build it.

Table 15.3 relates the development stages to procurement options. The asterisks indicate work that your organization should do. In any case, you should perform analysis to determine your needs, test for quality assurance, and prepopulate the database. For an in-house application, you also perform design and implementation. For an outsourced application, you should design the database, but you can off-load the remainder of design, as well as implementation. Most organizations perform their own training and application maintenance.

Development stage	Build an application in-house	Outsource application development
Analysis	*	*
Design	*	Partial. Do database design yourself. Outsource the rest.
Implementation	*	
Data conversion	*	*
Testing	*	Partial. Your organization and the vendor both do testing.
Training	*	*
Maintenance	*	*

Table 15.3 Development stage list. The asterisks indicate work that
your organization should do.

Analysis

Modeling is the focus of analysis (Figure 15.1). Analysis prepares a model of the application from the perspective of the real world. During analysis, you specify *what* must be done, not *how* it should be done. Analysis is a difficult task in its own right, and developers must fully understand it before addressing the additional complexities of design.

The preparation of a model and architecture must be interleaved for complex applications. The architecture helps to establish a model's scope. In turn, modeling reveals important issues of strategy to resolve. Thus there is much interplay between the construction of a model and the model's architecture, and they must happen together.

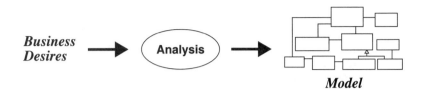

Figure 15.1 **Analysis**. The purpose of analysis is to construct models
that specify *what* must be done, not *how* it should be done.

During analysis, developers consider the available inputs and resolve ambiguities. Often business experts are not sure of the precise requirements and must refine them in tandem with software development. Modeling quickens the convergence between developers and business experts, because it is much faster to work with multiple iterations of models than with multiple implementations of code. Models highlight omissions and inconsistencies so that they can be resolved.

Developers begin analysis by modeling entities and relationships from the various input sources. As they elaborate and refine the model, it gradually becomes coherent. Once the model gels, developers need to reconsider and restructure it—to make the model more concise and enforce critical business rules. Models for operational applications are much different than those for analytical applications; Chapters 11–13 explain the differences.

In Chapter 9, I presented several database modeling notations and recommended that you use an ER notation for modeling, specifically the UML dialect.

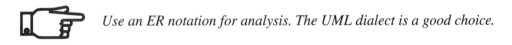

Use an ER notation for analysis. The UML dialect is a good choice.

Design

During design the focus shifts from an emphasis on the real world, to techniques for realizing the application (Figure 15.2). Developers address how a problem is to be solved, but they don't descend into the fine details of the target database and programming language. Thus, during design, developers should convert a model to relational database tables, for example, but they should defer the idiosyncrasies of a specific database manager, such as Oracle.

You must choose a specific data management approach—whether to use simple files (which suffice for some applications) or a database manager. Developers then determine the detailed data structures and algorithms that will realize the model from analysis.

Model

Figure 15.2 Design. During design developers address how a problem
is to be solved, but don't descend into fine details.

In principle, you have a choice of design notations. You can carry forward a
UML (or other ER dialect) model from analysis and augment it with design information such as primary keys, not null restrictions, and indexes. Or you can convert
to the IDEF1X notation, which is excellent for capturing relational database details.

I suggest that you use IDEF1X for design. The current UML tools are good at
modeling, but most have poor facilities for database design. (Most UML tools are
written for programmers.) In contrast, IDEF1X tools are excellent at database design. It is cumbersome to coordinate the use of a UML tool for modeling and an
IDEF1X tool for design, but in my opinion, this is the best compromise between the
need for intense unfettered thinking during analysis and database generation capabilities during design. (I comment further on tools in Chapter 17.)

 *Use an ER (non-UML) or IDEF1X notation for design. The current
UML tools are weak at designing relational databases.*

Implementation

Implementation is the stage for writing the actual code (Figure 15.3). It is at this
point that developers must deal with the nuances of the specific database manager
and programming languages that are being used to construct the system. Developers
should take the design model and drive it into the database structure. Once they have
established a sound database, they can implement programming logic and a user interface. Tools can generate the code for creating an empty database.

Empty tables   Screens

Figure 15.3 Implementation. Implementation is the stage for
writing the actual programming and database code.

Data Conversion

Data conversion adds existing data to a database (Figure 15.4) and is important for both operational and analytical applications. It is desirable to seed operational databases with data from overlapping applications. It is fundamental to data warehouses that they receive periodic updates to source data.

Empty tables   *Populated tables*

Figure 15.4 Data conversion. Data conversion adds existing data to a database.

Data conversion is often an intricate task. Source databases can be difficult to understand. In addition, the source data structure rarely matches the target data structure. Many source databases have data flaws that must be repaired. Chapter 12 covers data conversion in detail.

Testing

After implementation, the system is complete, but must be carefully tested before it can be commissioned for actual use. Hopefully, the ideas that inspired the original project have been nurtured through the previous stages by the use of models. Testers once again look at the original business requirements and verify that the system delivers the proper functionality. Testing can also uncover accidental errors (bugs) that have been introduced. If an application runs on multiple hardware and operating system platforms, it should be tested on all of them.

Training

An organization must train users so that it can benefit fully from an application. Training accelerates users on the software learning curve.

Maintenance

Once development is complete and a system has been deployed, it must be maintained for continued success. There are several kinds of maintenance. Bugs that remain in the original system will gradually appear during use and must be fixed. A successful application will also trigger requests for enhancements and a long-lived application will occasionally have to be restructured.

Models ease maintenance and transitions across changes in staff. A model expresses the business intent for an application that has been driven into the programming code, user interface, and database structure.

Software Development Life Cycle

Although the presentation of the software development stages has been linear, the practice need not be [Pressman-97]. There are four common approaches for building database applications.

Waterfall

The classic life-cycle paradigm is the waterfall approach. As Figure 15.5 shows, with this approach, developers perform the software development stages in a rigid linear sequence with no backtracking.

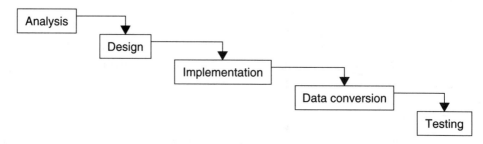

Figure 15.5 Waterfall approach. The waterfall approach is inflexible and unsuitable for most database application development.

The waterfall approach is suitable for well-understood applications with predictable outputs from analysis and design. It is also used in many contractual situations, especially for government projects (regardless of its suitability).

A waterfall is inappropriate for applications with substantial uncertainty in the requirements—which is most applications you will encounter. Too many organizations attempt to follow a waterfall when requirements are fluid. This leads to the familiar situation where developers complain about changing requirements, and the business complains about an inflexible information systems (IS) organization. A waterfall approach also does not deliver a useful system until completion. This makes it difficult to assess progress and correct a project that has gone awry.

  Except for applications with predictable outputs, do not use a waterfall approach.

Rapid Prototyping

With this approach (Figure 15.6) you quickly develop a portion of the software, use it, and evaluate it. You then incorporate what you have learned and repeat the cycle.

Eventually, you deliver the final prototype as the finished application or, after a few prototypes, switch to another approach. You must *quickly* cycle through prototypes (typically an iteration every two or three months) for this approach to succeed. Rapid prototyping focuses on the input of user interviews; if you can glean information from other input sources, you can reduce the number of prototypes.

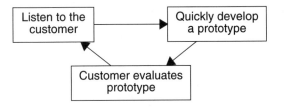

Figure 15.6 Rapid prototyping approach. Rapid prototyping facilitates software development by eliciting requirements from users.

Rapid prototyping promotes communication. You learn about the needs of the customer, and the customer learns what automation can provide. Thus, prototyping targets a core difficulty of software development—finding the true requirements. Rapid prototyping provides frequent checkpoints for assuring customers that development is going well. It also lets developers experiment with troublesome aspects of design and implementation. They can test a difficult algorithm and find if it works well before committing to a full implementation.

The prototype may be throwaway. Or it may be gradually elaborated until you achieve a working system. This is the weakness of rapid prototyping—often a prototype is unsuitable for enhancement, but you may receive business pressures to enhance it nonetheless. The key to success is to be prepared to discard early prototypes. Prototypes should be enhanced only if they are successful in the field and have a robust architecture.

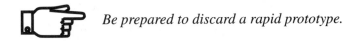 *Be prepared to discard a rapid prototype.*

Incremental Development

Incremental development (Figure 15.7) is similar to the waterfall approach, except that you partition the application and develop portions at a time. Multiple increments are delivered, and the accumulation becomes the finished application. (Contrast this with rapid prototyping where each deliverable replaces the preceding code.)

An advantage of incremental development is that you have frequent milestones. If you encounter difficulties, you can catch them early and adjust your practices.

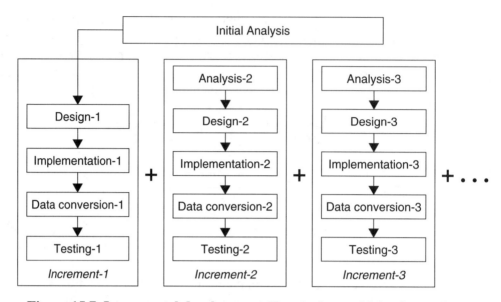

Figure 15.7 Incremental development. You deploy multiple pieces of operational software that combine to form the complete application.

The challenge is to find meaningful increments for development—breaking an application into pieces with few interdependencies. Ideally, the interfaces between the increments should be minimal and easy to define. Also you must perform much up-front analysis; otherwise, subsequent changes can disrupt earlier increments. Most applications require substantial infrastructure effort before useful increments of functionality become apparent to the user. A business may combine several increments before deployment to simplify logistics.

Fourth-Generation Language

A *fourth-generation language (4GL)* is a framework for straightforward database applications that provides screen layout, simple calculations, and reports. A 4GL raises the level of the implementation medium closer to that of analysis. Analysis work still remains, but less effort is needed for design and implementation. If your application fits the 4GL framework, developers can construct it rapidly with few errors.

The advantage of a 4GL is reuse: Multiple applications leverage the same 4GL software. Typically, a 4GL is purchased from a vendor, so your organization need not develop it. With skillful use, the performance of a 4GL application can be quite good.

The drawback of a 4GL is the rigidity of the framework. Developers become accustomed to the paradigm and may try to use it for inappropriate applications, such as those with complex computations. 4GLs also lack facilities for reusing application logic; developers must code similar forms repeatedly. 4GLs are sophisticated software and require an investment of time and effort to achieve proficiency.

Combining Approaches

You can combine the various approaches. For example, you might use rapid prototyping to flesh out requirements for difficult portions of incremental development. Sometimes, it is helpful to divide a large system into components and build the components with different approaches.

Table 15.4 summarizes the strengths and weaknesses of the software life-cycle approaches.

Approach	Strengths	Weaknesses
Waterfall	Suitable for applications with predictable outputs from analysis and design.	Copes poorly with fluid requirements. Does not deliver a useful system until completion.
Rapid prototyping	Elicits user requirements. Provides frequent milestones. Lets you experiment with troublesome development issues.	There may be business pressures to extend a fragile prototype. Code must often be thrown away.
Incremental development	Delivers useful portions of an application. Provides frequent milestones.	Some problems are hard to partition. Must complete infrastructure before delivering useful functionality.
Fourth-generation language	Developers can build applications rapidly with few errors.	Many applications do not fit the framework. A 4GL is yet another technology to learn.

Table 15.4 Comparison of life-cycle approaches. There are several good alternatives for coordinating the stages of software development.

Chapter Summary

This chapter has sketched out a process for building database applications. The outputs from development revolve around models and their manifestation in the finished system. Inputs vary widely across applications. You should be resourceful and take advantage of whatever inputs are available. Often, the most significant inputs are business documentation, user interviews, technical reviews, and related applications.

The inputs and outputs can be handled most effectively by using an organized development process with well-defined stages. It is critical to distinguish between analysis and design. Analysis is the phase of specification for determining the application requirements. Design is the phase of solution for devising a way to construct the software.

Given an overall process, you must also choose a life cycle. There are several options: waterfall (perform the stages in strict sequence), rapid prototyping (repeatedly develop the software and successively expand the scope), incremental development (break the application into pieces for which you use a waterfall or rapid prototyping), and a fourth-generation language (a framework that solves common database application tasks).

✔ **Document models**. Always supplement a model with an explanation, such as a data dictionary and a narrative.

✔ **Prepare your own models**. It is too risky to depend on another organization.

✔ **Also design the database in-house**. The database is critical to an application and does not take long to design.

✔ **Consider all input sources**. Don't dwell on user interviews to the exclusion of other input sources. There are many sources of requirements, and you should use them all.

✔ **Use an ER notation for analysis**. The UML dialect is a good choice.

✔ **Use an ER (non-UML) or IDEF1X notation for design**. The current UML tools are weak at designing relational databases.

✔ **Normally, avoid the waterfall life-cycle approach**. Consider the waterfall approach only for applications with predictable outputs.

✔ **Be prepared to discard a rapid prototype**. Enhance prototypes only if they are successful in the field and have a robust architecture.

Major recommendations for Chapter 15

References

[Pressman-97] Roger S Pressman. *Software Engineering: A Practitioner's Approach, Fourth Edition*. New York, New York: McGraw-Hill, 1997.

16

Acquisition Process

This chapter presents a systematic approach to evaluating and purchasing database application products from vendors. It is the counterpart to Chapter 15.

Outputs from Acquisition

The acquisition process yields several outputs.

- **Models**. A model can help you think clearly about a problem. Models for acquisition help you understand: (1) what you want (the requirements) and (2) the products the vendors are offering.

- **Data dictionary**. A data dictionary complements a model by defining important concepts, as well as giving examples and rationale.

- **Narrative**. A model is a form of documentation, but a model alone is not sufficient. Modelers should also provide a data dictionary and a written narrative. (They can fold the data dictionary into the narrative if they prefer.) The narrative should walk the reader through the model and explain subtleties and major decisions.

- **Converted data**. Users often want new applications prepopulated with basic data. They should not have to enter part names, customer names, addresses, phone numbers, and the like that are already known from other applications and standard sources of data. Data warehouses must receive periodic refreshes from operational databases.

- **Evaluation**. The acquisition process yields commentary on the various vendor products. Cursory evaluations are performed for the lesser products and thorough evaluations for the promising products.

Inputs to Acquisition

Technical reviews for acquisition differ considerably from those for development. Instead of evaluating a development effort that is underway, you evaluate multiple vendor products that are already built. The other inputs are the same as for development and are discussed in Chapter 15.

Stages of Acquisition

Acquisition for a major product (a product with more than $500,000 in license and deployment costs) has the following stages. You can simplify the process for a minor product or when you already have information. I elaborate on each stage in the following sections.

- **Find candidate products**. Browse the marketplace for potential products.
- **Document requirements**. Prepare a document that states your requirements. You can document requirements in parallel to finding candidate products and prescreening.
- **Prescreen candidate products**. With a cursory study, reduce the list of potential products to about six semifinalists.
- **Screen semifinalists**. Talk to the vendors and further reduce the list to two or three finalists.
- **Evaluate finalists**. Study the technical features, negotiate with the vendors, and make your final decision.
- **Data conversion**. Populate the application database with available data.
- **Training**. Help users master the new application.
- **Deployment**. Use the product. With purchased software, you should not expect a perfect fit to your business. You should be prepared to live with some limitations and to modify your business to fit the software.

Find Candidate Products

The first step in an evaluation is to compile a list of products that might meet your needs (Figure 16.1). It is important to be thorough and not to overlook quality products. Otherwise, you hobble the remainder of your evaluation.

Try to be creative in finding products and consider multiple information sources. Sources of product information include:

- **Publications**. Vendors often advertise in trade and technical magazines. Magazines also publish product evaluations. Some evaluations are objective, and oth-

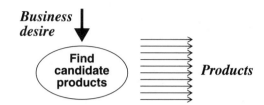

Figure 16.1 Find candidate products. The first step in an evaluation is to compile a list of products that might meet your needs.

ers are influenced by the magazine's vested interest in securing advertising from the vendor.

■ **The Web**. You can find some products by specifying relevant categories of software and using a search engine to browse the Web. For example, I did a search on "accounting software" with *www.profusion.com* and found many products.

■ **Trade shows**. You can attend a trade show in the area of interest. For example, many vendors attend trade shows for sales and marketing software in the hope of reaching prospective customers.

■ **Consultants**. You can retain a consultant who is an expert in your application area. Seek a consultant who is objective and does not have excessive business ties with a particular vendor.

 Cast a broad search to find candidate products.

Normally, you should rule out "vaporware"—hypothetical products that express the vendor's hopes for the future, but are not tangible at the current time. Hypothetical products are risky, and it is difficult to compare future promises with current reality. If you really want to consider a hypothetical product, delay your evaluation until the vendor actually *has* the product.

Document Requirements

Documenting requirements (Figure 16.2) lets you reach a consensus within your organization and inform the vendors. This step occurs in parallel to finding and pre-screening candidate products. The output is an RFP (request for proposal) or RFQ (request for quotation).

The process of documenting requirements should begin with an analysis model of the desired data. (See Chapter 15.) The model helps you understand the requirements, resolve conflicting opinions, and determine the proper scope. The different

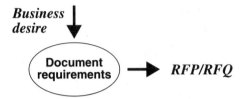

Figure 16.2 Document requirements. Document requirements to reach a consensus within your organization and to inform the vendors.

 It is still important to model requirements, even when you purchase a product.

application constituencies should all agree on the model. You also might want to prepare a high-level overview of your business process.

The next step is to establish the evaluation criteria and assign weights to them. It is important to distinguish between "musts" (the vendor must absolutely meet them) and "wants" (desirable features that you could possibly do without). Limit the "must" criteria so that you do not reject too many potential products. There are many kinds of criteria to consider.

- **Functionality**. The software must support important business logic.

- **User interface**. The interface should be satisfactory to your users. Otherwise, they will resist using the package, make more errors, and be less productive.

- **Platform**. Your business infrastructure will dictate the kinds of machines and operating systems on which the software must run. You may prefer a particular database manager, such as Oracle.

- **Architecture**. The vendor should be able to articulate the high-level structure of their software. You may prefer using a fat client, fat server, three-tier architecture, or TP monitor. (See Chapter 3.)

- **Performance**. The software should have a lively response for common operations. Users should not have to wait.

- **Security**. The software should protect data against failures and malicious intent.

- **Scalability**. A product should incrementally scale for additional users. Growth is problematic if you must replace hardware or switch to a different package.

- **Deployability**. Some packages are large and monolithic, because the vendor is trying to appeal to a wide variety of customers. Such packages can be difficult to deploy if much of the logic does not apply to your business.

■ **Documentation and training**. Documentation and on-line help should be clear. The vendor should provide training upon request.

Once you have an analysis model and selection criteria in hand, prepare an RFP/ RFQ. Tell the vendors what you want and the major criteria for selection. The RFP/ RFQ should ask questions to solicit information. I recommend that you include your model with the RFP/ RFQ so that vendors can better understand your requirements. You can then use the RFP/ RFQ to screen semifinalists, as I describe later.

Prescreen Candidate Products

Now you need to reduce the products under consideration to a manageable number—about six products (Figure 16.3). Reject the lesser products quickly, so that you have ample time to focus on the promising ones.

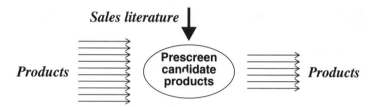

Figure 16.3 Prescreen candidate products. Reduce the products under consideration to a manageable number.

Your staff should conduct a paper study. They can review sales literature from publications, the Web, trade shows, and consultants. Have them consider just the major requirements—the five or ten most important criteria. Rate the candidate products as passing or failing the criteria. You have limited information at this point, and some of your perceptions may be wrong, so it is not worth too much effort.

You may not want to identify yourself to the vendors at this stage. Otherwise, you could receive nuisance calls and mailings for marginal products.

Screen Semifinalists

At this point, you should have about six significant products. You now need to learn more about them so that you can choose two or three finalists for the final evaluation (Figure 16.4). For this step, your organization needs to reach a consensus. During prescreening, you could make cursory decisions, but now you must be able to defend your choices. I recommend taking the following actions for each candidate vendor.

■ **Request detailed literature**. Unless the vendor looks very promising, reject them if they do not respond. Lack of response is one sign of poor customer service.

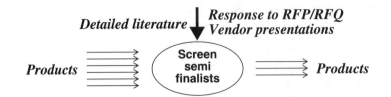

Figure 16.4 **Screen semifinalists**. Learn more about the products
to reduce the number under consideration.

- **Provide a copy of the RFP/RFQ**. Label the document as "company confidential," so that the vendors treat your requirements discreetly and do not disseminate them. Responding to inquiries is a bother for vendors. You must be able to assure them that you are serious about choosing a product.

- **Invite vendors to present the product**. Ask that they demonstrate live running software. Assess the functionality and user interface. Do not request evaluation copies at this time; defer that activity for the finalists.

- **Check the company's viability**. How long has the vendor been in business? What are their revenues, profitability, and number of employees? How large is their market share?

For the semifinalists, revisit your prescreening evaluation. Look more closely at the products, and consider additional criteria, say the 20 most important. Continue to reject products that fail any "must" criteria. Remember, however, that if you reject too many vendors, you may have to reconsider the "must" criteria. Keep the products with the best scores, and perform a sensitivity analysis to determine the effect of errors and uncertain weighting on the scores. Make sure that you are comfortable with the results.

It helps to have several people independently rate the products. They can then compare scores and agree on a group score. Separate scoring lets multiple people contribute, which leads to a better assessment.

 Have several persons independently rate each product. They can then all contribute, which leads to a better assessment.

Evaluate Finalists

You should have only two or three products left at this stage. These products will undergo your most thorough evaluation (Figure 16.5). Be careful and take your time. You may be investing quite a bit of money for the purchase and deployment costs. In addition, you forego the opportunity to choose another product. For each finalist, perform the following tasks.

When I worked at the GE R&D Center, lots of vendors would visit us and try to sell their products. One of our standard questions was to ask if they used their own products. About 50 percent of the vendors said "no" and had some lame excuse. We quickly ended these sessions and sent them on their way. If the software was not good enough for them, it was not good enough for us.

Business anecdote: Vendors should use their own software

Figure 16.5 Evaluate finalists. Probe the products deeply, and make your final decision.

■ **Request evaluation software**. If the software is difficult or confusing to install, that is a poor sign. Have users experiment with the software. Does the software have the proper functionality, and is it intuitive? Look at the on-line help and manuals. Are there routines for importing and exporting data for the database? Test the software on the required hardware platforms. You might want to send someone to the vendor's training classes.

   Check performance by running some representative benchmarks. If you have concurrent access, distributed data, or distributed computing, consider their effect on performance.

■ **Reverse engineer the database**. An evaluation copy gives you some feel for the software, but you still don't know how well it is built. For major acquisitions, it is well worth spending several weeks reverse engineering the finalists. Prepare a model of the product, and compare it against your requirements model. This helps you determine the database quality, which is a good indicator of the overall software quality. Look for surprises, such as an odd database design or a poor underlying model. Reverse engineering deepens your understanding of the product's capabilities and limitations. Chapter 20 has more details.

 Use reverse engineering to assess finalists for major purchases of database applications.

■ **Negotiate for purchase and support terms**. Will the vendor give you a discount? Reverse engineering gives you negotiating leverage. You learn about some of the product's flaws, which offset the vendor's claim of features.

Does the vendor have satisfactory support and consulting services? Do they have support via the Internet? Do they have any user groups for their product? If so, you may want to attend a user group meeting.

Try to keep a "poker face" in negotiating with vendors. You can get a better price and terms if the vendor cannot count on your business. It helps if you have at least two serious finalists; then, you don't have to pretend.

■ **Obtain customer references**. Request that each vendor provide customer references. Most vendors will readily do this. You can often obtain much information and surprising candor from references. Most references don't mind a polite, good-faith call about a product. After all, they purchase products and make reference calls themselves from time to time.

Check customer references. You can learn much with a small investment of time.

Now consider all the information, and score each product. By this time, the scores should be anticlimactic: You should have a good idea of which product is best. If the scores show that all the finalists are weak, you should reconsider buying a product (and instead develop it) or consider delaying purchase.

> A client used this acquisition process and found themselves with a vaporware product (a product that is an idea and does not yet exist) as a finalist. They discovered this when they visited the vendor. The vendor had deliberately blurred their current inadequate product with promises of the desirable product. Even with your best efforts, evaluation is still an imperfect science.

Business anecdote: Ferreting out hypothetical products

Data Conversion

Data conversion for purchased software is similar to that for development and was discussed in Chapter 15.

Training

Many vendors offer training for their products, which is often more economical than attempting to provide training on your own.

Deployment

Many vendor packages have user-definable fields and forms, and you can use them to a limited extent. However, it is not a good idea to modify a package heavily. There are obvious issues of cost and customization time, but modification also impedes your ability to accept vendor upgrades. You should use a package with minimal modification or not use it at all.

 Limit customizations of vendor software. Customizations cost time and money and make it harder for you to accept upgrades.

Chapter Summary

Even when you purchase software, models are still important. You need to under-stand requirements, reach consensus, and decide on scope. You need to be able to communicate this information to a vendor.

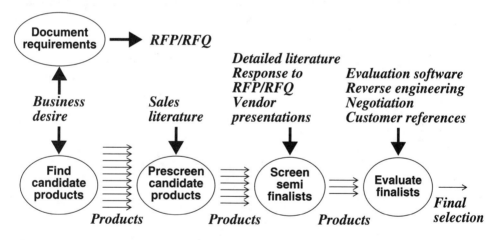

Figure 16.6 Overall acquisition process. A systematic evaluation
process will help you choose better vendor products.

I recommend a systematic evaluation process (Figure 16.6). First, perform a search and find candidate products. In parallel to the search, document your require-ments with a model and write a statement of requirements to give to the vendors (RFP/RFQ). For a large number of candidates, perform a quick paper study to re-duce the number to about six. Then gather more information from the vendors and reduce the number to two or three finalists. The finalists are worthy of a full evaluation in which you experiment with the software, reverse engineer its database, negotiate with the vendor, and check customer references. With a purchased product you still need to perform data conversion to seed the initial database and train users.

✔ **Broadly search for candidate products**. Try to be creative and consider multiple product information sources.

✔ **Use modeling**. Modeling is still important, even when you purchase a product. You need to understand requirements, resolve conflicting opinions, and determine scope.

✔ **Independently rate products**. Several people should separately rate each product. They can then all contribute, which leads to a better assessment.

✔ **Consider reverse engineering**. Use reverse engineering to assess database quality and better understand important products.

✔ **Check customer references**. You can learn much with a small investment of time.

✔ **Limit customizations of vendor software**. Customizations cost time and money and make it harder for you to accept upgrades.

Major recommendations for Chapter 16

17

Project Management

Successful software engineering not only requires a sound methodology, but also requires that you manage a project well.

Choosing the Right People

The key to any successful project is to have a clear staffing plan.

Project Staffing

Database applications involve multiple kinds of expertise; the most important are listed below. For a small project, the same person may fill several roles. For example, the same person might be the analyst, architect, and database designer. Not all roles are needed for all procurement options. If you are buying an application, for example, your project does not need a programmer. Table 17.1 shows the critical roles for the three procurement options: buy the application, build it in-house, and outsource development.

- **Executive sponsors**. The executive sponsors authorize and fund an application.

- **Users**. These are the people who will ultimately operate the software. Their willingness and ability to use the new software will determine whether it succeeds or fails.

- **Analysts**. Analysts capture and scrutinize requirements by constructing models. Analysts must work closely with users and application experts. They transition models to architects, database designers, and programmers.

    Analysts should understand modeling concepts, notations, and development processes. It is helpful if an analyst is familiar with the business or has related expe-

Organizational role	Purchase an application	Build an application in-house	Outsource application development
Executive sponsor	*	*	*
User	*	*	*
Analyst	*	*	*
Architect	Partial. Assess vendor infrastructure.	*	Partial. Work with contracted architects.
Database designer	Partial. Convert legacy data.	*	*
Programmer		*	
Project manager	Partial. Address deployment issues.	*	Partial. Monitor progress and address deployment issues.
Toolsmith		*	
DBA	*	*	*

Table 17.1 Role list. The appropriate roles depend on the procurement option.

rience. An analyst should be a good communicator and an active listener. A skilled analyst will have the ability to abstract the essential features of an application. It is helpful if an analyst is familiar with database design and reverse engineering.

■ **Architects**. Architects lead the procurement effort; they make the major design decisions and assess vendor infrastructure. Architects must understand how a new system interacts with other systems and anticipate and monitor system performance. The chief architect serves as the mediator between technologists and management. An architect must be attuned to the needs of the customer and is the customer's advocate in dealing with other technologists.

Architects must combine business understanding with technical knowledge of communications, hardware, and software. An architect typically is a seasoned person with a great deal of experience. Architects are often generalists, rather than experts in a technology area. However, they must still be able to recognize when special skills are needed and add them to the project team.

■ **Database designers**. Database designers prepare the database structures according to the analysis model. They should also take a first attempt at tuning the database. Database designers must work with architects and programmers in devising an approach for coupling programming code to the database. Database designers often must write scripts to convert legacy data.

All database designers should be able to read models and understand how to implement them well. Many database designers are already familiar with ER and IDEF1X models. Database designers must deeply understand relational database products and keep pace with emerging technology such as replication. They must be fluent with SQL and 4GLs (fourth-generation languages) and have some programming experience.

- **Programmers**. Programmers write the actual language code. They build on the outputs of analysts, architects, and database designers.

  Programmers should understand models and be familiar, although not necessarily proficient, with databases. They should be able to recognize when database queries can express logic better (less development effort, more flexibility, and faster performance) than programming code. Some programmers are responsible for preparing a user interface; they should be skilled at user interaction metaphors, as well as programming.

- **Project manager**. The project manager identifies tasks, assigns tasks to individuals, schedules completion dates, and monitors progress. The project manager must work closely with the architects.

- **Toolsmiths**. Toolsmiths provide tools to boost development productivity. They make recommendations for in-house tools and vendor products. On occasion, a toolsmith may develop a custom tool that is important to project success. For example, for one project I wrote ancillary software to read old reports and populate an initial database.

- **Database Administrators (DBAs)**. DBAs provide routine support for databases and deal with problems that arise. Some of their responsibilities are to authorize new users, add new disc space as needed, backup databases, and monitor performance.

When I was at GE R&D, I worked on a difficult bill-of-material application. I had the good fortune to lead this project along with Bill Premerlani. The project was a five-year effort, and we encountered a number of challenges along the way. I don't think either one of us could have succeeded as the sole architect. But by working together and playing off each other's ideas, we were able to make the project a big success.

Business anecdote: Two architects are best for difficult applications

Corporate Structure

As Figure 17.1 shows, a large organization can most effectively service demand by placing a few experts in a technology-oriented group that supports groups of developers organized by business area. Table 17.2 clarifies the respective roles of the technology and application groups.

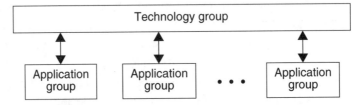

Figure 17.1 Corporate structure. A technology group can provide expertise for groups of developers organized by business area.

	Technology group	Application group
Perspective	The entire organization	A business area
Appropriate tasks	Promulgate standards and computing techniques; maintain enterprise models; support the application groups	Build applications; evaluate products for potential purchase
Required skill level	Expert with modeling and databases	Fluent with modeling and databases
Number of groups	One per organization	Many per organization
Size of group	Small to limit overhead	As many as needed to serve business area

Table 17.2 Technology vs. application groups. A large organization needs both kinds of groups.

The technology group takes the perspective of the entire organization. It promulgates standards and computing techniques, maintains enterprise models (see Chapter 21), and supports the application groups. You should place the best modelers and database experts in the technology group, so that their skills are available to everyone. The technology group should not build applications; this is the purpose of the application groups. Rather, the technology group should be the custodian of advanced skills. Keep this group small to limit overhead.

Application groups have a different role. Their purpose is to learn about the business and transfer knowledge across related applications. Application group members should work closely with their business counterparts. Developers should be fluent with modeling and databases, even though the most skilled modelers and database designers belong to the technology group. Application group members should do most of the work in evaluating products for potential purchase.

Some firms use a different organization; they place all modelers in a technology group and loan them out to perform modeling for application developers. I strongly advise against this arrangement. Modeling is such a stimulus to insight and dialog that it should be dispersed across an entire computing organization. (For that matter, it is also beneficial if some business and marketing staff learn about models.) Modeling is the lingua franca for software development and application developers should build models for themselves.

 Encourage all developers to learn to model.

Choosing the Right Application Scope

An application can be (and ideally should be) part of a broader vision. You should think in terms of suites of applications that interoperate. You can prepare an enterprise model (see Chapter 21) to get an understanding of the combined applications. The tools from the UNIX operating system are a good example of interoperating applications. Each tool is small and has a specific focus, but they can be connected in flexible ways to accomplish larger purposes.

 Try to avoid application stovepipes. Rather, build and purchase applications that contribute to a broader goal.

It is helpful if an application is not too big. However, the business sets the scope of an application, and you may not have much control over its size. If you have a large application (requiring a year or more of effort), you should keep developers on a tight leash and insist on frequent deliverables (every few months). You can then more readily determine their true progress. You can catch misunderstood requirements and development mistakes more quickly and waste less time and money. For this reason, I discourage the waterfall development life cycle and recommend rapid prototyping, incremental development, or a fourth-generation language instead. (See Chapter 15.)

Large applications can also be troublesome to purchase. You incur a large purchase and deployment cost, but may use only some of the many features. Sometimes, it is better to buy a more focused product.

Remember that a suitable project should deliver a major business benefit. The project should either provide a strong financial payback or deliver important "soft" benefits, such as greater flexibility or improved maintainability. If you cannot convincingly justify a project, it is best not to start it. Any project must have a clear definition of success.

Estimating Effort

For a purchased application, estimation is relatively simple; you need to understand requirements, evaluate products, purchase a product, and deploy the chosen product. For a newly built application, the time and cost are larger and more variable; you need an accurate estimate so that you can make a sound business decision. You can prepare an estimate several ways.

- **Itemization**. Break a project into small tasks that you can understand and accurately estimate. Many people underestimate software development effort, because they overlook tasks.

- **Analogy**. Compare your project with a similar application and estimate time and cost by analogy.

- **Formula**. Characterize your application and use a formula to estimate time and cost [Pressman-97, pages 120–125].

Always allow for contingencies. Too many estimates assume that all will go well. Expect to encounter some problems. If you understand a problem well and have experience, you can include a small contingency (10 percent). For a difficult problem, include a larger one (25 percent or more).

Beware of imposed estimates. A good estimate must reconcile business needs with technical realities. If there is a disconnect, requirements must be reduced or a different technical approach must be found. Both management and technologists must buy into a project estimate for it to be reliable.

Don't rush a schedule to compensate for delay. On several occasions, I have seen companies leisurely debate and then when they decide to do a project, try to compress the development schedule to make up for lost time.

Estimation errors are often caused by misunderstandings of scope. Technologists and customers can have different perceptions. Modeling helps to promote

Early in my career, I was being interviewed for a job. The company had an interesting project, the schedule was set by management, and they were behind schedule. Did I want to join their team? After the interview, I thanked them for their hospitality and went elsewhere.

Business anecdote: Avoid dictating a schedule

agreement by eliciting detail and making assumptions more obvious. Models make added requirements and "scope creep" more apparent.

Several factors affect the time and cost of software development. Estimates are inherently more accurate for straightforward applications as opposed to research applications. Furthermore, the quality of your staff greatly affects cost and schedule. The additional productivity of skilled staff usually exceeds their increased pay. Also with skilled developers, you can assign fewer persons to a project team and reduce coordination time.

You should staff a project deliberately and not just add developers when it seems to run late. You can seldom speed-up a project that is behind schedule by adding personnel. The increased staff hours for training and coordination often outweigh the incremental output. [Brooks-95, page 19]

The agreed-upon schedule should allow for dilution from other tasks. Your staff will have distractions and will not be able to spend 100 percent of their time on a specific project. In practice, it is difficult to get more than 50 percent dedicated time.

Figure 17.2 summarizes important estimation items.

* Allow for contingencies.

* Beware of imposed estimates.

* Don't rush a schedule to compensate for delay.

* Explicitly agree on scope with your customer.

* Consider variables such as application difficulty and staff quality.

* Staff a project deliberately and don't just add developers when it runs late.

* Allow for dilution from nonproject tasks.

Figure 17.2 Estimation list. Make sure you address these items.

Software Reviews

All projects should receive at least one formal review, and several reviews are ideal. The review should take place after the model and architecture are complete. For newly built applications, it is the last chance to correct mistakes before implementation. The review causes the whole organization to buy into the application, not just the developers. For purchased applications, a review session publicizes the evaluation process and what was learned.

A formal review has several benefits. It brings multiple minds and experiences to bear on a problem. It promotes conversation and becomes a learning experience, for both the presenters and the audience. Finally, a review broadens awareness, making the organization more resilient to personnel turnover and helping developers learn from related applications.

To put it bluntly, there is no downside to an occasional review. Reviews should require no more than a few days of preparatory effort. The purpose of the review is to assess the work, not the people involved.

The permissive approach is to regard review comments as merely advisory; technologists must listen to the advice, but they need not act on it. The more aggressive posture is to require a formal sign-off; senior staff must certify that a model and architecture are sound before a project can proceed. The aerospace community routinely requires such approval and has multiple reviews.

The review is intended for technologists, rather than management, so it should be attended mostly by staff experienced in related applications and technologies. Some managers and technically inclined business experts can attend, but they should not dominate a review.

Unfortunately, my experience is that many technologists are reluctant to subject their work to review. They are unaccustomed to receiving critical comments and do not realize the opportunity for learning, improving their project, and exchanging ideas. This is a shame. Management should encourage reviews and set the tone for a critical, uninhibited, and constructive discussion. They should make continued project funding contingent on holding a review.

 Management should require that all projects have at least one formal review session.

Tools

When possible, use tools to automate development. I can only generally discuss tools here, because products change rapidly, and a more specific discussion would quickly become dated. Avail yourself of any helpful products. On occasion, your staff may need to write a special-purpose tool if there is unusual logic and conventions to support.

Modeling Tools

Large applications (50 entity types or more) require a heavyweight modeling tool. The minor benefit of a tool is that it increases productivity. The major benefit is that a tool can deepen thinking. Tools help experts concentrate on the important abstractions and build better models. Tools help novices observe syntax and avoid common mistakes. Vendors Rational Rose and Paradigm Plus provide tools that support the UML notation (which I recommended in Chapter 9, because it is a clean, concise notation and a standard).

For small applications, you need not use a modeling tool. You can rely on paper and pencil or use a general-purpose graphics editor such as Microsoft's PowerPoint or Adobe's Framemaker. For example, I used a graphics editor to prepare the models in this book, so I could tightly control the layout.

Low-end tools such as Microsoft's VISIO standard edition automatically maintain connectivity and provide an intermediate option. For examples, entity boxes stay attached to relationship lines. A downside of low-end tools is that they have no intrinsic understanding of models and will let a person draw nonsensical constructs.

Table 17.3 summarizes the trade-offs for different kinds of modeling tools.

Kind of modeling tool	Strengths	Weaknesses
High-end tool (Rational Rose, Paradigm Plus)	Actively helps a person build a model. Analysts can build models in front of an audience.	High cost ($1500+ per seat). Takes time to become proficient.
Low-end tool (VISIO standard edition)	Low cost (about $100 per seat). Low learning curve. Maintains connectivity for a diagram.	Does not catch modeling errors.
Graphics editor (Framemaker, PowerPoint)	Can be low cost. Permits tight control of layout. Many persons are already skilled with these.	Does not catch modeling errors. Is tedious to maintain connectivity manually.
Paper and pencil	No cost. No learning curve.	Practical only for very small diagrams (fewer than 10 entity types).

Table 17.3 Trade-offs for modeling tools. There are several options for modeling tools that trade cost for power.

Database Design Tools

In principle, a developer should be able to prepare a database design directly from a UML model. However, in practice, most UML tools poorly support databases. Consequently, I recommend that you use separate tools for modeling and database design. It is easy to make accidental errors, so I do not recommend designing databases by hand.

One good option is to export a UML model to an IDEF1X tool such as Computer Associate's ERWin. (Don't let the name fool you. ERWin is not an ER tool, but instead supports the IDEF1X notation.) UML tools are good for modeling and thinking abstractly; IDEF1X tools are good for designing relational databases. IDEF1X tools can generate code to create the initial database structures.

 Use a UML tool for modeling and an IDEF1X tool for relational database design.

You will have to expend some effort to keep a UML model and an IDEF1X model consistent. The UML tools can export their model to an IDEF1X tool, but the resulting layout is clumsy, and most designers will want to clean it up. A designer must also enter database details. Consequently, when the designer revises the UML model, corresponding revisions must be made to the IDEF1X model, or the UML model must be reimported and the details entered again. Usually, it is easier to update the IDEF1X model.

This double maintenance is annoying and caused by current tool limitations. Nevertheless, when placed within the context of software development, the wasted effort is small. The benefits of clear thinking and a crisp design greatly outweigh the cost of duplicate work.

Another option is to use a tool that supports an ER dialect other than the UML. Some of these tools support database design well. This is not my choice, however, because the other ER dialects are more verbose than the UML. (See Chapter 9.) I believe that verbosity compromises the ability to think abstractly.

So far, I've discussed commercial design tools in terms of creating an empty database. Few tools support changes to the structure of a populated database. Database maintainers usually have to modify the database structure directly, rather than update via a model. However, they should still keep the model current so that they can think clearly about the database.

Overall Recommendation

In general, managers should not be heavy handed and force developers to use a specific modeling tool. Rather, they should be flexible and support a few tools. Remember, the overriding issue is to get your developers to model; the choice of tool is a secondary decision. Multiple tools will cause more redundant entry of models, but, once again, this is insignificant compared with modeling's benefits.

Standardizing on select tools has several benefits. Quantity purchases lead to better discounts. There is less support hassle, and it is easier to swap licenses across machines and developers. A common tool promotes information exchange.

There are also sound reasons for *not* standardizing on tools. The tool market is rapidly evolving. If your organization becomes too fond of a tool, it may miss out on improvements. Some developers will resist using tools if you dictate the choice.

A compromise is to support two or three modeling tools for application development. You then have most of the benefits of uniformity and can still keep pace with the evolution of the market and the individual tastes of your developers. Limit use to a single modeling tool for each application.

Regardless of the tools you choose, make sure that developers are careful with generated code and spot check it for correctness and efficiency. Some tools generate bad code with flaws that are subtle and difficult to catch. Also, if your developers pay attention to tool output, they will better understand what the tool is doing.

> I have used a number of tools over the years. Much to my surprise, some of the tools I have tested actually generate incorrect SQL code! The moral is to be careful with tools of any kind. Test them and carefully monitor the results.

Business anecdote: Tools can make errors

Chapter Summary

There are many project management issues for database applications. The appropriate staffing for a project will depend on whether you are purchasing software, building it yourself, or commissioning an outside party to build it for you.

There are several ways of preparing project estimates: itemization (break a project into small tasks), analogy (compare your project with a similar application), and formula (use a standard formula to estimate time and cost).

One way to increase the quality of your applications is via software reviews. Sadly, many organizations do not take advantage of reviews.

When possible, use tools to automate development. Modeling tools can help you construct better models. Database design tools improve productivity and avoid mistakes.

> ✔ **Encourage all developers to learn to model**. Budget adequate funds for training and mentoring to help them with the paradigm shift.
>
> ✔ **Beware of application stovepipes**. Instead, devise a broad software vision. Try to build and purchase applications that contribute to a broader goal.
>
> ✔ **Learn from software reviews**. Management should require that all projects have at least one formal review session.
>
> ✔ **Use tools to build models**. Use a UML tool for modeling and an IDEF1X tool for relational database design.
>
> ✔ **Limit the number of tool vendors**. It is reasonable to support two or three modeling tools for application development, but use a single tool for each application.

Major recommendations for Chapter 17

Resource Notes

[Reel-99] is a good article on general success factors in software projects.

[Humphrey-97] has lots of good advice on time management and avoiding defects in software. Humphrey's book is the voice of experience and is especially valuable for beginning developers.

References

[Brooks-95] Frederick P. Brooks, Jr. *The Mythical Man-Month, Anniversary Edition*. Reading, Massachusetts: Addison-Wesley, 1995.

[Humphrey-97] Watts S. Humphrey. *Introduction to the Personal Software Process*. Reading, Massachusetts: Addison-Wesley, 1997.

[Pressman-97] Roger S Pressman. *Software Engineering: A Practitioner's Approach, Fourth Edition*. New York, New York: McGraw-Hill, 1997.

[Reel-99] John S. Reel. Critical success factors in software projects. *IEEE Software*, May/June 1999.

Part 5

Advanced Technology

Part 5 concludes the book with a discussion of advanced topics that are highly relevant to database applications—both newly built and purchased.

Chapter 18 discusses distributed databases—databases that place data at multiple locations but hide the complexities from users and application programs.

Chapter 19 covers reverse engineering, which lets you build on the accomplishments of past projects, rather than start from scratch. With reverse engineering, you can salvage ideas, code, and data from obsolete applications.

In Chapter 20 I describe specifically how to use reverse engineering to assess vendor software. The basic idea is simple—database applications are focused about a database. Thus, if you can assess the quality of a database, you can reasonably infer the quality of the overall product.

Chapter 21 describes integration technology. Organizations obtain value not only from individual applications, but also from the synergy between them. You can integrate operational applications to reduce data proliferation, data conflict, and multiple entry. Integration also enables analytical applications and queries across the boundaries of individual operational applications.

Chapter 22 concludes with comments about object-oriented (OO) technology. Although OO technology is currently outside the mainstream of databases and data processing, many organizations are attempting to use OO languages and concepts with relational databases. There is a great deal of confusion about how to combine the two technologies.

18

Distributed Databases

Distributed databases often arise with industrial applications. Users are at different locations, and there are common data to synchronize and reconcile. Furthermore, sometimes updates must be coordinated among multiple databases. Distributed databases are useful for both operational and analytical applications.

Distributed Database Concepts

A *distributed database* is built on top of a computer network, rather than on a single computer. Data may be distributed over a local area network (LAN), a wide area network (WAN), or even an occasionally connected network. For example, traveling salespersons may copy part of a master database and periodically synchronize their data. Data are stored at different network sites; DBMS processing can occur at individual sites or combinations of sites.

Distributed databases have several advantages.

- **Synergy**. You can coordinate individual databases.

- **Modular growth**. You can incrementally add to database capacity.

- **Fault tolerance**. With replication, data remain available even if individual databases fail. Multiple copies of data protect against catastrophe.

- **Cheaper computing**. You have more flexibility in configuring your computing resources.

However, distributed database technology is complex, and problems can arise.

- **Security**. Local sites can provide protection independent of the overall database. Communication networks, on the other hand, can be prone to security breaches.

- **Data consistency**. References across site boundaries—a foreign key at one site that refers to a table at another site—are vulnerable to inconsistencies. Developers should try to avoid them.

- **Administration**. Distributed databases are more difficult to administer than DBMSs that run on a single computer.

DBMSs provide two complementary mechanisms for distributed data: two-phase commit and replication. Two-phase commit lets a DBMS coordinate updates to multiple data sources. Replication provides a mechanism for managing multiple copies of data.

Two-Phase-Commit Protocol

Consider a travel itinerary—a person might book a flight with one database, a rental car reservation with another database, and hotel reservations with additional databases. The traveler may wish to proceed only if all reservations can be made, even though the reservations involve several databases.

The ***two-phase-commit (2PC) protocol*** can coordinate such multidatabase transactions. 2PC ensures that they entirely commit or entirely abort. That is, the updates occur for all the databases or for none. As Figure 18.1 shows, the 2PC protocol centralizes the decision to commit, but gives each subordinate DBMS the right to veto. Different applications or DBMSs can coordinate different transactions.

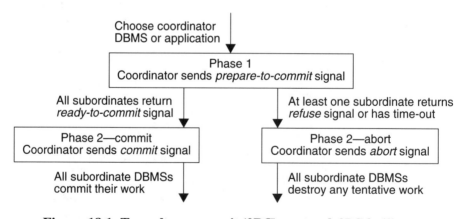

Figure 18.1 Two-phase-commit (2PC) protocol. 2PC facilitates transactions that span multiple databases.

For the first phase, the DBMSs prepare to commit. The coordinating DBMS (the coordinator) sends *prepare-to-commit* commands to all the subordinate DBMSs.

The first phase can terminate with a decision either to abort or to commit the transaction.

The coordinator decides to abort the transaction if any subordinate returns a *refuse* signal. A subordinate returns a *refuse* signal if it cannot write the transaction, such as if there is a conflict with another transaction or a violation of a database constraint. The first phase can also yield a decision to abort if a subordinate does not respond within the allotted time. This time-out guards against communication failures.

The coordinator decides to commit the transaction if all subordinates return a *ready-to-commit* signal.

Once the coordinator reaches a decision, it writes the decision in a safe place that is protected against the effect of failure. At this point, the outcome of the transaction is fixed, and the subordinate DBMSs can no longer influence it. The phase-2 commit terminates when all the subordinates have committed their part of the transaction and made it durable. The coordinator receives all the confirmations and can tell its client that the transaction has completed.

For some situations, destroying tentative work is not an option. For example, banks normally do not destroy transactions that are posted to accounts. However, they can define an action to compensate for a prior transaction, such as crediting an incorrect checking account fee back to the account.

Most RDBMSs and some third-party products support 2PC logic. 2PC has the following trade-offs.

- **Advantages**. It tightly synchronizes updates to data. Developers know that all data will be written or nothing will be written, which means that they are free to concentrate on other aspects of their applications.

- **Disadvantages**. Communication failures can impede database availability. Access to affected data is blocked while DBMSs wait for the signal to commit or abort. Interaction with the DBMSs also incurs a performance overhead.

 Use the two-phase commit (2PC) protocol only where necessary. The technology is complex, and products don't always support it adequately. Also, applications with 2PC can be difficult to test.

Replication

An alternative to the use of 2PC is **_replication_**, which maintains copies of data at various database locations. Users can read any copy, but the DBMS must propagate any updates to all copies. As an example, consider a a retail price list for products. Prices

For one project we had a data manager that did not support 2PC. Neverthe-less, we were able to finesse the situation by defining compensating transac-tions. We just wrote to the databases individually and ran compensating transactions if all the databases did not commit. The only flaw in our logic was that intermediate work could be seen before the entire transaction was finished, but the business could tolerate this.

The point of this story is that sometimes developers can work around product limitations.

Business anecdote: Finessing a product limitation

are read often, but updated only occasionally. The price list would be a good candi-date for replication and dissemination to multiple business locations.

Replication is not as rigorous as the 2PC protocol, but its performance is better, particularly for data that are often read, but seldom written. Replication has the fol-lowing trade-offs.

- **Advantages**. Despite system failures, data are likely to be available for reading and may be available for writing. Furthermore, replicates make reading of data more efficient, because there is no need to communicate with another DBMS. Multiple copies protect data against accidental loss.

- **Disadvantages**. Copies of data are not always exactly the same. This can be troublesome if your application requires precise data. Writing of data is less ef-ficient since multiple copies must be written and additional data transmitted over a network.

 Do not use replication for a mix of DBMS vendors. Replication is only supported for a network of databases from the same vendor.

Replication Approaches

The major RDBMS products support replication but vary in their approaches. With a **_peer-to-peer approach_**, any copy can be updated and changes are propagated to the other copies. With a **_master-slave approach_**, all updates must be performed via the master copy; the updates are then propagated to the slave copies. Peer-to-peer has the advantage of flexibility; any copy can be updated. However, two copies can receive coincident updates that clash, and typically, developers must write special code to handle this. The master-slave approach is more restrictive, but avoids coin-cident updates.

RDBMS products also vary in their update time lag. With immediate replication, an update is immediately propagated to the other copies. With periodic replication, updates are propagated after some time interval, such as once a day.

Ideally replicates should appear as a single copy. Replication is not intended to change the perceived contents of a database; rather, it is an artifact to help efficient operation. If the time lag is small, the copies are likely to be indistinguishable. On the other hand, a longer time lag lets changes be grouped, which improves performance. The exact balance of currency and performance depends on the needs of an application.

Locating Data

Distributed databases offer freedom in locating data, whether there is a single copy or several replicates. Generally speaking, a good distributed database design minimizes communication traffic. To arrive at a suitable design, developers should forecast the queries and updates to be executed from the various DBMS sites. Once a distributed database application is deployed, administrators can monitor database performance and move data around as needs evolve.

A good design also attempts to eliminate, or at least minimize, referential dependencies among sites. It is highly undesirable for a table at one site to reference a column at some other site, especially if there might be updates.

Communications Software

Developers can use a variety of techniques to communicate among distributed DBMSs.

■ **Custom programming**. You can always program a solution, but there is seldom a need to do so. Suitable logic is readily available and inexpensive compared to custom programming.

■ **SQL communication**. Distributed DBMSs have built-in logic that route commands and data as needed over a communications network. For example, a distributed RDBMS can access remote data by sending an SQL command over the network and receiving a table.

■ **TP monitors**. They have built-in logic for connecting clients and servers that can make it easier to manage distributed data.

■ **Object-oriented techniques**. The Object Management Group's CORBA, Microsoft's OLE, and Java Beans all make it easier to distribute data by invoking special programming code that connects clients and servers.

Chapter Summary

A distributed database is built on top of a computer network, rather than on a single computer. Distributed databases are important, because they facilitate modular growth, increase fault tolerance, and sometimes lower the cost of computing. There are two complementary mechanisms for dealing with distributed data: 2PC and replication.

The 2PC protocol coordinates the use of data that are stored in multiple databases. 2PC ensures that multidatabase transactions entirely commit or entirely abort.

The replication approach maintains copies of data at various database locations. Any copy can be freely read, but updates must be propagated to all copies. Major RDBMSs support replication but vary in their approaches.

Developers can use various techniques for communicating between distributed DBMSs—SQL communication, TP monitors, and OO techniques.

✔ **Use 2PC only where necessary**. The technology is complex and not always well supported by products. Also, applications with two-phase commit can be difficult to test.

✔ **Do not use replication for a mix of DBMS vendors**. Replication is only supported for a network of databases from the same vendor.

Major recommendations for Chapter 18

Resource Notes

[Bernstein-97] explains fine technical details of 2PC and replication. Chapter 16 of [Orfali-96] also explains the 2PC protocol.

References

[Bernstein-97] Philip A Bernstein and Eric Newcomer. *Principles of Transaction Processing*. San Francisco, California: Morgan Kaufmann, 1997.
[Orfali-96] Robert Orfali, Dan Harkey, and Jeri Edwards. *The Essential Client/Server Survival Guide, Second Edition*. New York, New York: John Wiley and Sons, 1996.

19

Reverse Engineering

Reverse engineering is the inverse to normal development; reverse engineers start with the actual application and work backward to deduce the requirements that spawned the software. Reverse engineering lets you salvage ideas and data from past systems for use by new systems. You can also evaluate candidate products in depth to more reliably determine the best ones.

Most reverse engineering involves operational applications. There is little need for reverse engineering of analytical applications—most data warehouses are relatively new, and their structure is much less complex than operational databases. In this chapter, I focus on how to use reverse engineering with newly developed applications. Chapter 20 addresses purchased applications.

Overview

With *reverse engineering*, you take an existing design and extract the underlying logical intent. There are several motives for reverse engineering a database.

- **Re-engineering**. *Re-engineering* is the process of redeveloping existing software systems. Re-engineering consists of three steps: reverse engineering, consideration of new requirements, and normal development. Re-engineering lets you salvage relevant ideas, data, and code from past systems, rather than start from scratch.

- **Vendor software assessment**. I routinely reverse engineer the databases of vendor software. The quality of the database design is an indicator of the quality of the software as a whole. An understanding of the concepts supported by the underlying database structure also lets you judge functionality claims better.

- ■ **Integration**. An understanding of encompassed software is a prerequisite for integration.

- ■ **Conversion of legacy data**. A person must understand the correspondence between the old database and the new database before converting data.

My experience is that you can reverse engineer a database independently of programming code. Databases are explicitly declared and more amenable to study. Furthermore, the data are generally the most stable part of an application. Reverse engineering a database alone is often sufficient.

 Use database reverse engineering to salvage from past applications and carry forward useful ideas and data.

Figure 19.1 contrasts reverse engineering with forward engineering (normal development).

Forward engineering	Reverse engineering
Given requirements, develop an application.	Given an application, deduce tentative requirements.
More certain. The developer has requirements and must deliver an application that implements them.	Less certain. An implementation can yield different requirements depending on the interpretation.
Prescriptive. Developers are told how to work.	Adaptive. The reverse engineer must find out what the developer actually did.
More mature. Skilled staff readily available.	Less mature. Skilled staff sparse.
Time consuming. Months to years of work.	Relatively rapid. Days to weeks of work.
Model must be correct and complete or the application will fail.	Model can be imperfect. Salvaging part of the information is still useful.
Process of creation. The system must change.	Process of examination. The system need not change.

Figure 19.1 Forward engineering vs. reverse engineering. Reverse engineering requires a different mindset.

Outputs from Reverse Engineering

Reverse engineering has several useful outputs. The exact outputs depend on your motive.

- **Models**. The quality of the model depends on the available inputs and the motive for reverse engineering. For example, you need a thorough model when converting legacy data, but a partial model can suffice when assessing vendor products. The model conveys the software's scope and intent.

- **Mappings**. Reverse engineers can tie model attributes to database fields, which is helpful for integrating applications and converting legacy data.

- **Logs**. Reverse engineers should record their observations and pending questions. A log documents decisions and rationale.

- **Evaluations**. Reverse engineers can explicitly judge the quality of a database, especially for vendor software. In this case, the judgment itself is the valuable product. I recommend assigning a grade that reflects the design's consistency and the extent of errors. (See Chapter 20.)

Inputs to Reverse Engineering

A complete process must consider all inputs. The available information varies widely across problems.

- **Database structure**. The database structure is normally the dominant input. It specifies the data structure and many constraints—precisely and explicitly. The structure varies according to the kind of DBMS, both by paradigm and product. Relational DBMSs (RDBMSs) have declarative structure that can be readily inspected. Network and hierarchical DBMSs express fewer constraints. COBOL files often contain extensive data declarations.

  Reverse engineering can be difficult, because information is often missing from the database structure. Reverse engineers must conjecture and augment the structure by considering other inputs.

- **Data**. If data are available, you can discover much of the data structure. A database structure may be badly flawed, yet the data may still be quite good. A thorough application program or disciplined users may yield data of better quality than the structure enforces. The downside with data is that they are much more time consuming to study than database structure.

  For large databases, you may have to sample the data to reach tentative conclusions, and then explore the full database for verification. Examination cannot prove many propositions, but the more data you encounter, the more likely will be the conclusion.

- **Queries**. You can scan application code and look for clues from queries that manipulate data. Relational database views can also be suggestive. For example, a join of two fields might indicate a foreign-to-candidate key relationship.

- **Forms and reports**. Suggestive titles and layouts can clarify a database structure. Form and report definitions are especially helpful if their binding to database structure is available. A more empirical approach is to enter known, unusual values to establish the binding between forms and the underlying structure.

- **Documentation**. Problems vary in their quality, quantity, and kind of documentation. Documentation provides context for reverse engineering. User manuals are especially helpful. Data dictionaries—lists of important entities and their definitions—may be available. Use data dictionaries with care, however, because they often become stale as the underlying database changes.

- **Application understanding**. If you understand an application well, you can make better inferences. Application experts may be available to answer questions and explain rationale. You may be able to leverage models from related applications.

Table 19.1 summarizes the strengths and weaknesses of the various input sources.

Input source	Strengths	Weaknesses
Database structure	Specifies data structure and constraints precisely and explicitly. Often available.	Information may be missing. Often has errors.
Data	Can clarify ambiguities in data structure.	Tedious to study.
Queries	Can clarify ambiguities in data structure.	May not be available.
Forms and reports	Provides meaningful names.	Can be tedious to establish binding with database.
Documentation	Provides context for reverse engineering.	Can be difficult to reconcile with database structure.
Application understanding	Provides context for reverse engineering.	Sometimes not available. Application experts are busy.

Table 19.1 Reverse engineering inputs. There are multiple kinds
of inputs with different trade-offs.

Stages of Reverse Engineering

With forward engineering, developers first analyze an application and prepare a model of its intent. Only then do they design the application—that is, choose strategies for solving the problem. Finally, they implement the application by writing the database and programming code.

As Figure 19.2 shows, you can organize reverse engineering on a similar basis. You start with an implementation of an application (primarily the database structure) and determine dependencies between fields. This yields a design model that you can then abstract and reconcile with other inputs. The ultimate result is an analysis model of the conceptual intent.

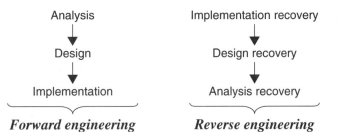

Figure 19.2 Forward engineering vs. reverse engineering. You can organize reverse engineering on a similar basis to forward engineering

You can reverse engineer by constructing models that describe the existing software and the presumed intent. This process has three main stages.

- **Implementation recovery**. Quickly learn about the application and prepare an initial model.

- **Design recovery**. Undo the mechanics of the database structure and resolve foreign key references.

- **Analysis recovery**. Remove design artifacts and eliminate any errors in the model.

Implementation Recovery

In implementation recovery, you prepare an initial model (Figure 19.3) that forms the basis for reverse engineering. Because the initial model will serve as a reference throughout reverse engineering, it should purely reflect the implementation and have no inferences.

The first task is to browse existing documentation and learn about an application. The resulting context clarifies the developer's intent and makes it easier to com-

Figure 19.3 Implementation recovery. Quickly learn about an
application and prepare an initial model.

municate with application experts. You should finish this task in a few hours. What
you learn is incidental to the actual reverse engineering, but it is important, because
it helps you notice more as you proceed.

The next step is to enter the database structure into a modeling tool—by typing
or automation. Some tools can read the system tables of an RDBMS and seed a model. If you use these tools, you should at least skim the database structure to get a feel
for the development style. There are four steps to converting database structures into
model structures.

- **Create tentative entity types**. Represent each physical data unit (COBOL
  record, IMS segment, CODASYL record type, or RDBMS table) as an entity
  type [Davis-95]. Give each entity type the same name as its corresponding physical data unit.

- **Create tentative relationship types**. For a CODASYL application, represent
  the set types as relationship types. Otherwise, defer relationship types until design.

- **Create tentative attributes**. The data elements in the legacy system become attributes of the entity types. Indicate not null restrictions, data types, and lengths
  if the information is available.

- **Note keys and indexes**. Note primary keys, candidate keys, and foreign keys if
  they happen to be defined. Otherwise, note unique and secondary indexes.

Design Recovery

During design recovery, you undo the mechanics of the database and perform only
straightforward actions (Figure 19.4). You should postpone conjecture and interpre-
tation until the analysis recovery stage. Typically, you can perform design recovery
autonomously, without help from application experts. During this stage, you resolve
three main issues.

- **Identity**. Most often, unique indexes will be defined for the candidate keys of
  the entity types. Otherwise, look for unique combinations of data; such data can
  suggest, but do not prove, a candidate key. You can also infer candidate keys by

Initial model   **Design model**

Figure 19.4 Design recovery. Undo the mechanics of the database structure.

considering names and conventions of style. A suspected foreign key may imply a corresponding candidate key.

■ **Foreign keys**. Foreign key (references from one table to another) determination is usually the most difficult aspect of design recovery. Foreign keys ultimately resolve to relationship types and generalizations in a model. Matching names and data types can suggest foreign keys. Some DBMSs, such as RDBMSs, let developers declare foreign keys and their referent, but (unfortunately) most legacy applications do not use this capability.

■ **Queries**. When queries are available, you can use them to refine your understanding of identity and foreign keys.

The final product of design recovery still reflects the DBMS paradigm and may include optimizations and errors. In practice, the model will seldom be complete. Portions of the structure may be confusing.

Analysis Recovery

The final phase is analysis recovery—interpret the model, refine it, and make it more abstract (Figure 19.5). It is primarily during this phase that you should consult with available application experts. Analysis recovery consists of four main tasks.

Design model   **Model**

Figure 19.5 Analysis recovery. Remove the artifacts of design,
and eliminate any errors in the model.

■ **Clarification**. Remove any remaining artifacts of design. For example, an analysis model need not include file and database access keys; they are merely design decisions and contain no essential information.

■ **Redundancy**. Normally remove derived data that optimize the database design or that were included for misguided reasons. You may need to examine data before determining that a data structure is a duplicate.

■ **Errors**. Eliminate any remaining database errors. I include this step during analysis, because you must thoroughly understand the database before concluding that the developer erred. In the earlier stages, an apparent error could instead have been a reasonable practice or the result of incompletely understanding the database you are reverse engineering.

■ **Model integration**. Multiple information sources can lead to multiple models. For example, it is common to have a reverse-engineered model from study of the structure and data. A forward-engineered model might be prepared from a user manual. The final analysis model must fuse any separate models.

The following table is from a legacy application. The *customer* table ambiguously assigns values to columns. For example, the city can be stored in any address field. Furthermore, city, state, and zip code are mixed. With such a design, it would be difficult to find the customers who live in the city of Chicago.

Customer table

customerName	address1	address2	address3
Moe	456 Chicago St.	Decatur, IL xxxxx	
Larry	198 Broadway Dr.	Suite 201	Chicago, IL xxxxx
Joe	123 Main St.	Cairo, IL xxxxx	
Shemp	Chicago, IL xxxxx		

Business anecdote: An example of database errors

Iteration

The reverse engineering process is, of course, somewhat idealistic and not quite as neatly divided as the three stages imply. In practice, there is much iteration and backtracking. Portions of a model may proceed more rapidly than others. You will also need to backtrack to correct occasional mistakes and oversights. Nevertheless, the process provides a useful starting point, even for complex problems.

Reverse Engineering Principles

Several broad principles govern the reverse engineering process.

- **Don't mistake hypotheses for conclusions**. Reverse engineering yields hypotheses. You must thoroughly understand the application before reaching firm conclusions.

- **Expect multiple interpretations**. There is no single answer as in forward engineering. Alternative interpretations of the database structure and data can yield different models. The more information that is available, the less judgments should vary among reverse engineers.

- **Don't be discouraged by approximate results**. It is worth a modest amount of time to extract 80 percent of an existing database's meaning. Reverse engineering injects reality into modeling and is more efficient than starting from scratch. You can use the typical forward engineering techniques (such as interviewing knowledgeable users) to obtain the remaining 20 percent. Many people find this lack of perfection uncomfortable, because it is a paradigm shift from forward engineering.

- **Expect odd constructs**. Database designers, even the experts, occasionally use uncommon constructs. In some cases, you won't be able to produce a complete, accurate model of the database, because that model never existed.

- **Watch for a consistent style**. Databases are typically designed using a consistent strategy, including consistent violations of good design practice. You should be able to deduce the underlying strategy.

Tools

Reverse engineering tools must blend their inferences with assertions from the reverse engineer. Reverse engineering is too complex and ambiguous for total automation. It is difficult to combine different kinds of inputs and cope with uncertainty. A suite of flexible, interactive, loosely coupled tools is most likely to succeed.

- **Modeling tools**. Such a tool helps you manage the evolving model. (See Chapter 17.)

- **Structure analysis tools**. Some tools claim that they can automatically generate a model from a database structure. In practice, commercial tools can handle only the clean designs—designs you will seldom encounter. Research tools do better, but they are still incomplete. DB-MAIN is an impressive research tool [Hainaut].

■ **Repository tools**. A repository holds information about models, database structure, and mappings [Blaha-98a]. A repository enables advanced queries and manages data so they do not become lost.

■ **Data analysis tools**. Tools can make inferences from data. For example, a tool could determine unique combinations of data and look for potential foreign key dependencies. Reverse engineers can also analyze data by writing custom SQL code.

Use reverse engineering tools, but expect to augment them with some manual effort.

Reverse Engineering Skills

No tool can replace skilled users, and reverse engineering requires a variety of skills.

■ **Proficiency with modeling**. Reverse engineers must be proficient with modeling. Many people have trouble learning how to model—how to abstract and realize an application indirectly through modeling rather than through direct coding. The ability to model is a prerequisite for reverse engineering.

■ **Familiarity with database design**. Reverse engineers must thoroughly understand forward engineering rules, so that they can quickly translate design idioms into modeling constructs. Interpreting database designs is complicated, because of the many optimizations and flaws that are found in practice. Proficiency with SQL also helps, especially for exploring data in relational databases.

■ **An ability to focus**. Reverse engineers cannot become mired in detail. They must be satisfied with quickly obtaining 80 to 90 percent of the available information. The remaining 10 to 20 percent is seldom worth the recovery effort. Reverse engineering is incidental to the primary task of developing an application, so you cannot afford to digress.

■ **Self-confidence**. Reverse engineers must be confident of their ability to second guess other designers. They will encounter some odd and incorrect designs.

Because reverse engineering is a difficult and specialized skill, it is not practical to disseminate it widely. Large organizations should cultivate a small group of experts to provide the skill for others as needed. These experts should be in the technology group. (See Chapter 17.) Small organizations should outsource reverse-engineering tasks. Figure 19.6 has an outsourcing list [Blaha-99].

✱	Proficiency with both modeling and databases
✱	Ability to show outputs from some past projects
✱	Willingness to commit to a fixed-price contract
✱	Conversant with key published work

Figure 19.6 Outsourcing list. A reverse engineering contractor should have these skills.

 Limit reverse engineering skills to a few experts. Reverse engineering is a difficult technology, so it is not practical to disseminate the skill widely.

Techniques for Learning Reverse Engineering

I suggest the following techniques for learning reverse engineering.

■ **Modeling and database design**. First, learn these prerequisite skills.

■ **Training and mentoring**. Those who thoroughly understand modeling and database design are ready to receive training in reverse engineering. It helps to work with a skilled mentor.

■ **Case studies**. [Hainaut] recommends self-contained case studies that can be mastered in a limited time. Multiple case studies are needed, because a single problem will not fully cover all the reverse engineering idioms and situations.

Estimating Effort

On average, it takes me about three weeks to reverse engineer a clean relational database with 500 tables. Most effort is manual—interacting with a modeling tool and writing documentation. Several factors affect the difficulty and expected time.

■ **Database size**. The reverse engineering effort is roughly proportional to the database size. For a relational database, the primary metric is the number of tables.

■ **Database errors**. It is more difficult to reverse engineer a database that is riddled with errors. Severe errors can double or triple your effort.

■ **Personal proficiency**. A novice requires more time than an expert, roughly six times longer.

- **Database paradigm**. COBOL takes more effort than a relational DBMS. Network and hierarchical databases take an intermediate effort.

- **Required outputs**. A thorough reverse engineering that produces a model requires more work. Reverse engineering that merely assesses the quality of the database design requires less work.

Reverse engineers must be able to limit their efforts. Project management determines how much time is justified, and reverse engineers must confine their activities to the authorized time. This is a different mindset than forward engineering and disconcerting to some. With forward engineering, the application must be complete, or it is not useful; with reverse engineering, partial salvage is still of value. You should continually reassess the benefits of reverse engineering as you proceed and stop when returns diminish.

Sometimes, it is best to reverse engineer only part of an application. For example, you may focus on a few themes or the interfaces to other applications.

Limit reverse engineering efforts so that they do not waste time.

Chapter Summary

Reverse engineering is the process of taking an existing design and extracting the underlying logical intent. There are various motives for reverse engineering, including re-engineering (redeveloping existing software), assessing vendor software, integrating applications, and converting legacy data. You can reverse engineer databases apart from programming code.

The purpose of reverse engineering determines the appropriate outputs. The primary outputs are models, mappings, logs, and evaluations. The database structure is usually the dominant input. Other inputs include data, queries, forms, reports, documentation, and application understanding.

The process for reverse engineering is the inverse of normal development. Reverse engineers start with an implementation and undo database mechanics to achieve a design model. They then abstract and reconcile the design model with other inputs to yield an analysis model. Reverse engineering is iterative and need not proceed in a strict waterfall. It is common for portions of a model to proceed more rapidly than others. Also, reverse engineers will find occasional mistakes and oversights that they must go back to rectify.

Here are several examples of relational databases that I reverse engineered and my level of effort.

- **A customer service application with 500 tables**. The database had a clean design, and I was not familiar with the application. It took one week to assess the database design. I did not take the time to construct a full model.

- **A mechanical engineering application with 150 tables**. The database had so many errors that I was unable to construct a complete model. It took one week to assess the database design and construct a partial model.

- **A mechanical engineering application with 400 tables**. I studied the database structure, data, and documentation. It took about two months to assess the database design and construct a full model. My efficiency was lower, because this was my first reverse engineering project.

- **A customer contact application with 100 tables**. I studied the database structure and documentation. The database had an unorthodox architecture and many errors. It took two weeks to assess the database design and construct a full model.

Business anecdote: Reverse engineering effort depends on multiple factors.

Reverse engineering tools are hampered by the intrinsic difficulty of reverse engineering. Unfortunately, conventional development practice is chaotic, and all kinds of styles and errors are found. It is difficult for tools to cope with the wide variation.

Reverse engineering requires a variety of skills and is difficult to learn. Because it is a specialty, an organization should not widely disperse it. Large firms should concentrate knowledge in a few experts; small firms should outsource the work. The length of the reverse engineering effort depends on several factors: database size, database errors, personal proficiency, database paradigm, and the desired outputs.

Resource Notes

[Blaha-98b] and [Batini-92] give more detail on the mechanics of database reverse engineering. [ER] and [WCRE] are good sources of general reverse engineering information. [Chikofsky-90] explains basic terminology.

> ✔ **Salvage from past applications**. Reverse engineering helps developers carry forward useful ideas and data.
>
> ✔ **Use reverse engineering tools**. Unfortunately, the tools are incomplete, so you will need to augment them with some manual effort.
>
> ✔ **Limit reverse engineering skills to a few experts**. Reverse engineering is a difficult technology, so it is not practical to disseminate the skill widely.
>
> ✔ **Limit reverse engineering effort**. Confine reverse engineers to a fixed amount of time (generally no more than a few weeks) and have them justify any additional effort.

Major recommendations for Chapter 19

References

[Batini-92] C. Batini, S. Ceri, and S. Navathe, *Conceptual Database Design*. Reading, Massachusetts: Benjamin/Cummings, 1992.

[Blaha-98a] Michael Blaha, David LaPlant, and Erica Marvak. Requirements for repository software. *Fifth Working Conference on Reverse Engineering*, October 1998, Honolulu, Hawaii, 164–173.

[Blaha-98b] Michael Blaha and William Premerlani. *Object-Oriented Modeling and Design for Database Applications*. Upper Saddle River, New Jersey: Prentice Hall, 1998.

[Blaha-99] Michael Blaha. The case for reverse engineering. *IEEE IT Professional 1*, 2 (March/April 1999), 35–41.

[Chikofsky-90] Elliot J. Chikofsky and James H. Cross II. Reverse engineering and design recovery: A taxonomy. *IEEE Software*, January 1990, 13–17.

[Davis-95] Kathi Hogshead Davis. August-II: A tool for step-by-step data model reverse engineering. *Second Working Conference on Reverse Engineering*, July 1995, Toronto, Ontario, 146–154.

[ER] Entity-Relationship Conference. These conferences have been sponsored for a number of years by the Entity-Relationship Institute.

[Hainaut] JL Hainaut and colleagues at University of Namur have written a number of informative papers (http://www.info.fundp.ac.be). Most of the papers are in English.

[WCRE] IEEE Working Conferences on Reverse Engineering (1993, 1995–present).

20

Assessing Vendor Software

This chapter continues the discussion of reverse engineering, but emphasizes its use for purchased products. As with Chapter 19, this chapter has little to say about analytical applications, because most purchased applications are operational. The chapter takes the perspective of a large organization buying the software (not the perspective of the software vendor offering it).

The reverse engineering assessment techniques apply only to vendor software built around a database—which includes most of the applications large organizations purchase. Also, vendors are more willing to divulge database structures than programming code.

Business Benefits

In the past, there have been four bases for evaluating software: functionality, cost, vendor stability, and the attractiveness of the user interface. Reverse engineering adds a fifth criterion: quality. You can discern how well the database of an application has been designed and conceived. You can assess the quality of both the database design and the conceptual model underlying the database. If a product has a flawed database, it is likely to be ruined and have messy programming. In contrast, a product with a sound database has quality that is likely to pervade other aspects of the software.

Unfortunately, many applications have flawed databases. Roughly half the databases I have studied have major errors. Some have dangling references to data that have been deleted. Others have severe conceptual misunderstandings that ripple through their structure. Therefore, you cannot assume correctness; you *must* check the database.

Aside from providing a means to assess software quality, reverse engineering has additional benefits.

- **Understanding**. Few vendors provide models to help you understand their application. However, the database structure is often there for the asking and you can use reverse engineering to construct your own models. Models can help you understand both the scope and content of a vendor product. You can set aside the sales claims and better judge the capabilities and limitations. You find out what is really being sold rather than just take a chance.

- **Negotiation**. The vendors emphasize their strengths. Reverse engineering makes you aware of some of their weaknesses, so you will have a stronger hand in negotiations.

- **Communication**. Reverse engineering can make it easier to talk with a vendor. The vendor may have their own assumptions, architecture, and mindset—all of which provide a context for their explanation of an application. If you aren't familiar with their context, it can be difficult to understand what they mean. With reverse engineering, you get inside the vendor's mind and can converse with their terminology.

- **Data conversion**. There is often legacy data to migrate to the vendor product. You must understand both the source and target before converting data.

The bottom line is that reverse engineering can deepen your understanding of vendor products and help you make better decisions. The payoff is striking when you consider that a software purchase and deployment can cost millions of dollars and that a reverse engineering assessment can be performed in as little as a few weeks.

Assessment Process

Chapter 16 presented a software acquisition process that starts with a search for potential products. You should then do a cursory paper study to reduce the list of products to about six semifinalists. The next step is to talk with the vendors in detail, after which you should be able to narrow your list to two or three finalists. The last step is to analyze the final products and negotiate with the vendor before deciding on the winning product.

Database reverse engineering is an important part of assessment. Without it, you cannot tell how well the software is built. You learn about software quality before committing to the product. You should routinely reverse engineer the finalists in any acquisition of a major database application (more than a $500,000 purchase and deployment cost).

☞ *Use reverse engineering to judge the finalists in any major acquisition of a database application.*

Database reverse engineering has become feasible, because most vendors now use a relational database. Relational databases are declarative; data structure and constraints are explicit, and less needs to be inferred than with other database paradigms.

Unfortunately, most vendor products ignore foreign keys. There are two reasons for this. First, many vendor applications are programmed to support the "lowest common denominator." They use only plain vanilla capabilities that nearly all DBMS releases support; since many of the old releases do not enforce foreign keys, the products avoid defining them. Second, many vendors do not understand such advanced database technology. They are skilled programmers, but may be only adequate database designers.

Reverse engineering of vendor software can be affected by business negotiation. For example, you may be unable to ask the vendor questions during price negotiation; a business doesn't want to tip its hand and indicate product preferences. This can make it more difficult to understand a database.

My client was choosing between two applications. The favored product had been marketed by a large vendor for many years. An alternative product had been marketed by a small vendor for only a few years.

We experimented with each product to help us decide. We found that the favored product required more training, was difficult to understand, and ran slower. Nevertheless, we were not sure which one to choose. It was possible that the poor results for the favored product could be explained by inexperienced support staff being assigned to our project. Maybe we had not configured the product properly.

When we reverse engineered the two databases, the choice became perfectly clear. The favored product had a solid database design, but badly flawed conceptualization. In contrast, the alternative product had both a clean model and clean database design. Our difficulty was clearly caused by the flaws in the favored product. Reverse engineering let us directly compare the intrinsic quality of the applications.

Business anecdote: Choosing between products

Grading a Database

The reverse engineering log records details about primary keys, candidate keys, foreign keys, nulls, indexes, and the like. However, although these details are useful, the log alone does not convey the overall result of an assessment. I have found it helpful to quantify a database evaluation with a grade. The grade reflects the consistency of the database and the extent of design and modeling errors.

Figure 20.1 quantifies the grading scale. "A" is the best grade, and "F" is the worst, with "B," "C," and "D" denoting intermediate quality. I normally assign grades only to vendor databases. In-house databases could also receive grades, but this might offend some developers. Furthermore, for an in-house database, the typical purpose is recovery of ideas and data—not assessment.

Grade	Explanation	Examples of Flaws
A	Clean	No major flaws. Style is reasonable and uniformly applied.
B	Structural flaws, but they do not affect the application	Inconsistent data types and lengths. Not-null constraints, candidate keys, and enumerations are not defined. Columns have cryptic names.
C	Major flaws that affect the application (bugs, slow performance, lack of extensibility)	Inconsistent approach to identity. Haphazard indexing. Foreign keys have mismatched data types.
D	Severe flaws that compromise the application	Primary keys are not readily apparent. Much unnecessary redundant data.
F	Appalling (the application does not run properly or runs only because of brute-force programming)	Deep conceptual errors in the model that underlies the database or gross errors in the database design.

Figure 20.1 Grading scale for databases. A grade reflects the consistency of the database and the extent of design and modeling errors.

There are several possible responses to a poor grade: Choose the vendor anyway and make the best of it, choose another vendor, forego the application, or build the software yourself.

I reverse engineered a database for an application and assigned it a grade of "F," because the database design was awful. Nevertheless, my client chose to purchase the product. There was a shortage of suitable products, and even this flawed application could deliver business benefit. Furthermore, the product had some technical merits apart from its deep database flaws. I recommended that my client shift to a better product if one became available.

The reverse engineering results alerted my client to the negative qualities of the database and they prepared a strategy to mitigate the consequences. Essentially, the poor design made it difficult to load legacy data. Also the database was prone to accumulating bad data and difficult to extend.

My client also used the negative evaluation to negotiate for a better price, terms, and conditions. Reverse engineering helped my client understand the vendor's architecture and communicate with the vendor about the product.

Business anecdote: A bad grade is not necessarily a veto

Ethics

When I reverse engineer vendor software, my purpose is not to uncover the vendor's secrets so that my client can re-create the software. First, that would be unethical. Second, reimplementation is usually uneconomical, and I would view it as a last resort. Rather, my purpose is to assess the software's merit, to get past the hidden assumptions and the sales claims. Reverse engineering deepens my understanding of a product and lets me communicate with a vendor.

Unfortunately, many persons still regard reverse engineering as sinister. They completely misunderstand the intent, perhaps because hardware reverse engineering is often done to re-create the product. However, this is *not* the case in database reverse engineering, and there is nothing at all wrong with a customer discovering what is truly for sale.

My clients openly ask vendors for their database structure and tell them why they want it. If the vendor refuses, my clients tell them they will be penalized in the evaluation. Most vendors acquiesce and settle for a nondisclosure agreement. I urge my clients to agree to reasonable nondisclosure terms.

Some vendors find reverse engineering threatening, but it is only threatening to the *inept* vendors. The *superb* vendors should welcome the technology; it makes their excellence visible for all to see in a manner that is much more credible than mere words or a sales ad. This kind of credibility cannot be bought.

Reverse engineering has further benefits for skilled vendors. When customers are assured of quality, they can justify paying a premium price, and they become more interested in collateral products. A customer will pay more for software that has fewer maintenance problems and is simpler to deploy.

Reverse engineering causes a shift in business practices and fosters a culture of openness. The vendors put forth their products for customers to judge. Reverse engineering exposes the strengths and weaknesses of products and causes an evolutionary bias toward excellence. Reverse engineering induces vendors to upgrade their software engineering practices so that they can survive the scrutiny.

Thus reverse engineering vendor software can benefit the entire software community. With widespread practice, the bias toward quality would build on what software engineering has already accomplished. Software engineering strives to improve software quality—precisely what vendor reverse engineering targets.

 Tell vendors why you are performing reverse engineering and formally ask for their database structure.

Industrial Response

I have found that most business leaders are not aware that they can use reverse engineering to assess vendor products, but they readily accept the notion once I explain it. The barrier is the confusion about how to practice the technology.

- **Modeling**. Many people don't understand how to model. Few can master the paradigm shift to develop software indirectly via models.

- **Databases**. Some people understand databases. Others do not.

- **Software engineering**. Many organizations lack a software development process. Many do not appreciate the need for such rigor.

- **Tools**. Tools don't help much. Reverse engineering tools are intrinsically complex, and commercial tools are weak.

The net result is that only informed organizations commission reverse engineering projects. Unfortunately, despite the need, it is slow to catch on. This dilemma is a challenge for the technical community.

Chapter Summary

Database reverse engineering is valuable not only for recovering information for newly built software, but also for assessing vendor products. Reverse engineering lets you discern how well the database of an application has been designed and conceived. The quality of the database is a good indicator of the quality of the software as a whole.

The business case for reverse engineering of vendor databases is compelling. A software purchase and deployment can cost millions of dollars; a reverse engineering assessment can be performed in as little as a few weeks. A thorough assessment can guide your purchase decisions, leading to reduced expenditures and better product choices. Reverse engineering of databases works only for database applications, but that describes a large body of commercial software.

Reverse engineering of vendor software offers a creative response to the "software crisis." With widespread practice, vendor reverse engineering would cause a bias toward quality. Database reverse engineering provides both a carrot and a stick. The excellence and flaws of various products become more apparent and more heavily influence product success and failure. This bias toward quality would complement the improvement that software engineering has been able to accomplish.

✔ **Use reverse engineering to assess products**. Use reverse engineering to judge the finalists in any major acquisition of a database application.

✔ **Be candid with vendors**. Tell vendors why you are performing reverse engineering, and formally ask for their database structure.

Major recommendations for Chapter 20

Resource Notes

Most of this chapter is based on [Blaha-98], [Blaha-99a], and [Blaha-99b].

Most organizations are unaware of the idea of reverse engineering for assessing vendor software. Nevertheless, occasional incidents of such work have been published. [Premerlani-93] describes several vendor databases studied at GE R&D. [Richards-97] describes experiences at Levi Strauss. [Aiken-99] discusses the reverse engineering of PeopleSoft, which helped the Virginia government better understand the package.

References

[Aiken-99] Peter Aiken, Ojelanki Ngwenyama, and Lewis Broome. Reverse engineering new systems for smooth implementation. *IEEE Software*. March/April 1999, 36–43.

[Blaha-98] Michael Blaha. On Reverse Engineering of Vendor Databases. *Fifth Working Conference on Reverse Engineering*, October 1998, Honolulu, Hawaii, 183–190.

[Blaha-99a] Michael Blaha. The case for reverse engineering. *IEEE IT Professional 1*, 2 (March/April 1999), 35–41.

[Blaha-99b] Michael Blaha. How to recognize database winners and losers. *IEEE IT Professional 1*, 3 (May/June 1999), 20–25.

[Premerlani-93] William Premerlani and Michael Blaha. An approach for reverse engineering of relational databases. *First Working Conference on Reverse Engineering*. May 1993, Baltimore, Maryland, 151–160.

[Richards-97] Dan Richards. Reverse engineering: What works, what doesn't. *Database Design Summit*, September 1997, San Diego, California.

21

Interacting Applications

Most operational applications are built for a specific business purpose. These "stovepipes" perform their given task, but are developed with little regard for other applications. Consequently, the applications work well individually, but do not collaborate for the overall benefit of a company. You can use one of two technical approaches to combine applications.

- **Data warehouses**. Periodically copy and reconcile operational data in a separate database (a data warehouse), so that it can be queried across application boundaries. The data are not live, but are consistent. Chapter 12 covers this approach.

- **Integration**. Propagate data between operational applications so that they need not be repeatedly entered. This chapter covers the ***integration*** approach.

Overview

The application-centric development that has caused "stovepipes" has significant advantages. Applications are justified by a business need. Application-centric development is focused on servicing the business need and quickly realizing the potential payback. Projects become more manageable, and it is easier to define and measure success.

Nevertheless, as applications increase in size and complexity, organizations are finding the limitations of application-centric development. There are many business motives for integrating applications.

- **Cost reduction**. It is wasteful for applications to acquire the same data repeatedly. It is also costly to maintain a patchwork of interfaces. Integration technol-

This is the third book I have published with Prentice Hall. They dutifully send me a royalty check every six months. The payment depends on book sales via the various channels. There are different royalty rates for U.S. sales, Canadian sales, mail order, and other categories. Book clubs and some foreign printings yield a single payment, regardless of the number of copies sold. The different channels have different time delays for reporting.

Prentice Hall computes royalties with an application that collects data from the systems for the various sales channels. Unfortunately, there is no application that can tell authors the total number of books that have been sold.

This example is typical of many industrial situations. Applications can provide only the information for which they were designed. It is problematic to go beyond the rigid predefined services. Integration technology seeks to combine applications for greater flexibility.

Business anecdote: Limitations of stovepipes

ogy can reduce multiple data entry and provide a disciplined approach to connecting applications.

- **Data consistency**. It is difficult to ensure that data are correct, consistent, and timely. By reconciling differences, integration can improve the quality of data in individual application databases.

- **Greater flexibility**. Applications should enable, not inhibit, business decisions. Applications are inflexible when they are balkanized and changes have an unknown effect on other applications. Integration technology can reduce the stasis of a network of applications, simplifying changes and making the effects more predictable.

- **Enabling analytical applications**. Integration reconciles differences between operational applications, which is a prerequisite for a data warehouse.

- **Mergers and reorganizations**. Integration technology makes it easier to consolidate applications for business mergers and reorganizations.

I recommend the following process for integrating applications.

- **Application modeling**. Model each application. Chapters 8–10 describe the issues in this step.

- **Enterprise modeling**. Build an enterprise model from important portions of the application models. An enterprise model spans applications and provides a focus for integration.

- **Integration techniques**. Decide how to relate application models to each other and to an enterprise model.

- **Identity applications**. Augment the integration architecture by rigorously enforcing the accuracy and consistency of the concepts essential to your business.

- **Data exchange format**. Use XML as the data format for applications that exchange files.

Enterprise Modeling

An *__enterprise model__* describes an entire organization or some major aspect of an organization. An enterprise model abstracts multiple applications, combining and reconciling their logical content. It also gives you a high-level understanding of the relationship between applications and the processing that must occur to exchange data. Finally, it provides infrastructure for integration.

There may be multiple tiers of enterprise models, especially for large organizations. For example, in Figure 21.1, finance, engineering, manufacturing, and sales may each have their own enterprise model. Reconciling these intermediate models yields the overall enterprise model. For simplicity, the rest of this chapter considers only a single enterprise model.

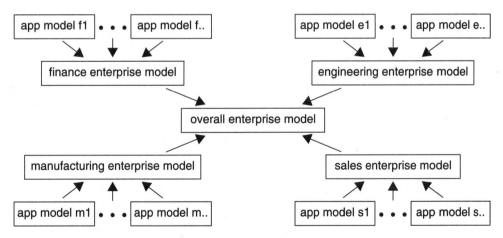

Figure 21.1 Enterprise models. There may be multiple tiers of enterprise models.

Top-down vs. Bottom-up Modeling

In principle, there are two approaches to building an enterprise model—top-down or bottom-up. With the top-down approach, you construct a high-level model of the organization and then elaborate until you have sufficient detail. In contrast, the bottom-up approach synthesizes an enterprise model from the models of relevant applications.

The top-down approach yields a coherent model; the bottom-up approach must cope with disjointed applications built over time. Essentially, top-down modeling provides a clean start apart from the problems of the applications.

But top-down modeling has disadvantages. The most serious is that it can lack focus and become an obscure exercise without value to an organization. A top-down model may also lack the detail needed for integration.

I recommend that you prepare an enterprise model mostly bottom-up. The applications are important to an organization and have the business information, so use them to drive construction. You should successively rationalize applications with an enterprise model and add their information. I do not favor top-down construction, because there is too much risk that the modeling effort will become disconnected from reality. However, it is appropriate to guide the construction of an enterprise model with a top-down vision.

 Build an enterprise model from the models of relevant applications. Guide the model with a top-down vision, but build the model bottom-up.

Scope

An enterprise model should not include everything in application models, or it will become too large. Instead, it should include only concepts (entity types, relationship types, and attributes) that appear in multiple application models, plus possibly a few other key concepts. You should avoid duplication and be sure to reconcile overlapping concepts. This reconciliation is often difficult, because applications can express concepts in different ways.

An enterprise model should contain little more than the intersection of relevant applications.

You should construct an enterprise model by reconciling models rather than database structures. It is just too difficult to construct an enterprise model directly from database structures and simultaneously address the artifacts of implementation, as well as different conceptualizations. If application models are unavailable, you will first need to perform reverse engineering. (See Chapter 19.)

I learned the hard way about limiting the size of an enterprise model. Several developers and I were building an enterprise model from the full contents of applications models. The client chose this approach, and I did not object, because it was not apparent that it was wrong. As applications were added, the enterprise model became increasingly unwieldy, and we found it difficult to reconcile overlapping concepts. Eventually, the effort was discontinued. In retrospect, the size of the enterprise model was much of the problem.

Business anecdote: Limiting the size of an enterprise model

Managing an Enterprise Model

Despite the basic need, many managers fear that enterprise modeling will get out of hand and become wasteful. I share this concern and have some suggestions. First, constrain your enterprise modeling resources—for a large organization, about one person-equivalent per year from three part-time modelers should suffice. Second, involve enterprise modelers with application projects to ground them with reality. Finally, subject enterprise models to periodic reviews.

Most organizations have trouble building enterprise models. Some models I have seen are poor and ill conceived. Others are of high quality, but too large in scope. Enterprise modeling requires proficient developers.

It is difficult to keep an enterprise model consistent with changes to application models. I have no good solution to this problem. Ideally, tools should manage correspondences between models and warn developers about inconsistencies [Blaha-98b]. However, current commercial tools lack such a capability. Limiting the size of an enterprise model lessens the problem. My best advice is to track changes to application models carefully. Sometimes a spreadsheet can help maintain correspondences between enterprise and application constructs.

Unlike with application models, you should limit enterprise modeling to a single tool. Only a few people will be building an enterprise model, and it is awkward to have multiple tools. Figure 21.2 summarizes techniques for managing an enterprise model.

Integration Techniques

There are several techniques for connecting applications. In practice, you need not choose a single technique. In fact, I normally combine techniques.

* Constrain enterprise modeling resources.

* Involve modelers with application projects to ground them with reality.

* Subject enterprise models to periodic reviews.

* Obtain proficient modelers.

* Carefully track application changes, and propagate them to enterprise models.

* Limit enterprise modeling to a single tool.

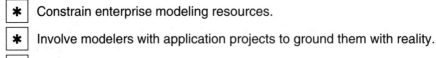

Figure 21.2 Enterprise modeling list. Be sure to address these items.

Master Database

An obvious approach to integration is to require that all applications store data in a single master database, denoted by the solid line cylinder in Figure 21.3. Each application then operates on its own portion of the master database (dotted line cylinders). The master database subsumes and thoroughly integrates the individual applications.

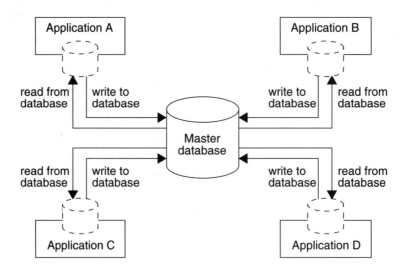

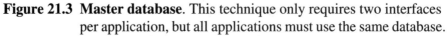

Figure 21.3 Master database. This technique only requires two interfaces per application, but all applications must use the same database.

There are many advantages of integration with one database. The thorough integration is readily apparent to the end user; by definition, there are few inconsistencies between applications. With a single database, there is no unplanned redundant data. The deep understanding that is needed to achieve the master database improves the extensibility and quality of applications.

Unfortunately, you can normally create a master database only for small groups of applications. It is impractical for a large group, because you must revise or rewrite too many applications. Also, you aren't likely to get a multivendor consensus on a single model. Thus in industrial settings, you must cope with multiple databases, each with its own particular model.

Point-to-Point Interfaces

Another obvious integration approach—and the one most often used—is to connect pairs of applications directly. In Figure 21.4, there are two interfaces for each pair of applications that must exchange data. One interface reads from the first application and writes to the second; the other interface reads from the second application and writes to the first. The integration mechanism for point-to-point integration does not require an enterprise model, although an enterprise model might still make it easier to understand and seed new application models.

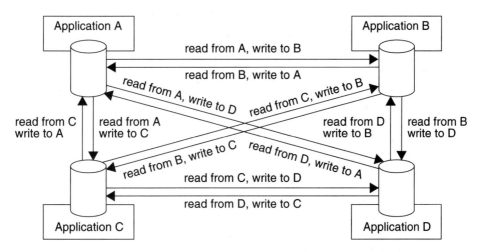

Figure 21.4 Point-to-point integration. This technique is commonly used, but for 50 applications, it can mean 2,450 interfaces!

There are advantages to point-to-point integration. It is straightforward to understand and implement; the developer must deal with only two applications at a time. There is little disruption to ongoing business activities, because you can run each application in isolation and then integrate them when the interfaces become available. Point-to-point integration is often the preferred approach when there is little commonality among applications or there are few of them. Some vendors provide point-to-point interfaces between their software and selected other packages.

However, there are severe drawbacks to the widespread use of point-to-point integration. The most serious is that the interfaces create a large web of dependencies. If n is the number of applications, there could be as many as $n(n-1)$ interfaces (Figure 21.5). Maintaining the interfaces can become more difficult than maintaining the applications. A few point-to-point interfaces are certainly acceptable, but many more rapidly become impractical.

Number of applications	Possible number of point-to-point interfaces
5	20
10	90
50	2,450
100	9,900
500	249,500

Figure 21.5 Explosive growth. Point-to-point integration leads to explosive growth in the number of interfaces.

Not every pair of applications will exchange data, so there could be fewer than $n(n-1)$ interfaces. With n applications, however, enough applications will exchange data for point-to-point integration to suffer explosive growth in the number of interfaces.

Indirect Integration

The third approach, indirect integration, is the most complex, but it provides the backbone of a robust, scalable integration strategy. In Figure 21.6, applications communicate indirectly via the enterprise database, rather than directly with each other. The figure shows the enterprise database with dotted lines, because it need not be a physical database—it could be a transient store for passing actual data or a translator of read and write requests. Unlike the master database approach, indirect integration does not modify applications and instead introduces an integration layer.

The most significant advantage of indirect integration is scalability; for each new application, you add only two interfaces to the enterprise database—one for reading and one for writing. Thus, if you have 10 applications, you have only 20 interfaces. This contrasts starkly with point-to-point integration, where you could have

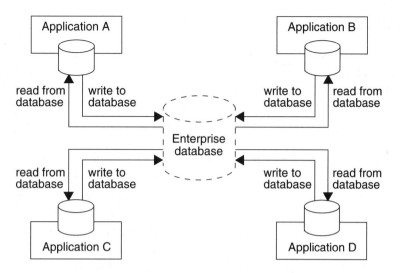

Figure 21.6 Indirect integration. Indirect integration via an enterprise database requires *2n* interfaces.

90 interfaces for 10 applications. Furthermore, indirect integration does not disrupt applications to achieve integration, which happens in the master database approach. Indirect integration is clearly the preferred technique for coping with numerous applications.

The biggest disadvantage of indirect integration is complexity; the indirection requires special software. However, you must accept the complexity if you want an integration technique that handles many applications. Indirect integration is more difficult when application models and their implementations are greatly dissimilar.

Hybrid Approach

The best approach combines the three techniques. Indirect integration should be the backbone strategy, but can be supplemented with master databases and point-to-point integration. Point-to-point integration can be helpful for applications with a high volume of data exchange. A master database is suitable for clusters of closely related applications, especially those from the same vendor.

 Use indirect integration as the backbone integration strategy augmented by selected use of point-to-point integration and master databases.

Identity Applications

Proper use of the integration techniques will yield an integration architecture that is flexible, robust, and linearly scalable with the number of applications. However, integration is still difficult. You have the enterprise-modeling problem of determining the precise correspondence of data and the operational problem of how to exchange data. You can further reduce the complexity of integration by establishing several identity applications.

An ***identity application*** is a dedicated application that enforces the accuracy and consistency of a key entity type, such as *customer*, *part*, and *contract*. (These vary according to your business.) You should use identity applications as a resource for all other applications. Thus, for example, an identity application could service all requests to create a new customer. An identity application simplifies integration by providing an anchor point that cuts across applications.

Consider a customer identity application. If each application can individually name customers, you could encounter many variations, such as *AT&T*, *A.T.&T.*, and *American Telephone and Telegraph*. This kind of variation makes it difficult to find data. In practice, integration does not fully occur and information is lost for some queries. In contrast, a customer identity application would dictate the precise name for a company, and all applications would use the same name. It is then much easier to find customer data. Subsequent queries on other entity types might still fail to match fully, but at least integration is less complex.

Ideally, the customer identity application should create all new customers. However, vendor applications may not let you exercise that much control. In any case, an identity application could at least check that a customer created in one application is consistent with occurrences of the same customer in other applications.

 Use a small number of identity applications to make integration less complex.

Data Exchange Format

The eXtensible Markup Language (XML) offers a format for data exchange that can facilitate integration both within and outside a company. For example, a participating merchant might want to periodically send an airline a transaction file to post against frequent flyer accounts. The merchant's information systems can generate an XML file, and the airline can subsequently process it.

XML was created as a successor to HTML. HTML combines content and presentation. In contrast, XML focuses on content and lets another language (eXtensible Stylesheet Language, XSL) handle presentation. This separation permits multiple presentation formats (such as for desktop computers, palmtops, and audio devices) to be generated from the same XML file.

An XML document is self-contained, having both data and its description. Figure 21.7 shows a sample XML document for the frequent flyer scenario. The first line specifies the version of XML; the second line specifies the document type definition (DTD) file (to be discussed). The remainder shows a merchant post consisting of a merchant name and two activities. Each activity has a date, customer name, frequent flyer account, and point award.

```
<?xml version="1.0"?>
<!DOCTYPE merchantPostDefn SYSTEM "merchantPostDefn.dtd">
<merchantPost>
    <merchantName>ABC Company</merchantName>
    <activity
        <date>2001-01-20</date>
        <customer>James Smith</customer>
        <frequentFlyerAcct>A123456</frequentFlyerAcct>
        <points>500</points>
    </activity>
    <activity>
        <date>2001-01-20</date>
        <customer>John Doe</customer>
        <frequentFlyerAcct>B234567</frequentFlyerAcct>
        <points>250</points>
    </activity>
</merchantPost>
```

Figure 21.7 XML example. XML provides a standard data exchange format.

Figure 21.8 defines the *merchantPostDefn* DTD referenced in the second line of Figure 21.7. A document type definition (DTD) constrains the data in an XML document to improve data quality. The data in an XML document must conform to the DTD or an XML processor will reject it. Figure 21.8 states that a *merchantPostDefn* has one merchant name and one or more activities (the plus suffix). An activity then has one each of *date*, *customer*, *frequentFlyerAcct*, and *points*. All fields are entered as character data (the *PCDATA* specification).

XML has several advantages. It is a vendor-neutral standard that the World Wide Web Consortium (W3C) maintains. XML tools are readily and freely available to

```
<!ELEMENT merchantPostDefn ( merchantName activity+ )>
<!ELEMENT merchantName (#PCDATA)>
<!ELEMENT activity ( date customer frequentFlyerAcct points )>
<!ELEMENT date (#PCDATA)>
<!ELEMENT customer (#PCDATA)>
<!ELEMENT frequentFlyerAcct (#PCDATA)>
<!ELEMENT points (#PCDATA)>
```

Figure 21.8 Document type definition (DTD) example. A DTD
constrains the data that an XML document can store.

generate files, read files, and verify content. XML makes it easier for applications to exchange data, eliminating the need to deal with proprietary data formats.

Even though XML is helpful, it is not a panacea for integrating applications. There is still a need for agreed-on DTDs. Figure 21.8 is a simple DTD; more complex DTDs can be devised via structural modeling. Without accepted DTDs, it can be difficult to translate between different application data representations.

 Use XML to format data that are passed among applications through intermediate files.

Chapter Summary

Most operational applications are built for a specific business purpose with little regard for other applications. This leads to multiple and inconsistent data entry. The resulting web of interfaces can be more difficult to maintain than the original applications. Integration technology improves this situation by providing a systematic approach to connecting applications.

A key step in successful integration is enterprise modeling. An enterprise model describes an entire organization or some major aspect. An enterprise model calls attention to overlapping data among the various applications.

There are several possible integration techniques. Indirect integration should be the backbone strategy, but you can supplement it with master databases and point-to-point integration.

Identity applications complement the integration techniques and make integration less complex. Identity applications enforce the accuracy and consistency of important entities, such as customer, part, and contract. An identity application provides an anchor point that cuts across applications.

In many cases, data are moved among applications via intermediate files. The XML standard provides a uniform means for representing the data in the files and simplifying processing.

✔ **Build an enterprise model from the models of relevant applications**. Guide the model with a top-down vision, but build the model bottom-up.

✔ **Limit the size of an enterprise model**. An enterprise model should contain little more than the intersection of relevant applications.

✔ **Use indirect integration as the backbone integration strategy**. Supplement it with selected use of point-to-point integration and master databases.

✔ **Use identity applications**. A small number of identity applications can make integration less complex.

✔ **Use XML**. Use XML to format data that are passed among applications through intermediate files.

Major recommendations for Chapter 21

Resource Notes

[Blaha-98a] has further technical details about integrating applications. Charles Goldfarb is the creator of a prior language (SGML) on which XML is based. [Goldfarb-00] thoroughly explains XML and illustrates its use.

References

[Blaha-98a] Michael Blaha and William Premerlani. *Object-Oriented Modeling and Design for Database Applications*. Upper Saddle River, New Jersey: Prentice Hall, 1998.

[Blaha-98b] Michael Blaha, David LaPlant, and Erica Marvak. Requirements for repository software. *Fifth Working Conference on Reverse Engineering*, October 1998, Honolulu, Hawaii, 164–173.

[Goldfarb-00] Charles F. Goldfarb and Paul Prescod. *The XML Handbook, Second Edition*. Upper Saddle River, New Jersey: Prentice Hall, 2000.

22

Object-Oriented Technology

Object-oriented (OO) technology organizes systems as collections of interacting objects that combine data and behavior. This contrasts with conventional procedural software in which data structure and behavior are only loosely connected.

Many database practitioners regard OO technology as irrelevant, because the literature focuses on OO programming. This stereotype is unfortunate, because OO technology is more than programming. For example, OO technology also applies to hardware, user interfaces, software engineering, and databases. Furthermore, OO technology and RDBMSs complement each other, and you can use the same model to develop both programming code and the relational database structure.

Unified Modeling Language (UML)

The UML [Booch-99] [Rumbaugh-99] is a general-purpose visual modeling language. The programming community has endorsed the UML, and it is making inroads with the database community as well. The UML has been standardized by the Object Management Group (OMG), a nonprofit organization with more than 500 members, which was established to promote OO standards.

The UML has several kind of models. Chapter 9 presented the UML object model which is essentially just an ER model. The other kinds of UML models are intended mostly for programming.

The UML is a notation, not a software development methodology. A methodology has two aspects: concepts and process. The UML deals with concepts, but lacks a process. This omission is intentional. It is more difficult to standardize a process than a notation, and the appropriate process varies with the application. Databases, real-time software, engineering problems, and user interfaces, for example, have different needs.

UML Object Model

In Chapter 9, I explained the UML object model using ER jargon, because ER is broadly accepted in the database community. I now present the same model (repeated as Figure 22.1), but describe it using OO jargon, which is what you will find in the UML literature. This should give you some idea of how ER and OO terminology correspond.

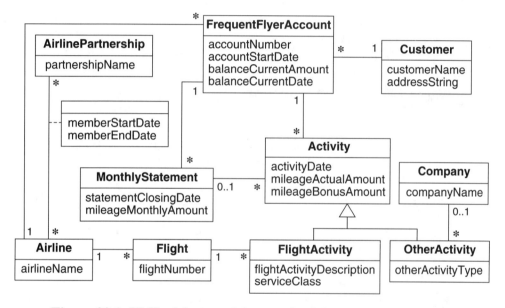

Figure 22.1 UML object model example. OO concepts are helpful
for developing database applications.

Object models are built from three basic constructs: classes, associations, and generalizations. Each box in the figure with a bold font name denotes a class. An *__object__* is a concept, abstraction, or thing that can be individually identified and has meaning for an application. A *__class__* is a description of a group of objects with similar properties (attributes), behavior (programming code), meaning, and relationships to other objects. Thus, class *Airline* describes objects *United Airlines*, *Lufthansa*, and *Air New Zealand*. The figure has ten classes.

The diagram has 20 attributes which are shown in the lower portion of the boxes. Attributes include *accountNumber*, *accountStartDate*, and *serviceClass*. An *__attribute__* describes values that can be stored.

The figure has nine associations, each of which is indicated by a series of one or more lines between classes. (The lines connected to the triangle are another construct to be discussed shortly.) The line between *FrequentFlyerAccount* and *Customer* is one of the associations. A ***link*** is a physical or conceptual connection between objects. An ***association*** is a description of a group of links with similar properties, behavior, and meaning. Associations are the glue that connects the classes.

Attributes *memberStartDate* and *memberEndDate* describe the association between *Airline* and *AirlinePartnership*. These attributes clearly belong to the association and not the related classes. They are connected to the association with a dotted line. The airlines in a partnership may start and end their membership on different dates. All other attributes in the figure describe classes.

Multiplicity is indicated at each end of an association—the "*", "1", and "0..1" annotations in the figure. ***Multiplicity*** is the number of occurrences of a class that may connect to a single occurrence of a related class. The association between *Customer* and *FrequentFlyerAccount*, for example, has one-to-many multiplicity. Each account pertains to only one customer, but one customer can have many (zero or more) accounts. The "*" is UML notation for "many." The figure also illustrates at-most-one multiplicity (0..1). An activity appears in at most one monthly statement, but may not be in a monthly statement if it has not been reported yet.

The final concept in the figure, generalization, is shown with a triangle. ***Generalization*** organizes classes by their similarities and differences. An activity can be a flight activity or some other activity. The attributes, behavior, and associations for the *Activity* class pertain to all activities. In contrast, only a *FlightActivity* may have a description, service class, and reference to a flight. Only an *OtherActivity* may have an *otherActivityType* (indicating if the occurrence is a credit card purchase, car rental, or hotel stay) and a reference to a company. The apex of the triangle connects to the class with the general information (the ***superclass***). Lines connect the base of the triangle to the other classes with specific information (the ***subclasses***).

Figure 22.2 summarizes the correspondence between OO and ER concepts.

OO Concepts and Databases

Relational Databases

I believe OO technology has great promise for improving the way we conceive and deliver software. However, although it is starting to take hold in the programming community, it has had less success with the database community to date. I believe this mixed success is caused by the heavy programming emphasis in the OO literature and the cultural differences between programmers and database practitioners.

ER concept	OO concept
Entity	Object
Entity type	Class
Relationship	Link
Relationship type	Association
Multiplicity	Multiplicity
Attribute	Attribute
Generalization	Generalization

Figure 22.2 Comparison of concepts. ER concepts have corresponding
OO concepts.

Many people assume that OO concepts and relational databases do not fit together. The reality is quite to the contrary! With skillful use, a relational database can provide an excellent implementation for OO models. I do it all the time. You can use the
same OO model to develop programming code and the relational database structure.

The UML provides the basis for unifying relational databases and OO technology. The UML object model is an ER model; ER models have been widely used to
design relational databases and are starting to be used to design programs. Relational
databases can incorporate programming code directly through stored procedures.

OO Databases

Two motivations have led to the development of OO-DBMSs.

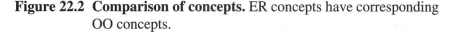

Recently, I encountered an odd situation that illustrates the marketplace confusion with OO technology. A major RDBMS vendor formed a new OO programming group for contract application work. I met some of these people
and found much to my surprise that they knew little about databases. Their
approach to applications was to write programming code and minimize the
use of a DBMS. The vendor wanted OO technology, but had no idea how to
combine it with an RDBMS.

Given that at least one RDBMS vendor has a muddled understanding of
OO technology, it is no surprise that practitioners find it confusing.

Business anecdote: Confusion about melding OO technology with databases

- **Programmer frustration with relational databases**. Many programmers don't understand RDBMSs and want something more familiar. RDBMSs are declarative (queries describe properties that requested data must satisfy), while most languages are imperative (stated as a sequence of steps). Furthermore, RDBMSs awkwardly combine with most languages and programmers prefer a DBMS with a more seamless interface.

  This is a poor reason for choosing an OO-DBMS. The reality is that RDBMSs dominate the marketplace now and will for the foreseeable future. Programmers should not be using an OO-DBMS out of frustration; they should learn to deal with RDBMSs. RDBMS products are much more mature and have proven features for reliability, scalability, and administration.

- **Need for special features**. RDBMSs lack the power that some advanced applications need. OO-DBMSs offer advanced features, like rich data types and quick navigation of data structures, and they let you access low-level primitives.

  This is a good reason for choosing an OO-DBMS. If you have an advanced application that is critical to your business, using an OO-DBMS can make it easier to develop. Engineering applications, multimedia systems, and artificial intelligence software can sometimes benefit from the use of an OO-DBMS.

 Do not use an OO-DBMS merely to avoid dealing with an RDBMS. Use an OO-DBMS only for critical applications that require advanced features.

OO Extensions to SQL

Vendors and the SQL standard committee have been seeking to add OO extensions to RDBMSs. Two of the most prominent additions are abstract data types and references.

- **Abstract data types (ADTs)**. Conventional RDBMSs have limited data types; they support numbers, strings, dates, and little else. ADTs let a database store any type of data, such as geographic coordinates, pictures, and audio clips. An ADT may also have operations bundled with it. An audio clip, for example, may have an operation to go to a specified location. The vendors have given ADTs various names, such as Oracle cartridges and Informix data blades.

  ADTs are a good idea and extend the power of RDBMSs. They also tie you to a vendor, because their details are beyond the SQL standard. You should use ADTs only when their benefit is compelling.

Abstract data types are product specific. Use them only when their benefit is compelling.

■ **References**. A reference is a field that contains the address of a record (a pointer). Consider the stock ownership example from Chapter 6 (repeated as Figure 22.3). An RDBMS can find the *stockAmount*, *personName*, and *companyName* by joining the three tables. In contrast, if you replace *personID* and *companyID* with references, you would not need joins. Rather, the RDBMS would traverse the references to the appropriate person and company for each *stockAmount*. The intent of SQL references is to support fast navigation and object-orientation.

Unfortunately, the SQL standards committee made a mistake when they added references. References are theoretically unsound, add complexity, and do not add power [Date-98]. There are better techniques to improve performance, such as careful indexing and product-specific tuning. Fortunately, references are grafted on to SQL, so you can easily ignore them.

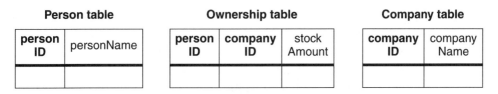

Person table		Ownership table			Company table	
person ID	personName	**person ID**	**company ID**	stock Amount	**company ID**	company Name

Figure 22.3 Stock ownership example from Chapter 6

SQL references are a bad idea. Do not use them under any circumstances.

Two extensions for RDBMSs would make them easier to use with OO techniques. These capabilities would be useful additions to both products and the SQL standard.

■ **Extend referential integrity actions to support generalization**. RDBMSs can automatically maintain consistency between a foreign key and its primary-key referent. For the example in Chapter 11 (Figure 11.8), the *on delete cascade* clause (constraint *fk_act1*) causes all corresponding *Activity* records to be automatically deleted when a *FrequentFlyerAccount* record is deleted. Similarly, the *on delete no action* clause (constraint *fk_otherAct2*) prevents deletion of a company if there is a referencing *OtherActivity*.

The current referential integrity mechanism is one-way. To support generalization properly, it should be two-way. A superclass (the entity type with general data) record then depends on a subclass (an entity type with specific data) record, and a subclass record depends on a superclass record.

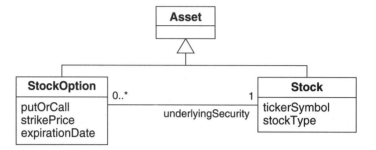

Figure 22.4 A UML model. SQL should be extended with two-way
referential integrity to support generalization properly.

Figure 22.4 is an excerpt from the financial case study in [Blaha-98] that illustrates the need for two-way referential integrity. The purpose of the *Asset* superclass is to unify some common data and behavior that the excerpt does not show. An asset can be a stock or a stock option. A stock can have many stock options written against it. For example, IBM stock can have put and call options written for various strike prices and expiration dates.

For operational applications, the usual implementation of generalization is to map the superclass and subclasses each to a table. You can use referential integrity to make the records of *StockOption* and *Stock* depend on *Asset*. The deletion of an *Asset* record then cascades to the deletion of the appropriate subclass record, *StockOption* or *Stock*. You can also use referential integrity to cause the deletion of a *Stock* to cascade to the deletion of the related *StockOption* records.

Now the problem is as follows. The deletion of an *Asset* (that happens to be a *Stock*) cascades to cause the deletion of the *Stock* record. Deletion of the *Stock* record then cascades to cause the deletion of any *StockOption* records. But now referential integrity breaks down; deleting a *StockOption* record does *not* cause the deletion of an *Asset* record. The deletion cascade goes only downward, from the superclass to the subclasses. For proper behavior, it should go both ways.

The workaround with one-way referential integrity is to do more programming (and consequently to do more work and risk more bugs). In the case study, we had to write additional code first to check for the existence of associated stock options and then to delete them before deleting a stock.

■ **Support partitioning of records across tables**. The meaning of ordinary generalization (the only form I cover in this book) is that each superclass record has at most one subclass record. Current RDBMSs cannot readily enforce this constraint. For example, there is nothing to prevent the following situation. A stock could be entered in the *Asset* table with an ID of 18, in the *Stock* table with an ID of 18, and also in the *StockOption* table with an ID of 18. Once again, you must do additional programming, instead of writing a simple declarative constraint, to ensure proper behavior.

Components

Components are currently a hot area of OO technology. ***Components*** are software building blocks that you can flexibly combine to build applications and large systems. Microsoft's OLE/DCOM technology, OMG's CORBA, and Java Beans provide communications infrastructure for linking components.

Components are a good idea—I endorse the aims and the technology—but they do not obviate the need to conceive a database well and design it properly. Components package programming code into meaningful units with a crisp, coherent focus. Typically, you must combine multiple components to realize an application. Components that interact with a database are more interconnected than the literature might lead you to believe. Often, you must express relationships among the components in the database or your application will be missing information.

For example, information about companies pervades many applications. A company must be related to the relevant employees, orders, parts, locations, invoices—whatever relationships are important for an application—or a database will not be fully functional. Individual components for companies, employees, orders, parts, locations, and invoices could lack the critical relationships. Thus, even though components are crisp, coherent, and generally have a small focus, you must still model the database with a broad perspective and capture dependencies between objects. It is best to regard components as small views into a holistic database.

 Be wary of dependencies between components that interact with a database.

Chapter Summary

The combination of OO and database technologies is relatively new, so it is not surprising to see some flaws and immaturities. The marketplace is rapidly evolving as it begins to rationalize the two technologies.

The UML has a number of models, one of which (the object model) is an ER model. ER models are widely used and accepted by database practitioners. As I demonstrated by repeating the explanation of the model from Chapter 9 using OO terminology, there is a correspondence between ER and OO concepts.

The latest SQL standard has added OO extensions to RDBMSs. This is a worthwhile goal. One addition is abstract data types; these are powerful, but should be used with caution to avoid dependency on a specific product. The other major addition, references, is ill advised and candidly a mistake, reflecting the general confusion about how to combine OO technology properly with RDBMSs. I noted two extensions from which both products and the SQL standard could benefit.

Many applications are now starting to incorporate components. However, components that store data in a database are often not distinct and will have relationships. This is contrary to the hype of components—that they are rigorously separated and can be freely mixed and matched.

✔ **Use OO-DBMSs selectively**. Do not use an OO-DBMS merely to avoid dealing with an RDBMS. Use it for critical applications that require advanced features.

✔ **Be careful with abstract data types**. Abstract data types are product specific. Use them only when their benefit is compelling.

✔ **Avoid SQL references**. SQL references are a bad idea. Do not use them under any circumstances.

✔ **Be careful with components**. Components that interact with a database can have hidden dependencies.

Major recommendations for Chapter 22

Resource Notes

[Blaha-98] has additional information on the mechanics of implementing OO models with relational databases.

References

[Blaha-98] Michael Blaha and William Premerlani. *Object-Oriented Modeling and Design for Database Applications.* Upper Saddle River, New Jersey: Prentice Hall, 1998.
[Booch-99] Grady Booch, James Rumbaugh, and Ivar Jacobson. *UML User's Guide.* Reading, Massachusetts: Addison-Wesley.

[Date-98] CJ Date. Don't mix pointers and relations! Presentation at *Third Annual Object/Relational Summit* sponsored by Miller Freeman. Washington DC, September 16–19, 1998.

[Rumbaugh-99] James Rumbaugh, Ivar Jacobson, and Grady Booch. *UML Reference Manual*. Reading, Massachusetts: Addison-Wesley.

Appendix

Glossary

abstract data type an extended data type for storing unusual data, such as geographic coordinates, pictures, and audio clips.

analytical application an application that emphasizes complex queries that read large quantities of data. Analytical applications enable organizations to make strategic decisions. (Contrast with *operational application*.)

API an acronym for *Application Programming Interface*. A set of procedures that provide the functionality of an application.

architecture the high-level plan or strategy for building an application.

attribute a description of values that can be stored in a database.

BLOB an acronym for *Binary Large OBject*. The BLOB data type lets a value of almost any size be stored in a database.

bus architecture (of a data warehouse) a data warehouse with consistent dimensions across fact tables.

business rule a statement of business logic that often can be expressed in a relational database with SQL constraints.

candidate key a combination of columns that uniquely identifies each row in a table. The combination must be minimal and not include any columns that are not needed for unique identification. No column in a candidate key can be null.

client the requester of client-server services. (Contrast with *server*.)

client-server computing an architecture for which a resource, the server, provides computation for multiple requesters, the clients. One client can also access multiple servers.

CODASYL an acronym for *COmmittee for DAta SYstem Languages*. A standard for network databases.

cookie a record in a special file that contains keywords and simple values. Used to retain simple data for a Web client.

COTS an acronym for *Commercial Off The Shelf*. A software package available for purchase from a vendor.

data dictionary a list of definitions, examples, and rationale for important concepts.

data independence a desirable quality of a query language. A person specifies the desired data and the DBMS determines how to get it. SQL largely, but not fully, realizes this goal.

data mart a portion of a data warehouse. A data mart can be built more quickly and yields quicker payback than a full data warehouse. Often, a data mart is built to satisfy the needs of a department.

data mining the discovery of subtle trends and patterns in large quantities of data, often by using artificial intelligence techniques.

data warehouse a database dedicated to decision-support applications.

database a permanent, self-descriptive store of data that is contained in one or more files.

database application an application that uses a DBMS to handle its long-lived data.

database management system the software for managing access to a database.

database manager see *database management system.*

DBA an acronym for *DataBase Administrator*. A DBA is responsible for routine tasks such as backup, security monitoring, and performance monitoring.

DBMS an acronym for *DataBase Management System*. Software that manages access to a database.

declarative constraint a constraint that is expressed as a statement, rather than as a series of programming steps.

denormalization the violation of normal forms. Developers should only violate them for good cause, such as to increase performance for a bottleneck. (See *normal form.*)

dependent entity an entity that can exist only if some other entity also exists. Also called *weak entity.* (Contrast with *independent entity.*)

dimension (for a data warehouse) a basis for facts. Sample dimensions are date, location, product, customer, sales person, and store. (Contrast with *fact.*)

discriminator an attribute that indicates the appropriate specific record for each general record in a generalization.

distributed database a database built on top of a computer network, rather than on a single computer.

DTD an acronym for *Document Type Definition*. A DTD constrains the data in an XML document, thereby improving data quality.

enterprise model a model that describes an entire organization or some major aspect of an organization. An enterprise model combines and reconciles the logical content of multiple applications.

entity a concept, abstraction, or thing that can be individually identified and is relevant to an application.

entity type a description of a group of entities with similar properties, meaning, and relationships to other entities.

ER an acronym for *Entity Relationship*. The classical approach to modeling invented by Peter Chen. You note entities from the real world, describe them, and observe relationships among them.

fact (for a data warehouse) a measure of the performance of a business. Sample facts are sales, budget, profit, and inventory. (Contrast with *dimension*.)

fat client a client that provides most of the application logic, as well as the user interface. (Contrast with *fat server.*)

fat server a server that provides most of the application logic in addition to data management services. (Contrast with *fat client.*)

file a means for primitive storage and retrieval that is provided by computer operating systems.

foreign key a reference to a candidate key (normally a reference to a primary key) and is the glue that binds tables.

fourth-generation language (4GL) a framework for straightforward database applications that provides screen layout, simple calculations, and reports.

generalization an organization of entity types by their similarities and differences.

groupware software that manages unstructured information for collaborating users. Groupware organizes data into documents that consist of items.

hierarchical database a database that is organized as a collection of inverted trees of records. The inverted trees may be of arbitrary depth. IBM's IMS product is the most prominent hierarchical DBMS.

HTML an acronym for *Hyper Text Markup Language*. A language for presenting and formatting data. Often used for conveying documents over the Internet.

independent entity an entity that can exist on its own. Also called *strong entity.* (Contrast with *dependent entity.*)

index a data structure that quickly locates records according to column values. An index is typically implemented as a sequence of levels with increasing precision. An index typically has a wide fan-out at each level, often a factor of 50 or more.

integration the propagation of common data between applications.

Internet a worldwide communications infrastructure for connecting clients and servers.

join the combination of two RDBMS tables on the basis of a comparison of values, often on the equality of values.

metadata the description of data.

methodology a specific systematic approach to the development, operation, and maintenance of software.

model an abstraction of something that lets you thoroughly understand it. A model provides a roadmap for a database.

multidimensional database a database that is organized about facts that relate to dimensions. Intended for use with data warehouses.

multiplicity the number of occurrences of an entity type that may connect to a single occurrence of a related entity type. Sometimes called *cardinality* or *connectivity.*

n-tier architecture a combination of applications, each of which has a three-tier architecture. The applications invoke each other, causing an arbitrary number of tiers.

network database a database that is organized as a collection of records that are related with pointers. Most network DBMSs adhere to the CODASYL standard. Do not confuse *network* databases with communication *networks.* These are different uses of the term *network.*

normal form a guideline for relational database design that increases data consistency. As tables satisfy higher levels of normal forms, they are less likely to store redundant and contradictory data.

null a special value denoting that a value is unknown or not applicable.

object-oriented database a database that is perceived as objects that mix data and programming behavior.

object-oriented technology an organization of systems as collections of interacting objects that combine data and behavior.

object-relational database a relational database in which some data can be perceived as objects.

object-relational DBMS a relational DBMS with added OO features. Some OO features in current products are technically unsound.

OLAP an acronym for *On-Line Analytical Processing*.

OLTP an acronym for *On-Line Transaction Processing*.

on-line analytical processing decision-support applications that use a data warehouse. (Contrast with *on-line transaction processing*.)

on-line transaction processing operational applications that are performed on line, while the user waits. (Contrast with *on-line analytical processing*.)

one-tier architecture an architecture that combines data management, application logic, and the user interface into a single executable file. (Contrast with *two-tier* and *three-tier architectures*.)

OO an acronym for *Object-Oriented*.

operational application an application that involves the routine and critical operations of a business. (Contrast with *analytical application*.)

primary key a candidate key that is preferentially used to access the records in a table. Each table should normally have exactly one primary key.

RDBMS an acronym for *Relational DBMS*.

record a group of values that a database stores together. The tables of a relational database consist of many rows—each row is called a record. Groups of values in hierarchical and network databases are also called records.

relational database a database in which the data are perceived as tables.

relational DBMS a DBMS that manages tables of data and associated structures that increase the functionality and performance of tables.

relationship a physical or conceptual connection between entities.

relationship type a description of a group of relationships with similar properties and meaning.

replication a database approach that maintains copies of data at various database locations and keeps them consistent.

reverse engineering the process of taking an existing design and extracting the underlying logical content.

schema the structure of the data in a database.

security physical and logical protection of data.

server the provider of client-server services. (Contrast with *client*.)

software engineering a systematic, disciplined, quantifiable approach to the development, operation, and maintenance of software.

SQL an acronym for *Structured Query Language*. The standard language for accessing a relational database.

star structure (for a data warehouse) a database design that focuses on facts, each of which relates to many dimensions.

stored procedure programming code that is stored in a database.

strong entity see *independent entity*.

structural model a definition of the data that can be stored and retrieved for a database.

system tables (of a relational database) the definition of the database structure that is also stored in the database.

three-tier architecture an architecture that separates data management, application logic, and the user interface into three separate layers. (Contrast with *one-tier* and *two-tier architectures*.)

TP monitor an acronym for *Transaction-Processing* monitor. Software for building applications that process transactions reliably, efficiently, and economically.

transaction a group of commands that succeed or fail as an indivisible unit of work. An entire transaction is written to a database or nothing is written.

trigger a database command that executes on some specified occurrence.

two-phase commit (2PC) protocol a technique that coordinates multidatabase transactions. 2PC ensures that they entirely commit or entirely abort.

two-tier architecture an architecture that organizes an application into two layers. One layer focuses on the user interface; the other on data management services. Application logic may be in either or both layers. (Contrast with *one-tier* and *three-tier architectures*.)

UML an acronym for *Unified Modeling Language*. The UML was developed by Booch, Rumbaugh, and Jacobson for modeling applications.

URL an acronym for *Unified Resource Locator*. URLs provide a general-purpose naming scheme for Internet resources.

view a table that an RDBMS dynamically computes from a query stored in the database.

weak entity see *dependent entity*.

Web the worldwide communications network used to connect clients and servers for the Internet.

XML an acronym for *eXtensible Markup Language*. XML provides a standard representation for data enabling more flexible presentation of data and less complex data exchange.

Index

X

XML 224–226

Z

Zachman framework 84

Key Recommendations: Part 4

✔ **Use a methodology**. Your organization should have a disciplined and reproducible approach to obtaining software.

✔ **Use a tailored methodology**. You will have greater success if you use a methodology specific to database applications, rather than a general-purpose one.

✔ **Document models**. Always supplement a model with an explanation, such as a data dictionary and a narrative.

✔ **Prepare your own models**. It is too risky to depend on another organization.

✔ **Also design the database in-house**. The database is critical to an application and does not take long to design.

✔ **Consider all input sources**. Don't dwell on user interviews to the exclusion of other input sources. There are many sources of requirements, and you should use them all.

✔ **Normally avoid the waterfall life-cycle approach**. Consider the waterfall approach only for applications with predictable outputs.

✔ **Be prepared to discard a rapid prototype**. Enhance prototypes only if they are successful in the field and have a robust architecture.

✔ **Broadly search for candidate products**. Try to be creative and consider multiple product information sources.

✔ **Independently rate products**. Several people should separately rate each product. They can then all contribute, which leads to a better assessment.

✔ **Check customer references**. You can learn much with a small investment of time.

✔ **Encourage all developers to learn to model**. Budget adequate funds for training and mentoring to help them with the paradigm shift.

✔ **Learn from software reviews**. Management should require that all projects have at least one formal review session.

✔ **Use tools to build models**. Use a UML tool for modeling and an IDEF1X tool for relational database design.

✔ **Limit the number of tool vendors**. It is reasonable to support two or three modeling tools for application development, but use a single tool for each application.